9/21

Matter of Conscience

Written by

Bruce Neckels

AUTHOR'S NOTE:

Knowing that, in the words of Antonio Munoz Molina, "A drop of fiction taints everything as fictional," the stories and conversations in this book reflect my recollection of events. Some names have been changed to protect the privacy of those depicted. Dialogue has been re-created from memory, and though much has been paraphrased, the essence is accurate.

ISBN: 978–1–64316-236-2

Cover design by Sylvia Haber, Perpetuart
Author photograph by Hakan Erses.

"Very special thanks to the Publish Wholesale team for
your assistance, patience and understanding"

authorpartner@publishwholesale.com

I've lost many friends and family members over the years – too numerous to mention them all. Therefore, I'm naming only those who were part of my life and meant so much to me during the time frame of this book.

IN MEMORY OF:

Susan Arnell Boyd
Ann Brebner
Dan Caldwell
Rick Cluchey
David Ireland
Allan Pimental
Ken Whelan

SPECIAL THANKS TO:

Rita Runyan
Kara Kennedy
Anthony Crane
Peter Langs
Bess Scher

"Having known and lived through Bruce's story as a friend, it is a privilege to read such a well written, compelling book. His story portrays a young man faced with a dilemma, and finally forced to make a choice. 'This book should be read NOW."
Frances Hill. (Founding Artistic Director Urban Stages, OFF Broadway theater New York)

"Some may ask: "'How can a former Marine and combat veteran of the Vietnam War endorse a book by a "Conscientious Objector'"? The answer is simple. Bruce Neckels is a man who showed courage and commitment in his beliefs by going to prison. He didn't hide; he didn't create false exemptions; he took the punishment his government mandated. One of the founding principles of our nation is the right of each individual to stand up for their belief. The rest of us, whether we agree with them or not, should support that individual's right to express their belief. - James Reynolds

FOREWORD

T heodore Roosevelt once said – "Recognition belongs to the man who confronts the great challenge of life - whose face is marked by sweat, tears, and blood, and by daring greatly knows the triumph of high achievement." Bruce Neckels refusal to violate his conscience protesting the Vietnam War, is an inspiration in today's culture of mendacity. His remarkable Memoir shows how one lives and what one fights for, no matter the cost of personal suffering – defines the man. MATTER OF CONSCIENCE recreates a shameful era in American History doing greater damage to our future than relocating Japanese citizens, Congressional witch hunts, the Hollywood Blacklist, and Watergate. Bruce Neckels incisive writing brings alive a protesting culture of love, friendship, loyalty, drugs, music, alienation, and pain. Above all, his book describes the barbaric dehumanizing American Prison system, where sadism, massive incarceration, and the criminalization of dissent destroys the future of generations of our nation's disadvantaged young.

Bruce Neckels quarrel with the land he loves gives new meaning to patriotism.

Norman Weissman, author of:
The Patriot
My Exuberant Voyage

DEDICATED TO MY DAUGHER ERIN:

When I began writing this, you were two months away from your ninth birthday. You are now a twenty-seven-year-old college graduate, working on a career of your own. Even though you've just recently taken a considerable interest in the book, you let me know years ago that you understand and accept what I went through. I just wanted you to know that when I chose to go to prison as a conscientious objector against the Vietnam War, I was neither coward nor hero. It was a stand that I had to take based on observations, encounters, and information I had gathered which helped redefine my ideology and who I was.

TO MY WIFE WENDY:

Thank you for 40 years and still counting, of love, loyalty, honesty, friendship, support – and for reminding me when I was putting my energy in the wrong places, to focus back on what was most important…this book. I don't know where I'd be without you.

ACKNOWLEDGEMENTS

Thanks first to Dalton Trumbo, who I had the privilege of meeting in 1969 and whose book "Johnny Got His Gun" changed my life.

To Mohammed Ali, whose stand against the Vietnam War showed me that you have to put your conscience and your ass on the line when it means something. I would like to thank my dear friend, James Reynolds, an ex-Vietnam vet who engaged in combat for eight months on a daily basis, and lived to still think and have nightmares about it - for his relentless encouragement to write my story. Thanks to so many people who supported and visited me during the time I had to spend in that "shithole" called the San Francisco County Jail: Terry, Joanne, Al, Marsha; Amy, Heather, and my dear late friends, Susan and Dan.

And while at Safford Federal Prison, stuck in the middle of the desert, a thousand miles away from home - thank you, Amy - the first to come visit me. To Susan, Mark, Frances, David; and to my dearest friends in life, Terry and Joanne - thanks for taking the time to come visit me at SFP. It wasn't an easy place to find. To Colette for your undying support. Mail-call is the most anxious moment of the day in prison—someone reaching out to me from the outside, from home—assuring me that I was being thought of. And every day, I had at least one letter from you. Thanks to Colette's late friend Andrew, a prominent New York attorney, who reached out to help me. His efforts, phone calls, and letters were a great source of encouragement. I so deeply regret that I never got to meet him personally.

Thanks to the Vietnam Vets who I met after prison, while touring college campuses all over the United States and Canada, performing as an actor in a prison drama, "The Cage." It was great relating our experiences to each other. Thanks for respecting what I had to do, because I certainly respected you. We all got screwed on this one.

I can't mention "the Cage" without giving a special thank you to the late Rick Cluchey, author of the play, for giving me one of the greatest eye-opening experiences I've ever had in my life, not to mention 45 years of friendship.

And finally, I guess I have to thank the late Judge Samuel Conti for sentencing me to prison. Without his decision, *Matter of Conscience* would not be possible.

CONTENTS

"Two roads diverged ..... and I took the one less traveled by, and that has made all the difference."
Robert Frost –

Two roads diverged... both dangerous... one choice... and no turning back.
Bruce Neckels–

PROLOGUE

Saturday, June 26, 1971

It was a gruesome ride - that 1,000-mile trip from the San Francisco County Jail to Safford Federal Prison in Safford, Arizona. Sitting with two other prisoners in the back seat of a 1970 Ford LTD 4-door sedan - squeezed together, handcuffed and leg-ironed. Traveling between Blythe, California, and Tucson, Arizona, going 90 miles an hour with the windows rolled down and the outside temperature at 110 degrees, that heat wave blasting in my face. Yes, the car had air-conditioning. But the FBI officer who owned that car, a former Marine Corps Sergeant, was administering a dose of his own personal punishment.

I sat quietly, acting as though it didn't bother me one bit. We asked the Agents if they would turn on the radio. To our surprise, they did. And how ironic that the song playing was James Taylor singing "You've Got A Friend." That was painful. No, not a damn thing was going right. I was at the lowest point in my life and I wouldn't be calling out anybody's name because no one was going to come running to save me.

On June 11, 1971, at 11:00 a.m., I walked into the Northern District Court in San Francisco, California, to receive my sentencing for "Refusing to Submit to Induction." I had refused in 1969, when the Vietnam conflict was at its peak, and San Francisco had been the Mecca for draft resisters and pot smokers. I could get anything from probation to five years in prison. I'd already eliminated probation because President Richard Nixon had recently appointed the judge I was about to face on the recommendation of California Governor, Ronald Reagan. Orders from Nixon were to crack down on pot smokers and draft resistors. At the same time, there was an opening in the United States Supreme Court, and this judge was being considered for the position. So his objective was to show Nixon how tough he could be. Almost everyone who faced him went to prison. In fact, a jailhouse doctor at S.F. County told me he threw his own nephew in jail for six months, because the kid got busted on pot. In another case, some young lady inside her home, at her kitchen window, was smoking a joint. She was spotted by someone taking an evening stroll, who called the police. They quickly moved in and busted this "criminal" while she was chopping carrots. They found remnants of a marijuana cigarette. The lady faced Judge Samuel Conti and was promptly given jail time. Never as much as a parking ticket, and he wouldn't cut her an ounce of slack for less thana gram of pot.

Affectionately known as "Hanging Sam," "Maximum Sam," I had read about this guy months earlier, in the San Francisco Chronicle. "2-Year Terms For 4 Draft Refusers" My heart was pounding and my adrenaline pumping as I read the story.[xxxxxx], attorney for [xxxxx], termed draft refusal *"a crime of conscience, a crime with no person as a victim." Judge Conti disagreed. "He chose not to go, so someone else had to go and perhaps today, that person is maimed or dead."*[1]

With that kind of sound logic, what chance did I have? No chance in hell. I was sentenced to two years in a federal prison.

As I sat in the holding cell behind the courtroom, handcuffed and leg-ironed, my thoughts went to the movie "Camelot" - King Arthur, pacing the battlefield before dawn, his final moments of peace and reflection as he prepared to do battle with best friend, Lancelot. Trying to make sense of it all, Arthur begs for Merlin to appear, wanting to know why this was happening. Where did it all start? That's what I was feeling... "Oh, Merlin... How the fuck did I get here?"

Chapter One
"The times they are a changin" – Bob Dylan

The decade of the 1960's was insane—Civil War, Part II.I doubt that even to this day, the people who lived through it understand why the hell we were thrown into a war that made no sense—a war that tore this country apart, turning children and parents against each other, brother against brother, friend against friend, youth against establishment—leaving politicians on all levels declaring verbal war against their own people and gambling their careers on whether or not they supported the Vietnam War.

For those young enough to not even have a clue about the 60's and Vietnam, it was an undeclared war. America had a Cold War - Capitalism vs. Communism thing happening in the 1950's, and with Communist China next door to Vietnam, who had just defeated the French colonists, President Dwight D. Eisenhower introduced his "Domino Theory" that if the commies marched through Vietnam, we could expect a collapse of Southeast Asia. Better find an anti-communist Vietnamese leader fast, move in and involve ourselves in a fight which had up to that point, been domestic and going on for 2,000 years—I won't even go back to B.C.. American involvement with that country began when we promised to assist Ho Chi Minh after World War II, then stabbed him in the back. More on that later.

Blacks (they were called "blacks" back then) were sent into the jungles of Viet Nam thousands of miles away to fight for their country, while their brothers and sisters were being hosed down, beaten, and murdered for having the nerve to fight for something called "civil rights." Young black children were spit at, cursed, and assaulted for trying to go to "white" schools. I was attending Merced Junior College, in Merced, California, in 1963-65. Everything was still pretty innocent then. But with John Kennedy's assassination on November 22, 1963, and an escalation of troops in Vietnam - from 16,000 in 1963, to almost 400,000 by the end of 1965 - the loss of baby boomer innocence had reared its ugly head.

On the music scene, the Beatles had landed in America in February of 1964, and changed what was still the infant stage of rock and roll music. Within months after they arrived, they controlled the first five positions of the singles charts in Billboard magazine. At one point they owned eight of the top ten of the week. However, they generously left studio space for The Ventures, The Ronettes, The Righteous Brothers, and The Supremes, to sign off on their careers—and they even let the Beach Boys finish up with their surfing thing, although in October of 1966, the BB's showed their staying power with the release of "Good Vibrations," one of the greatest hit singles of all times. But it was really their last hurrah, and by the end of 1968, the Beach Boys were pretty much an oldies act and a future cover band favorite. Though, to put them in historical rock and roll perspective, no band has ever come close to touching their chord structures and harmonies. But the Beatles officially put Elvis, Little Richard, Fats Domino, and Chuck Berry on the back burners and opened the door for Britain's second invasion of the Colonies—sans redcoats - with the likes of Dave Clark Five, Peter and Gordon, Gerry and the Pacemakers, Herman's Hermits and of course, one of the greatest bands that ever existed, The Rolling Stones. This second "invasion" was much more successful, and not one life was lost in anger, only drug overdoses. I had yet to appreciate a young man from Minnesota whose lyrics would inspire us all and take us through the 60's... Bob Dylan.

So there I was, playing junior college basketball and golf. I was a shorthaired Republican conservative who found it clever and daring when four of my buddies dressed up in black turtlenecks, combed their hair down in front of their foreheads, and sang "I Wanna Hold Your Hand." But I was always overly impressed back then.

And with months away from graduation, I still didn't have a clue what I was going to do. I knew I'd go to a four-year college—but as to where, and what to major in, I was lost. What I did know was that America's involvement in Vietnam was stepping up, the lessons of Dienbienphu apparently forgotten, or to put it more bluntly, never learned. And in February 26 of 1965, just after President Lyndon Johnson began his "Rolling Thunder" bombing campaign, he offered this comforting quote: *"I don't think anything is going to be as bad as* *losing, and I don't see any way of winning. "[2]*That being the case, I wasn't ready to die for nothing, and neither were any of my friends. And with the strains of Bob Dylan warning us all that "...the times they are a-changin'," I needed to get accepted somewhere fast. I decided to approach my choice of college in a very rational, logical way: Where do I want to live for the next 2-3 years? Answer... San Francisco. One of my boyhood buddies was already living there, attending college, and had been selling me on it. And I'd been to San Francisco on three different occasions:1958, my first pro football game—The 49ers and Y.A. Tittle against the Vince Lombardi-led Green Bay Packers; In 1959, I saw my first professional baseball game at the old Seals Stadium—the San Francisco Giants playing the Milwaukee Braves: Willie Mays, Hank Aaron, Eddie Matthews. Warren Spahn vs. Johnny Antonelli. And in 1962, when my girlfriend and I drove up for the day with another couple. While the other boy was looking for a famous magic shop on Lombard Street, this small-town boy found the magic of the city.

I went to the school library and began skimming through the handbooks of San Francisco's two major colleges: The University of San Francisco; and San Francisco State. USF? There was nothing there that interested me as far as selecting a major, and besides, it was a Catholic college—and I wasn't Catholic! As a little boy, growing up and living with a Ukrainian grandmother for the first nine years of my life, I went to St. Paul's Greek Orthodox Church. I sang and prayed in Ukrainian. I guess that could qualify me for being Catholic—but an incident at St. Paul's when I was seven years old, caused me to fall off the religious grid.

I opened up the San Francisco State handbook and began searching for any major that might interest me. I was quickly nearing the end and losing hope, until I reached a section titled "Radio-Television Broadcasting." Now that sounded like fun. I could be a DJ, spinning rock songs; or a TV talk show host - maybe one day take over "The Tonight Show Starring Johnny Carson." Johnny was eventually going to get bored doing that. Somebody would have to fill his spot. Why not me?

And so I applied at San Francisco State. Fortunately, two of my friends from Merced Junior College didn't know where they wanted to go either. I sold them on living in San Francisco; they applied; and within weeks, we were all accepted and on our way to live in the City by the Bay. Little did I know at the time, that my entire life, philosophy (what little I had of one), and beliefs would be turned on its ass.

The Times They Are a 'Changin'

Chapter Two

San Francisco: Future home of my heart...and my soul.

I t was early afternoon and overcast as we crossed the San Francisco-Oakland Bay Bridge. The view was breathtaking: The "Port of San Francisco" sign on the pier below the harbor clock; Coit Tower; Alcatraz off to my right, and the Golden Gate Bridge in the far distance; the smell of the salt air, Petula Clark singing "Downtown" over the radio. This was it! I was officially on my own.

We pulled up to our apartment on Ocean Avenue, just three blocks down from City College of San Francisco, where this kid named O.J. Simpson was playing football. City College was right next to the streetcar terminal. And on Ocean Avenue, were tracks that ran the bell-clanging electric streetcars, to this day, music to my ears. And with S.F. State an easy walking half-mile away; the Tower Theatre and Zanzibar Night Club only two blocks down the street; and a deli two doors away (owned by a Asian who let us buy on credit), I had food, recreation, and educational facilities all lined up. Next step: pre-registration tomorrow morning.

It wasn't one of the major campuses in the country. But with the butterflies in my stomach, it might as well have been Stanford or Michigan to a skinny, naïve, 21 year-old, San Joaquin Valley boy. I stood on the corner of 19th Avenue and Junipero Serra Boulevard for several minutes, just staring across the campus of San Francisco State College, unaware that I was looking at one of the major anti-war, political hotbeds of America. The main sidewalk was a downward slope, cutting between Administration and classroom buildings on the left, and five acres of sprawling, green grass, punctuated with giant eucalyptus and pine trees on the right. I began my slow walk through the campus, taking in the scenery, the students... The excitement grew even more when I reached the front of a brand new building with the words, "Radio-Television Broadcasting." Once inside, I saw that the Drama department shared the hallways to the left of the main entrance.

5

Straight ahead were the doors to R-TV. I entered and found myself looking at a small room to the left of the hallway, with a lighted sign, "KRTG." It was the campus radio station that broadcast to all the dorms and on-campus frat and sorority houses. Even though school hadn't officially started, there was already a student DJ sitting at the control board spinning records. Blasting over the speakers was Len Barry's "1-2-3."Only hit he ever had, but man, the idea that I'd put myself in a world where I could be sitting behind a mike and turntable, spinning records, had my heart pumping.

Quinn Millar was my Advisor. Good-looking man, impeccably dressed—he had a new sport jacket for every day of the week.

"What can I do for you, Mr. Neckels?"

"I want to take over the Johnny Carson Show," I replied.

"You'll probably need a little more experience. So, you want to be in front of the camera?"

"Yes," I replied. "But it doesn't have to be Carson. I'd like to be a sports announcer, too, or maybe even a radio DJ."

And so I signed up for Introduction to Radio-Television, a course that would put me in the studio learning and trying everything: pushing a camera, floor directing, technical directing, directing, operating a sound boom, and even some on-camera announcing. In addition, I had courses in Television Business Law; Television Writing, and History of Film. By total mistake and lack of funds, and parents who couldn't afford to send me to a four year college immediately after high school, I had stumbled on the right way to do college: get all the electives out of the way in junior college; save a fortune in tuition; then spend my last two or three years taking subjects which only pertained to, or supplemented my major. I couldn't wait to get started

Before going home that day, I stopped by "The Commons" (cafeteria) to grab a coke and check out the coeds. Pretty quiet, nothing excited me, so I started up the sidewalk, passing.... Jesus H. Christ.... Who are these people!!?I'd never seen such weird, disgusting, sleazy looking kids in my life! Long, straggly, dirty hair, with headbands, turquoise bracelets, beads around their necks—and I'm talking about the guys! Some were barefoot; others wore moccasins; their jeans flared out at the cuff—bell-bottoms, with holes in the knees. Threading the loops were huge, thick belts with buckles that could be used for weapons. They wore skimpy Fruit-of-the-Loom undershirts that were multi-colored—tie-dyed. And the girls didn't look any better. I noticed some of them didn't shave under their arms. They were obviously homeless or lost. No school would ever allow students to dress like this. I know! I subscribed to Playboy Magazine. I saw how the college guys dressed: Sport jackets with leather on the elbows, sweaters over shirts with a necktie knot barely visible; nice slacks, argyle socks, and loafers. Hell, I was on my way to Bruce Barry's on 19th Avenue to dress as closely to that look as I could afford.

And that's about as naive and ignorant as I was. Little did I know that these "love children" were going to change the look of America, start a revolution, support an anti-war campaign, the likes of which this country had never seen... and in less than two years, take me right along with them. In fact, I would keep going where 99.999% of them would never dare follow.... Prison.

Bay Bridge to the psychedelic mainland

The Commons: backdrop for organizing and protest speeches.

Who in hell ARE these people?

Chapter Three

September, 1965... What's a nice boy from North Dakota doing here?

U p until now, I'd never been one to take a lot of chances. I grew up with a Ukrainian grandmother in the small town of Belfield, North Dakota, for the first nine years of my life. Anna Shypkoski was her name. Born Anna Jesuchep in Austria, in 1894, of Ukrainian parents, story has it that her family moved back to the Ukraine when Anna was a young girl. She worked as a servant at a palace, scrubbing floors, polishing silverware, and harvesting potato crops. Apparently the Jesucheps and the Olynuk family were very tight, so Anna was promised in marriage to one Prokop Olynuk. But Prokop packed his bags and moved to America around 1909, promising Anna they'd be married as soon as she set foot on United States soil. So Anna and her sister, Polly, left the Ukraine in 1910, arriving in North Dakota, where Anna promptly looked up her assigned soul mate. Surprise, surprise - Prokop was married! Whatever happened to good old arranged marriages?

Anna and Polly were on their own. They lived together until Polly met Adolph Gauther and married him. And one enchanted evening a few years later, Anna met Dimitro Shypkoski. I don't know what the occasion was—they either met at a Greek Orthodox Church, or at a bar. Knowing my grandmother's love for Four Roses Whiskey in her later years, she had to have developed a taste for it at some point in her life. Why not at a bar one night when a handsome young man introduced himself, and bought her a shot of Four Roses? Either way, they did end up at St. Peter and Paul's Greek Orthodox Church and got married. Anna then stayed pregnant for the next five years, giving birth to four daughters and a son. One of the daughters, Janet, was my mother. Who would I be on this earth today, had Prokop kept his promise and waited for Anna to show up?

In 1941 my mother married a handsome man, Howard Neckels. They had two children: My sister Bonnie, born in 1942; and me, 1944.

But two years later, they were divorced. My dad took off for California with me, and my mom stayed in North Dakota with my sister. But for some reason, he came back, they switched kids and Dad went back to California. Weird, when I think about it. Seems natural that dad would keep the son, and mother would keep the daughter. But that arrangement had a lot to do with my development. Having no fatherly influence as a driving force in my early years, I had no one to show me how to be tough; never give up; how to throw a ball, catch a ball, shoot a ball—fight, fight, fight; win, win, win—all necessary items in a small boy's survival kit to success. So I learned it all on my own with no paternal guidance whatsoever - other than my movie screen role models at the Belfield Theater: John Wayne, Audie Murphy, Robert Mitchum, Richard Widmark, Burt Lancaster; and I have to single these two out: Gary Cooper and Randolph Scott. Hey, who knew, right? And surprisingly, I excelled at tackle football. And I loved to play war. The creek by my Aunt Polly and Uncle Adolph's house, and the wide-open field next to it, were my battlefields. I fought in every war and defeated knights, Indians, Confederate rebels, Japanese, and Germans. It's where I rode along-side Roy Rogers, and Dale Evans. I saved both their lives many times—probably why Dale had such a crush on me. But I always let Roy have her.

I rarely saw my mother. She was a schoolteacher, but had to find work in Grand Forks, on the other side of the state. There was one school in Belfield - first grade through high school - so teaching jobs were at a premium. For nine months out of the year, she lived in a dinky trailer, and in the dead of those cold North Dakota winters. Mom sent what little extra money she could to my grandma, and it was used for the bare necessities. I didn't get new shoes until the soles came apart and I was tripping over the front of them. I had very little in clothes, and in the winter, one pair of snow boots and one jacket, a couple of long sleeve cotton shirts; long underwear; one pair of mittens, and a scarf.

Seeing mom at Christmas, Easter, and during the summer were my favorite times, though it was no summer vacation for her. She would immediately get a job as a waitress in order to keep the money coming in. But she found time to teach me the more gentle things... reading, speaking proper English, trying to cut through the Ukrainian accent I'd developed being around my grandmother all the time. And she taught me how to sing and whistle. At four years old, I could carry a tune. There was many a warm, humid, summer night, when my mother and I would sit on the front porch, look up at the stars, and sing. *Someone's In the Kitchen With Dinah; You Are My Sunshine; Goodnight, Irene,* and *Twinkle, Twinkle, Little Star.*

By the time I finished fourth grade, my mother had married for her third time, and moved to Hayward, California. Her husband drove a truck for Convoy, hauling cars throughout the western United States. Mom was pregnant at the time, and living with her sister, brother-in-law and their two sons. Little did I know, but clandestine plans had been made for me, Anna, and my four year-old half-sister, Linda (by my mom's second marriage, also living with us)to go to California that summer after school, "to visit." The real scoop was that I wouldn't be coming back. Grandma was getting to old to handle me, and now that Mom was married again, with a husband to support her, it was time for me to live with parents. All parties agreed to withhold that information from me because they knew if I found out I was going to leave my grandmother, I'd have never gotten on that Southern Pacific passenger train. They would've been right. I loved my grandmother with all my heart—forget about the times she beat the living shit out of me—this lady was my best friend. We did everything together: went to the movies; to church every Sunday; we worked in the garden. Everything I learned about love in my early years, I learned from her.

We arrived in California after a three-day train ride in June, 1954. My mother was days away from delivering a baby. She was in no condition to mastermind the plan to keep me here, and get Anna back to North Dakota. So to assist in this effort, my father, his third wife (Opal), and my sister, Bonnie, were called in from Merced. The idea was for me to go visit them for a week, then return to Hayward in time to go back to North Dakota with my grandmother. I didn't want to go. I wept uncontrollably as my grandmother hugged and kissed me, spoke softly to me in Ukrainian, telling me it was just for a week. She packed my little suitcase and walked me to the car. As we pulled away, I looked out the back window. Anna was standing in the street still waving goodbye. There was such finality. I'm sure I sensed it. One week later, 7:00 a.m. Saturday morning, after a miserable week in Merced with that family, I sat out on the curb with my little suitcase at my side, waiting for my uncle to come driving up to take me back to Hayward. After sitting there for an hour, my dad came out, surprised, and I'm sure, disappointed, that I wanted out that badly. And that's when he said:

"Oh, I forgot to tell you. Your grandmother called last night. They won't be able to come pick you up till next week." He saw my dejection.

"Was it that bad here?" He asked. I replied that it was - while he and my step-mom were working, my sister and two stepsisters had me doing dishes, shaking rugs, running to the market—doing all the chores they were supposed to be doing. Thinking he was helping, my dad told his wife and she gave the girls hell, which was what my life became the next week. But along came another Saturday morning, and while everyone was still asleep, I packed my suitcase, went outside, and sat on the curb, waiting for my ride back to Hayward. After a while, my Dad came out.

"There's a telephone call for you. It's your grandma."

Which meant she was still in Hayward. She's sure as hell not at a gas station on the corner of Highway 99 and G, calling for directions. But that's okay. As long as she wants to tell me they're on their way, I'll take it.

But Anna wasn't on her way. She was calling from Walla Walla, Washington, where she was visiting a friend. My heart sank. And even when she told me in very broken English that she'd come for me soon, I didn't need a translator to tell me otherwise. I hung up and wept quietly, while my dad stood there sheepishly.

"Well, maybe we should enroll you in school here... in case she can't get back."

Enough already! Jesus, I'm two weeks away from my tenth birthday, but I'm not stupid. This was the plan all along. And poor Anna had to come up with the bullshit excuses. Nobody had the courage to tell me the truth. And all the hushed, angry sotto voce talks my dad and step-mom had outside in the backyard, must have been about dad wanting me to live here... not with my mom. And for Opal, a fourth child was not part of the bargain.

And so, for the next nine years, I lived with my dad, step-mom, sister, and two stepsisters. And there was no question who ruled that house.... Opal ... through fear. There was just too much rage, anger, and screaming to appreciate the good moments we had. Dad never gave his stamp of approval on anything without checking with her first. As he admitted to me years later, he'd been married twice already, felt like a failure, and didn't want to fail again. But laying back was so counterproductive. I was afraid to ever voice an opinion about anything, for fear I'd see the rolling of her eyes, followed by a punctuated, "Jeeesus Cheeee-rist! That's stupid!" It got so bad after a while, that I rarely raised my hand in class, because I was afraid if I was wrong, other kids and the teacher would, of course... think I was stupid. I watched them have physical fights; I heard the screaming, the crashing of objects; seeing my dad with fingernail marks scratched across his chest. She even came at him with a fireplace poker one night. This woman was a piranha-gator. Picture someone with bright red hair, who looked like Lucille Ball, with eyes like Marty Feldman's when she got real angry... which seemed to be her dominating attitude.

I had several opportunities to go live with my mom. But I felt so sorry for my father; I didn't have the heart to leave him. He needed me more than my mother did. Both stepsisters got pregnant and married, or married and pregnant, just to get the hell out of that house. And my sister refused to leave mom one summer when we both went to visit her. So I eventually had to go it alone, which was actually a little better. Opal was working nights as a cocktail waitress. My dad owned his own bar called the Fireside Inn, on 17th Street. And with me going to school during the day, I didn't have to put up with either one of them much. Finally, in the fall of 1962, just when I started classes at Modesto Junior College (for one year then transferred to Merced), Opal yelled up at me from downstairs, that she was leaving my father.

"Oh... okay. Good luck." I yelled back

What was I supposed to say? Beg her to reconsider? I hated her every day of my life for nine years. I hated always feeling I had to agree with her just so she'd like me that day. I sold my soul to her just to have a moment's peace... and a warm, gentle voice, with a pleasant smile. Later on that day, my father came home, asked me if I'd heard the news. I replied that I had, then made it short and sweet.

"You don't need me anymore." I moved out.

And that's the baggage I brought with me to San Francisco in September, 1965:I didn't like anyone raising their voice or yelling at me; I didn't stick up for myself; I was afraid to offer an opinion; afraid to guess at an answer. I played killer defense for the Merced College Blue Devils basketball team. I was a deadly free throw shooter; had a good outside shot... but don't give me the ball when the game was on the line, unless it was the free throw line. And, I came with 21 years of never going into a dentist's office. Belfield, North Dakota didn't have a dentist in town. Luckily, I ate so many fresh vegetables out of the garden my grandmother planted, that I didn't have a cavity. But between 10 and 17 years old, living with my dad and step-mom, I had eight. During the next four years, I picked up four more. So taking my fear of going to the dentist, and the fear that my parents would get mad at me for having to spend the money for fillings, I foolishly avoided the subject... until September 1965.... the beginning of my multiple epiphanies. I began litter-bugging my mind's emotional pathways with baggage I didn't want anymore. It was time to throw out what I didn't need.

Me at 8 years old

Me at 17

Anna Shypkoski , 1962

Identical to the home where I grew up.
(Note the outdoor toilet in the back. No fun on a freezing
North Dakota winter night)

Main Street – early 50's

Doesn't look much different today. Cars are newer.

Grandma Anna's favorite watering hole.
Was John and Joe's back in the 50's

Belfield Theater - since I didn't live with a father until I was ten,
here's where I found my male role models...on screen.

Chapter Four
911:A hiccup to my memoir

T here was a lyric from Joni Mitchell's song, "Woodstock" – something about seeing death bombers in the sky. September 11, 2001. An early riser, I grabbed a cup of coffee, got the paper, then turned on my TV to see that the North Tower of the World Trade Center had been hit by an airplane - then watched in horror as a second plane crashed into the South Tower. Minutes later they announced that a third plane crashed into the Pentagon; and yet a fourth plane has gone down in the fields of Pennsylvania. Except for this one, the other three were obviously suicide missions. And I doubt if they were Timothy McVeigh sympathizers. Since an attack had already been made on the Trade Center underground garage in 1993, this has to be another Middle-Eastern terrorist attack. The Pennsylvania plane must have been headed for the Capitol Building or the White House. I wondered where else we'd be hit today.

As I sat there glued to my television, I got the chills as I recalled a Sunday morning in 1976. I was doing a national sales convention tour for Datsun, and one of our shows took us to Newark, New Jersey. After the show finished that Saturday night, our tech man, Greg, wanted to drive into New York and go to the World Trade Center. I wanted to see it, too, so the next morning, we got up at 6:00 a.m. and drove into the city. The streets were empty; parking was easy. So we went into the WTC and up to the viewing tower. As Greg and I stood there looking out across the Hudson River toward New Jersey, I happened to spot an airplane way off in the distance heading south. I stared at it for a few seconds then said:

"One day terrorists are going to ram planes into these buildings."

#

It's later in the day, and no other incidents occurred... not even in Los Angeles. How can they not attack this city? Unless the terrorists assigned to the West Coast watched those planes go into the WTC in a ball of flame, and have reconsidered their fate. But for now, both North and South Towers no longer exist. They collapsed; each floor pancaked the one below it all the way to the ground, like vertical dominos. Thousands of people were dead - crushed or vaporized. The planes were all filled to capacity with fuel. Body parts and human ashes were found at least ten blocks away from the WTC. We pretty much know who our enemies are. And it is payback time. America wants justice. America wants revenge! I'm a peaceful man, yet my initial response is, I want revenge.

But for now, who wants to read about a Conscientious Objector of the Vietnam era? We are about to enter a new war - for the first time in 50 years - a just war, not at all like the Vietnam Conflict. American civilians—mothers, fathers, sons, daughters, friends, fiancés—all slaughtered while working at their desks, and looking forward to the weekend—coaching their sons' or daughters' baseball or soccer teams; going to the movies, a fall picnic, a birthday party.... a birth. People who had plans to get together with their friends for a barbecue, attend a play, or just watch TV. Instead, in a matter of minutes, thousands ceased to be, and millions would never be the same again. America will not sit down at any negotiating table on this one. We're going to kill somebody.

As for my story... I must table it for a while—a week, a month, a year—until the bad timing becomes better bad timing.

#

Or not....

Two days later, in the early evening of September 13, I was shopping at a nearby mall. I decided to walk over to Jamba Juice and get myself a 2-ounce shot of wheat grass. It was a beautiful, balmy evening – people sitting outside drinking lattes and juices, talking about the same thing. It was now clear that the suicide terrorists were indeed Middle Eastern, part of the al-Queda terrorist network started in the 1980's by a narrow-minded Muslim fundamentalist misfit, Osama bin Laden, who justified this mass murder by invoking religion and declaring a holy war between Islam and the Western world – placing his morality above mankind's.

I passed a table in time to overhear two college guys talking. Both looked like football players. One was wearing a Yankee cap, the other a UCLA sweatshirt. This was their conversation:

"Man, you fuckin' know we're gonna send thousands of guys over there."

"I know. This is gonna go on for years... like when Russia was in Afghanistan. They were there for what, ten years? And they lost thousands of guys."

"Hey, if the same thing happens to us, you know they'll bring back the draft. And I fuckin' ain't going. I'll go to prison first."

"Ahhh, I don't know about that –"

"I'm not shittin' ya. I'll go to prison!"

"I might head for Canada," said the other one.

As I stood there listening to these guys, I flashed back to 1968, when I began to question what I would do if I were drafted. But 33 years later this was the last thing I ever expected to hear. Not when our own soil was attacked. This was Pearl Harbor all over again. But Hawaii wasn't even a state in 1941. These sleaze balls hit the mainland. New York, gateway to the American dream. WTC: symbol of global economy. The Pentagon, symbol for military strength. Even those who could only grab on to the caboose of America's gravy train were better off here than most people on the planet. How could anyone say "hell no, I won't go!" But war is war, declared or not. Life is life. Death is death. These two realized that they have one life on this earthly plain, and whatever the reason was that we were attacked, had nothing to do with them. What did our leaders—politicians, military, big business—do over the past several decades to instill such hatred? Who put these two boys in a position to have to defend their country? Why are we going to war? Why are they choosing not to go? Perhaps my timing for this story is right. Maybe I can draw comparisons, or show that there's more to patriotism than picking up a gun without knowing why you're really fighting for your country. And is your "country" today what you had hoped for sixty years ago?

Chapter Five
You're a good man, Charlie Brown

So I've laid out the negative baggage I brought with me to San Francisco State from years past. And the only words ever spoken to me at this point in my life that were truth to my ears, happened while I was in my first year at Modesto Junior College, in 1962. My counselor was a man named Charlie Brown—his real name. Stocky man, either slightly balding or a flat-top haircut, can't quite remember which. He had the forearms of a steel-worker. There was a slight Southern drawl to his voice. He looked like a marine drill-sergeant. He taught biology, but I would've guessed metal or auto shop. One thing I did know in the fifteen minutes I spent with him... the man broke my balls. He got on me harder in fifteen minutes than my father did in the nine years I lived with him. Charlie asked me a lot of questions, trying to size me up and see where my head was at. And of course, me—I was trying to be nice and not say something "stupid." I wanted to please him so he'd like me. But Charlie saw right through it:

Charlie:18 years old, right, Neckels?

Me: Uh... yes sir.

Charlie: Do you think young men like yourself in America should be allowed to vote when they're 18years old?

Me: Uh... well, no, I don't think we understand or pay enough attention to politics yet. We're concentrating more on college and stuff.

Charlie: (dryly)Yeah, stuff... I see what you mean. Well, do you think everybody in America over 21, understands politics enough to vote?

Me: No –

Charlie:(interrupting) I'll bet there's some smart sixteen year-old high school kids taking debate classes, who know more about politics and current events, than 80 % of people over 21. Should they be allowed to vote?

Me:(Now getting hot under the collar, and feeling beads of sweat starting to form): Yeah, well, no. I think 16 is too young for most... 16 year olds to vote. And yeah... people over 21 should still be allowed to vote. It's up to them to learn about who or what they're voting for.

Charlie: But not if you're 18?

Me: No... I still think 21.

Charlie:(studying me. Now I'm totally coming unglued) Uh-huh. Well, Neckels, don't you think that if 18's old enough to fight, it should be old enough to vote?

Me: Yeah, you're right. Now I see what you mean.

Charlie: No you don't. Fighting and voting are two different things! One has nothing to do with the other."

NOW.... Had I said, "Hey, fuck you, Charlie Brown! If I've got two presidential candidates running for office, and one of them wants to stop a war; the other wants to escalate, and I'm 18 years old—and my life depends on whether I go to war or live in peace, then I demand the right to cast my vote!" ... I probably could have scored some points. But instead, I said:

"Yeah, okay... you're right."

Charlie Brown stared placidly at me for a few moments, then:

"Neckels, do you know what your problem is...?" And here came that moment of eye-opening truth:

"You raise too much corn, and not enough hell."

And so, moving forward to 1965, I'm one week into school. Mr. Corn Grower here is already overloaded with the endless possibilities stemming from a career in Radio-Television-Film. And that's when Charlie Brown #2 came into my life.

#

Dr. Arthur Hough was my professor for "Introduction to Radio-Television." I loved this guy. He looked like Fidel Castro. Dark complexion, curly, black hair, deep, chalky voice—very articulate—and always walked into class smoking a thick cigar, which would never fly today. And in a class of about 30 students, he selected me as the kid he was going to teach to "raise hell." He divided his class into three groups: A, B, and C. A was going to put on an FM radio show. FM was very fledgling back then, comprised of news and talk show formats. B group would do a full-on AM rock radio program; and C group, where I was placed, would put on a radio drama. Not just any radio drama. H.G. Wells, "The War of the Worlds." The same show Orson Wells and John Houseman did in New York, when they produced "Mercury Theatre On the Air." For those of you not familiar with that fatal evening: On Sunday night, October 31st, 1938, these guys scared the living shit out of the entire East Coast. What was supposed to be a Halloween prank was so vivid and realistic in its description of an invasion of space creatures landing in Grover's Mill, New Jersey, that thousands of listeners went into an absolute panic. And even though the Mercury Theatre clearly announced that the broadcast was fictional, those who didn't get that important piece of information evacuated their homes, fleeing for their lives. Fatal auto accidents occurred, as a result. Some even committed suicide rather than face an uncertain, horrible death at the tentacles of alien beings.

I sat there eagerly hoping I would get the lead role as announcer, who takes the audience through the invasion. Hough sat us down in a circle then:

"First, we need someone to direct this show..... Neckels."

Holy Christ! I went into shock. Did he just say "Neckels?!"Hough stared deeply into my eyes and right through me, waiting.

"I've never directed before," I said—like that was going to get me out of it.

"Well, this is your debut," said Hough. "Get your team together, cast it, get your sound people, your effects people, your actors, and get to work. You go up three weeks from today, 10 a.m.." He got up and walked out of the room, leaving me with nine people I didn't even know, all staring at me. I can't explain what happened next. I just started talking and it was making sense. "Okay, let's see how many roles there are, we'll have to double up on characters... Who wants to do sound effects...? Okay, I'll help with that. What's your name? Sandy? Hi, Sandy—so take note of all the effects we'll be needing. We can get crowd noises and explosions from the effects library." I was rattling off orders like I knew what I was talking about.

It's not like I blew in with the morning Bay Area fog without any leadership skills. I was Student Body President of my high school; I was on the very first board of officers during the first year of Merced College. I wasn't always afraid to voice my own opinion. I was the only officer who voted against the mascot name, "Blue Devils." Seemed too... demonic. No, I wasn't a wuss—I just never wanted to rock any boat. Even as a six year old boy in North Dakota, I knew when to take the bull by the horns, or in this case, a tree by its branches.

#

It was late December, and grandma and I still didn't have a Christmas tree. My mother had gone straight to Montana from her teaching job, to visit her brother. She promised we'd go get a tree as soon as she arrived back in Belfield. But I wanted that tree and Christmas was just around the corner. So one morning, I got up early, dressed warmly, and snuck out the door. I knew that the Red Owl store had a stack of Christmas trees in their basement. I walked in and told the man behind the counter that I wanted to pick out a tree and take it home. I had no money so he charged it to my grandma's account, after which I went down into his basement and picked out the tree all by myself. I'm sure it was a nice one, but by the time I finished dragging it home, it looked like the Christmas tree from Charles Shultz's "Merry Christmas, Charlie Brown." Grandma was furious, but we put it up and decorated what branches were left. So yes... there were times I could be very proactive.

#

The radio show was great. A few problems, like one of the two mikes going dead on us. I didn't have the sense for the first 10 minutes to gather everyone around one mike. But once it became clear to me, we did a good job – 6 on a scale of 10. Hough was pleased. After cast and crew had left the room, he sat me down and we talked about my mistakes. Every time I tried to justify what happened, he'd stop me dead in my tracks and tell me what I could have done. The critique finished, he lit his cigar, blew smoke in my face, and said, "Good job, Neckels." He then turned out the lights in the classroom, and left, closing the door behind him. I sat there in total darkness, with a big smile on my face. That's when the light bulb went on inside my head. I had just learned something especially important that would help me for life: An excuse isn't worth a damn. I told Hough about that moment a year later. He stared at me, nodded, and repeated softly, "An excuse isn't worth a damn... yeah... I like that, Neckels."

My second awakening came during that very same time I was directing "War of The Worlds." We still had regular classroom assignments to do and were working on delivering radio commercials. All were given a 30-second piece of commercial copy–mine was some brand of butter–and had to sit opposite a tape recorder, in front of the entire class, and deliver the spot in exactly 30 seconds. Hough gave me the "action" sign and I got through it. After I took my seat, Hough went to the tape recorder, rewound it, and played it—my voice—on that tape recorder—selling a product.

Up until the judge sentenced me to prison six years later, it was the longest 30 seconds of my life. I just plain stunk. I was colorless—flat, monotone, lifeless. My enunciation was embarrassing. Hough even put his hand to his mouth and pretended to yawn, like he needed to drive the point home. After my 30 seconds mercifully came to an end, all Hough could say was... "That's terrible." I had no excuse. He was right. I knew what I had to do. I needed help. Sounds easy, but I was someone who had always been afraid to ask for help. Even when I was playing high school and junior college golf, and my game going to hell. I developed a slice I couldn't get rid of. Do you think I had the sense to go to a coach and ask for help? No, I tried to fix it myself, and couldn't. And having a bad temper didn't help. But this was different. I was working on a career.

The bell rang, and I was off and running, too ashamed to look at anyone or say a word. I walked down the hallway and made a right turn to the drama department, to the door where a beginning drama class was still in session. I watched as novice thespians were doing mirror exercises (facing opposite each other while one student copied the slow motions of the other). It looked silly, but who was I to talk? I'd just made a complete ass out of myself.

Class ended, and as students filed out, I went in, and introduced myself to Thomas Terrell, the drama instructor. He was very elegant looking, with a beautiful head of well-groomed white hair, very soft-spoken, and he carried himself with great pride. I liked him the second I looked at him.

"I was wondering if it's too late for me to enroll in your class?" I asked. "I'm not a drama major. I'm Radio-TV, but I just heard my voice on a tape recorder, and I'm humiliated. I need to find something that will help me loosen up. Do you have room?"

Terrell laughed. Normally, late enrollment ended last Friday, but he saw my desperation and appreciated that it meant so much to me that I sought him out.

"You will be required to perform in scenes from two plays this semester," he said. I agreed, and he handed me a registration card. I filled it out, went to the office, and fifteen minutes later, I was taking Beginning Drama. Me! Drama—something I had considered to be quite sissified in high school. But for the first time, I tossed aside fear of showing weakness, and opened my soul and feelings for everyone to observe... more importantly, for me to observe.

It was great. Awkward, intimidating, embarrassing—until I began to see that drama class as an art studio, and myself as a marble stone—an alter ego that I could start chipping away at, to discover what was inside, what was already there, just screaming to be let out. I had been an actor all along. I knew pain, abandonment, love, hate, phoniness, jealousy, betrayal, lying, cheating, stealing, rage—because I had felt or done them all, or had them done to me. But the epiphany was knowing that these were now my tools, and not weapons of mass destruction against myself—and that I now had a "method" if you'll pardon the expression, of applying these emotions and experiences to characters. I went from faking honesty on stage, to having great moments of real honesty. For the first time, I went from being narrow-minded, to believing that anything and everything was possible. As Hamlet said to Horatio:" There are more thing in heaven and earth ,Horatio, than are dreamt of in your philosophy." (William Shakespeare). And even though I never had a thought that I could claim was totally my own, I began to examine more than just one side. I learned to create a history for my character before he ever set foot on stage; to understand what got him to that point in time. Then I became bold enough to recreate my own history—and to try and understand why I behaved as I did. I even tried to put myself in the place of a stepmother I'd hated every day of my life for nine years—who yelled and screamed, showed rage, impatience, cruelty, and thoughtlessness. Time to set aside all bitterness aside.

#

She was thirty-one years old when I dropped into her life. She'd been married once, divorced, and left with two daughters—one beginning fifth grade, the other, starting her freshman year in high school. Then she met and married my father, who had a daughter starting junior high school. Now there were three children to manage. And suddenly, I came into the picture - A nine-year boy with the manners of a little pig. Who chewed with his mouth open, and held a fork the way a golfer gripped a club - high maintenance, to be sure. I was not part of the bargain for this lady, whose life was becoming a nightmare. Whatever hopes and dreams she had for the future—and who bothered to ask her or even care what those were—had all turned into a career of child management, while holding down a job, coming home and cooking dinner. She didn't ask for this. Yes, she could have accepted responsibility, accepted her choice—and dealt with it in a nicer way. But not having read Dr. Spock, she chose what was really quite the norm, i.e., children were an abnormal species who did not deserve an opinion; who should speak only when spoken to, and to never ask why. This new awareness I was into, forced me to look at the flip side. There were good times; she did have kinder moments; aside from the cruel times, she could be a very nice person. I know she was very proud of me and my accomplishments in school and sports. She taught me the right things, but for the wrong reasons – more to accommodate her than to teach me a life lesson. Take ironing, for

29

example. Instead of gently saying to me, "Bruce you're a freshman in high school now, and you're going to start getting more interested in girls, dating, going to dances and the movies – and I might not always be around in case you need a shirt or pair of pants pressed. So I want to teach you how to iron in case an emergency comes along." It would've been embarrassing to me, I'm sure. But instead, one night when I was upstairs in my room doing homework, she screamed from the foot of the stairs to get downstairs and come to the kitchen. did, and there was an ironing board, iron and one of my shirts ready to be pressed.

"I'm sick and tired of ironing your clothes. It's time for you to start doing it yourself."

It was humiliating to me, and all I could do to keep from crying as I was being instructed. And it didn't help when one of my neighbor buddies came knocking at my back door, saw what I was doing, and started howling with laughter. However, months later, he needed a shirt ironed because he was meeting his girlfriend at the movies and didn't have a pressed shirt. He paid me a quarter to iron one for him.

And on the subject of clothes, rarely did I ever get new clothes, but whatever she could pick up at rummage sales. Nothing ever fit. I looked like a clown whenever I went to school, and it was embarrassing. She could have taken me with her and at least put those faded out pair jeans against me to make sure they weren't four sizes too big.

And whenever I went to visit my mom – Christmas, Easter, and summer vacation, she never failed to indignantly say: "I'm sure you're going to tell your mother how cruel and mean I am." And upon my return: "Well, did you tell your mother what a rotten person I am?" I always lied and said no.

By the time I was a senior in high school, I knew I was going to get no financial help for college. So during the school year, I worked as the marquee boy/doorman/usher at the Merced Theatre. And after graduation, I got a job with the Merced Irrigation District to make more money. Well, that did it for Opal. She wanted me to start paying room and board, but I needed that money to go to college. And when my dad took my side, she hid the mayonnaise so I couldn't use it to make sandwiches for my lunch. One time I found it hidden under the kitchen sink behind a can of Ajax and dish soap. Other times, the bread would be hidden.

The bad times far outweighed the good - so much for putting bitterness aside. I still couldn't let her off the hook and forgive. Yet did I ever once stop to think she might have been manic-depressive? Thyroid problems? Monthly hormonal issues? No. As far as I was concerned, she fucked up during the years I was trying to form a working philosophy of life. But I did manage to learn two things: One, that I can't do psycho-therapy on myself; and two - it was now my choice to either use that past misery to affect the rest of my life - as an excuse for failure - or do some damage control, and understand that the time is now, not yesterday. And that worked.... Sort of.

At least I was on the road to finding my inner voice. I was observing and studying people... and at San Francisco State in 1966-68... there was a lot to observe. From the filthy, disgusting hippies, who made me want to run home and take a shower, to the irony of the Students for a Democratic Society (SDS) sharing the main campus sidewalk next to an Army recruiting table—and one day, still early in the semester, a guy standing on a small platform stage, about a foot high off the ground. He had a mustache and beard; his hair, curly and down to his shoulders—rather snarly and dirty looking – a typical looking hippie. Except that he wore an army jacket and combat boots. Well, one combat boot. He was missing a leg. Propped up on crutches, he was yelling to no one in particular, about something horrifying he'd recently experienced in a far-off land. A place called Vietnam.

It was noon and I was finished with classes for the day. I had homework to do before going to work. School was barely two months old and I had already gotten a nighttime job at the Wells Fargo Operations Center on 50 First St. It was a great place for a college student to get a job. They were open 24 hours a day. It was their main check-processing center for all of Northern California. You could damn near pick your hours, depending on how much time you could spare and how much money you needed to make to get buy. For me, 4:00 p.m. - 9:00 p.m., Monday through Friday, gave me 25 hours a week, enough to go to school, do homework, pay my share of the rent,

31

utilities and food, and go see my weekly dose of "The Sound of Music." I had a crush on Julie Andrews.

I really wanted to walk away from that one-legged vet standing on that platform. But he wouldn't let me go. His words froze me in my tracks. I even forgot that I was feeling self-conscious, standing there, wearing my Bruce Barry powder blue sport coat, pale yellow shirt with color coordinated tie, slacks and loafers. All around me were the latest hippie fashions... and a weird smelling smoke that was drifting past my nostrils.

"We don't belong there, man... We don't even know who we're fighting. One day my unit went through this village. We gave people candy and cigarettes. They thanked us, smiled big at us, you know, like they loved us. Couple nights later, out on maneuvers, we engage in a firefight. After the VC scattered, we checked out casualties, and guess what, man? Some of 'em were the same peasants we saw at the villages. So we don't know who our enemies are. I'm sure one of the people I gave a cigarette to one day, planted the mine that blew off my leg.... (pointing at the army recruiters sitting at a table) Those guys are here to kill you, man. Ask any of 'em to tell you why we're there and they can't. They just give you some shit like, 'When your country calls you, you serve.' Or, 'We're there to stop the spread of communism.' Well, don't believe that shit, man. If they call you up, don't go. We can't win that war, because we're not just fighting North Vietnam, we're fighting Red China, and they've got millions of men... and they'll keep sending them, and sending them. And it's their land. They know every inch of it. They've got miles and miles of tunnels and caves. Booby traps hidden everywhere. We don't know how to fight that kind of guerilla warfare. And bombing them ain't gonna do shit, man. They just hide in their caves and tunnels, and come out after it's over.... And another thing, man... Our government's lying to you about body counts. We're not killing as many as you're hearing on the news, man...."(unknown Vietnam Vet speaker. San Francisco State College. October, 1965. Paraphrased by B. Neckels)

Jesus Christ! After he concluded his oration, I knew one thing for sure: I had to stay in college, and hopefully, by the time I graduated— in one year—this war would miraculously be over.

Three months later, sometime in early 1966, I heard that one of my boyhood neighbors had been killed in Vietnam. They found his body in four different pieces, tied to four different trees. Psychological warfare at its best. To this day, I don't know how much of that was true. I wasn't about to visit his parents and ask them to tell me all about it? I needed to learn more about Vietnam and find out why the hell we were even there. Time to enroll in another class that wasn't being offered at SFS: Vietnam 101, for no credit.

Mercury Theater's production of War of the Worlds,
directed by Orson Wells -slightly better than mine

Chapter Six
Peeling a layer of my conservative skin

My first year was over. What an eye-opener. I pulled off a B average, which wasn't bad, considering I was working five nights a week, and spent a hunk of "homework time" rehearsing for plays. I got an A in Beginning Drama, and found out I was a pretty damn good actor. I played The Gentleman Caller in Glass Menagerie, and Ernest in The Importance of Being Ernest. The bug had bitten, and even though I knew I'd get a degree in Radio-TV, I also knew I was going down another road after I got it. Instead of a nice high-paying job in some TV studio, as a cameraman, TD—whatever - I was opting for the insecurity and rejection of acting.

During the summer of 1966, after my first year at State, one of my roommates and I headed out on our own—which was sort of a chicken-shit thing to do to one of my other roommates for which I deeply apologize. But I was paid back.

My part of the rent for our apartment on Ocean Avenue had been $44.00 a month. But now I was on my way to Twin Peaks and a beautiful view of the city. The rent was $165.00 a month. My roommate, who had won an auto accident settlement against Merced County, was willing to pay a hundred dollars if I could come up with the sixty-five. It was do-able, so I accepted. One month later, he moved back home to Merced. He needed to save money because he wanted to marry his high-school sweetheart, coincidently the best friend of my high school sweetheart, who was attending college across the bay at Berkeley—but who had dumped me for some other guy. So there I was, alone in San Francisco, without my girlfriend and my roommate—living in a fancy one-bedroom apartment with a view. $165.00 a month, plus electricity and phone. Total monthly expenses: About $220.00. I was clearing about $260.00. So the remainder went for food and bus fares. I lived on Rice-A-Roni, that San Francisco treat, hamburger, shredded wheat, and Bugs Bunny Kool-Aid—and I stole the Kool-Aid whenever I could. In all fairness to my father, he called me every couple of weeks, asking if I needed any money. I turned down his help every time. I regret taking that away from him. It was my immature way of paying him back for the miserable nine years I lived with that hellcat he married.

I didn't really want a roommate, especially in a one-bedroom apartment. So I applied for more hours at Wells Fargo, but there were no immediate openings. I was determined to stick it out. I hadn't really ventured out that much during school, and since fifty cents a day on a streetcar or muni bus could get me anywhere in the city, I became a local sight-seer. I went everywhere alone and just took my time: Fisherman's Wharf, Ghirardelli Square, the Cannery, Golden Gate park, downtown, Palace of Fine Arts in the Marina District—I loved the Marina district. Flat, but right there next to the Bay, looking straight ahead at Alcatraz Island, and to the left, the beautiful Golden Gate Bridge. And then one day I hopped on a streetcar called the "N Judah" line, not quite sure where it was taking me. I got off at Buena Vista Park and just started walking. Before I knew it, I was standing on the corner of Haight-Ashbury, the hippie counter-culture/acid-head capitol of America. What a freak show! People dressed in clown outfits, fringe, leather, bell bottoms, granny dresses, headbands—music seemed to be pouring out from everywhere. This was the time of garage bands—there must have been a thousand in the Bay Area alone. It was Fantasyville. Get your buddies together, load up on beer, wine, whiskey, and weed, find an empty garage space or an old Victorian to rent for cheap—and maybe, just maybe, if your sound was different enough—you might cut a record and get it played on the Tom Donahue show. Tom was the man. "Big Daddy" they called him. One of San Francisco AM radio's top DJ's. But Tom had a vision of where all this was going. He quit AM, started spinning songs on a progressive FM station, and introduced his own record label. If a band could get to him, and if he liked you enough to help you cut a record—guaranteed he'd be playing it. No doubt about it – Tom Donahue was the Father of FM Rock Radio.[3]Little did I realize at the time, that holed up in one of these musical orifices, I could have been listening in the early, unrecorded sounds of Jefferson Airplane, Big Brother and the Holding Company, Moby Grape, Country Joe and the Fish, Quicksilver Messenger Service, and God knows who else?

I hung out for a couple of hours, checking out store windows filled with psychedelic band posters, buttons, beads, bongs, hash pipes—but still too innocent to understand what bongs and hash pipes were for. I must have turned down fifty requests for "change."

"Hey, brother, spare some change?"

"No, all I got is bus fare back home."

I wasn't lying either. I was probably as poor as they were. Okay, so maybe I had a ten-dollar bill in my wallet. But every time I said no, I was answered back by one of the four-patented phrases of the times: "Far out." "I can dig it." "Love you, brother." "Peace, brother."

I decided to head back to Twin Peaks and my one-bedroom pad with a view that I couldn't afford. But something caught my eye in a shop window. I stared at it for a minute or two, trying to convince myself that I didn't need it, that I should use the money for food. However, I decided that it was time to move out to edge city, so I went inside. When I came out, I was carrying a chain necklace with a nickel attached to it. But it wasn't just any nickel. It had been stamped out with some kind of metal cutter. The middle of the coin was a peace sign. Though the establishment still had a firm hold on me, I had just opened the door and peaked into the world of rebellion.

Chapter Seven
Hi Diddle-Dee-Dee –

"**D**ah dum, da-dum, da-dum.""You know the song.I just didn't want to have to pay royalties for five words. But it was written by Walter Catlett for Walt Disney's "Pinnochio."

By autumn, student protest over the Vietnam War was escalating as rapidly as the war itself. We were into thousands of our young men dying, and still, we weren't quite sure why. I was entering my senior year at San Francisco State, and already thinking about what to do when I graduated. I would certainly be drafted but now the idea of reluctantly doing my duty didn't seem like such a done deal. The image of Audie Murphy standing on a burning tank, machine-gunning the shit out of attacking Germans in "To Hell and Back," was no longer inspiring. Nor was "The Longest Day," even though I swear to God, if there is such thing as reincarnation, I got killed on Omaha Beach in my last life, before I even hit the sand. And I'm not saying that to set up any kind of justification as to why I became a conscientious objector in my current life. It's just my lifelong fascination with D-Day, and a feeling I was there.

Before the month of September 1966 was up, SDS students were entering classrooms - my Broadcast Communications class being one of them—and announcing that they were shutting down the school in protest of the Vietnam War. I walked through the campus, amidst the San Francisco Police wearing flack jackets and plastic-visored helmets. And though I was more pro-establishment, I found this to be rather exciting. A part of me was hoping that these student "rebels" had enough collective voice to stop the war before I graduated. But I had no time to lend a hand in their efforts. I was carrying a full load at school, including more drama classes. The acting bug had bitten me. And now I had a full-time job at the Wells Fargo Operations Center. My hours were from 11:00 p.m. – 7:00 a.m., Monday through Friday. I was dead-ass exhausted. Between this schedule, I found enough time to do homework. I slept on weekends.

Yet somehow I managed to get my acting career started. In the spring of 1967, on the advice of R-TV professor, Quinn Millar, I went to visit the Brebner Casting Agency. Quinn felt it was a good way for me to supplement my income by doing extra work on movies and commercials. Extras are background atmosphere—people in scenes who don't have dialogue. The Brebner Agency was the only game in town. If you wanted a shot in show business while living in San Francisco, this was it. I called and made an appointment. I was about to enter another source of personal growth and transformation. Not only would my confidence level and ability to perform under extreme duress, be tested—but I would meet new friends who would help me open my mind.

I looked damn good in my powder blue sport jacket, which was now a year old. So I wore that, along with a white shirt, tie, black slacks, and black shoes—and walked into the Brebner Agency. I remember it was about four o'clock in the afternoon. 1615 Polk Street. I had to walk up these narrow stairs into offices that weren't at all plush. When I entered the door into the waiting/reception room, I couldn't believe what I was seeing: All these sleazy, dirty looking hippies! They'd taken every seat available, and were sitting and lying all over the floor, filling out applications. I had to step over them just to get to the front desk and announce my appointment.

"Mrs. Brebner will be with you shortly," I was told by the receptionist. She handed me an application to fill out while I was waiting. I found a place in the corner and just stared at these hippies. Obviously, they were looking to make a few bucks, too. I smiled. I didn't care how long I had to wait, this Mrs. Brebner was going to select me, because I was the only one in there who had the sense to dress properly. I was without question the most hygienically clean person there. And to guarantee that I was the new golden boy around here, I brought a resume. It didn't have much on it—my educational status; scenes from the two plays I did the previous year in drama class, plus the declaration that I wanted to do TV commercials and eventually get speaking parts in movies. But looking around the room, I clearly had more experience than these dirt bags lying all over the floor.

And that's how naive I was. I didn't even have the sense to realize that these hippies were there because they were being seen for roles as... what else? Hippies! A movie was being cast which required street, park, and restaurant scenes to be filled with hippies. And within a week, I'd be working with them.

"Bruce Neckels!" The receptionist called out. Once again, I tiptoed over this carpet of human sleaze and into the main office. I was led into a small conference room.

"Ann will be with you in a few minutes," I was told.... again.

So I sat down in front of this empty desk and waited. Within a minute this lovely looking woman with white hair came bursting into the room. I stood as she introduced herself. She was British, and had the most beautiful accent. She carried herself like a queen and I could tell instantly that she deserved the respect of one.

"Hello, I'm Ann Brebner. Sit down." This lady was in a hurry. "What can I do for you?" She asked. I handed her my resume and told her exactly what it said: that I was majoring in Radio-TV, minoring in drama, and that I wanted to do TV commercials and speaking parts. It took her all of five seconds to glance through my resume.

"You don't have enough experience, yet. Call me on Monday, after four o'clock."

And with that, she got up and walked out of the room. What the fuck was it with people leaving me sitting alone in a room? At least she didn't turn out the lights the way Dr. Hough did.

I called her on Monday, at one minute after four. "Call me tomorrow," she said and hung up. Jesus! Was she in a hurry or just testing my determination? I called the next day and to my sheer joy was told to report to the Travel Lodge at the Wharf Wednesday morning at 7:00 a.m. My film career was about to begin.

I was an army private... I couldn't believe it. My first role as an extra, and they put me in an army uniform. A whole bus load of extras were driven to Golden Gate Park, to be in a scene being filmed at the Japanese Tea Gardens. The movie was "Petulia," starring George C. Scott and Julie Christie. Weird how the mind works. I can't remember what I had for lunch last Tuesday, but I remember being paired up with another extra also wearing an army uniform. His name was Alan

Gidly. He had a thick Australian accent. A real character—very funny guy. He was killed in a car accident several years later. But it was such a rush that day—seeing Scott in person; the lights; the 35mm. Panavision camera. For a brief moment, I forgot about the scary fact that in two months, I would be graduating from College, and that my draft status would be "I-A" - eligible to be drafted into the armed services. This army uniform I was wearing could become all too real. Not to mention that my anti-war sentiments had been kicked up another notch by the fact that I'd attended the "Human Be-In" at Golden Gate Park on January 14, 1967.It was the first time the mass media really began to take notice of the hippie counter-culture opposing the Vietnam War. I had gone with my new room-mate Sig Vandenberg, very conservative, but who did have a curious mind. On a lark we decided what the hell—let's go experience this event.

And it was great. Thousands of people showed up to hear music from The Grateful Dead, Jefferson Airplane, Quicksilver Messenger Service. Poet Allen Ginsberg was there; comedian Dick Gregory – all 96 pounds of him. He was on a hunger strike. And we stood 20 feet away from the stage and watched an older "hippie" named Timothy Leary, utter those immortal words, "Tune in, turn on, and drop out.". They were serving up free food and free LSD—I wasn't ready for the LSD yet. Little did Sig and I realize, but we had helped break in the new year for what was forever to be known as "The Summer of Love." A few months later down the coast came one of the greatest musical events ever—The Monterey Pop Jazz Festival, and the emergence of Jimi Hendrix, Janis Joplin and Big Brother, Otis Redding, and The Mamas and the Papas. M&P, who along with record producer Lou Adler, produced the event. Any musician, who was somebody, either performed or was on the festival board—I believe the Beatles and the Beach Boys also helped put it on. Then a couple of months later came the Beatles release of Sgt. Peppers Lonely Hearts Club Band, and the "Summer of Love" had hit its apex.[4]

This might have been from 1968

Not sure of year - 1966, 1967

There I am – top left, with a grey circle drawn around me.
When I brought the photo in tight, no doubt it was me.

Chapter Eight
June 2, 1967...

T his was not a good time to be graduating from college. Every draft board was on top of the situation, and I-A eligibility status reports were flying through the U.S. Postal Service like cheap ad mailers. I wasn't out of school a week when mine came. You see, we were running way behind schedule winning the Vietnam conflict. In less than four years, we had major setbacks—the most important, of course – 15,000 young men had come home in body bags. We had over half a million young men in Vietnam, and in America, demonstrations were ramping up. In 1967, 70,000 people marched down Fifth Avenue in New York, in support of our troops in Vietnam. Martin Luther King countered with his anti-Vietnam war march in New York. In San Francisco, another protest march took place down Market Street. And 50,000 demonstrated against the war at Lincoln Memorial in Washington, D.C.. The protest lines between the "hawks" and the "doves" were no longer so clear-cut. Now there were businessmen, politicians, teachers, and clean-cut mothers, walking alongside hippies. Many of these mothers had already buried their dead sons, and even more mothers did not want to go down that same road. There were too many scared and angry Americans who did not like what they were seeing as they ate dinner every night while watching their first ever televised war on the evening news. Yet less than one percent of them even had a clue why we were there, and what we hoped to gain. Including me. However, I was now starting to pay damn close attention.

Yet the thought of becoming a conscientious objector to the war still hadn't entered my mind. The two options I considered within my realm of do-ability were to continue going to college and getting a Master's Degree, or joining a National Guard or Army Reserve unit. Well, forget the latter. A few phone calls and I soon learned that everybody from 17 - 25 years of age had the same idea in mind, and Reserve/Guard units everywhere had at least a six month waiting list. I made an appointment with my draft board in Merced to appeal my I-A status. I remember the meeting lasted a few minutes and weeks later, was granted another "stay." College was no longer a place to acquire an education for a good paying career. It was a fucking sanctuary.

I spent that summer in San Francisco, glued to my television watching fires and rioting in Detroit. Two African Americans who'd returned home from Vietnam were given a welcome back party in some joint in the black district. The cops busted in, got rough, and all hell broke loose. By the time it was over, 43 people lay dead; 1,189 injured, and over 7,000 arrested.[5]Welcome home, boys! It was bad enough to have been pawns in a war thousands of miles away. But to come back and be used as an excuse to expose police brutality and poverty, to remind LBJ that his idea of a "Great Society" had failed!?Not only was Johnson escalating war in Vietnam, he was now sending thousands of troops into Detroit. This whole situation symbolized how so many blacks from places like Detroit and other inner cities, made up a huge number of kids dying in Vietnam. And for what? To come home to this? It seemed as though this country was coming apart. I'd earned my Bachelor of Arts Degree in Radio-TV-Film, but had no intention of becoming a radio operator in the jungles of Vietnam. And even though I wasn't aware of it, getting drafted in the summer of 1967 would have put me in Fort Ord Army Training Base in time to finish basic at the end of the year. The downside to being a college graduate? I could be made a 1st Lieutenant, and with more bad luck, be assigned to a unit heading for Vietnam—just in time for the January, 1968 Tet Offensive. The life expectancy of a 1st Lieutenant in Vietnam, from what I heard and what I can't verify, was approximately 22 minutes. I could be dead within one year.

But what really scared the shit out of me happened just a couple of days after the Tet Offensive began. It became known as "The Shot Seen 'Round the World." On February1, 1968, General Nguyen Ngoc Loan, a South Vietnamese chief of the national police force, had just found out that Viet Cong guerillas murdered one of his officers, the officer's wife and their six children. A young man suspected of being a Viet Cong officer was captured and brought before Loan. In front of an NBC news team and AP photographer, Eddie Adams, with no questions asked, Loan put his pistol up against the prisoner's head and fired a bullet point blank into his temple. To watch that kid hit the ground and see a stream of blood pouring out of that hole in his head is a visual I'll never forget.[6]

It was time to do some serious reading about this place called Vietnam.

Anti-war Demonstration - New York...

Washington D.C.

San Francisco

Eddie Adams photo

Chapter Nine
Vietnam 101

S ince this is not intended to be a history lesson on Vietnam, I won't delve too deeply. That's not to discredit author Hal Dareff, whose book, "The Story of Vietnam" I'll be using as my main reference. Mr. Dareff wrote a wonderful, concise book, which I've owned in paperback form since 1967, never intending to use it in a book of my own. And if you were to see the condition of it today, it is browned out, worn out, tattered, and in two pieces. So....

Vietnam, originally known as "Nam-Viet," had fought for its independence thousands of years before Christ. Their main foe was China, and victories were scarce. It was the local lords—ergo, small armies—fighting the central government—always a mismatch. And even when the Vietnamese managed to drive China out, the victory was short lived—couple of years tops. China would then come back, kick their ass, and reclaim the title. The ruling leader of Vietnam would lose his head, or in the case of the ruling Trung sisters, Trung Trac and Trung Nhi - commit suicide out of shame. This was in 42 A.D. and to this day the sisters are as honored as France's Joan of Arc.

I worked my way through the 8th Century when the Vietnamese aristocrats finally had an epiphany and realized they needed the support of all the people, including peasants, who never took part in the battles. It was time to stop treating them like slaves, and fight for freedom with a vested interest. So lord and peasant fought together side by side. They didn't care if they had to fight for a thousand years to make it happen - something worth remembering once I started making my split-page good points-bad points analysis about going to Vietnam.

In the 10th Century, Vietnamese peasants finally toppled China's ruthless Tang Dynasty. But the peasants didn't really have time to enjoy it because a united Vietnamese army was ready for a civil war, and for the next two hundred years, the Trinh family of the North, fought the Nguyen (pronounced "nuhWin") family in the south. The

Nguyens were mightier and always won because they fought on their own turf. And to make things a little tougher on the Trinh's, the Nguyens built two giant walls amidst the brutal terrain. These walls are close to the 17th parallel, which separated the North from the South until 1976.

By the end of the 15th Century, Portuguese explorer Vasco da Gama discovered the Asian continent, and for a brief moment Portugal was the only beneficiary to the rich trade. But soon all of Europe would follow: Spain, the Dutch, England, France, and thus began the division of North and South Vietnam by outside European forces. By the mid 17th Century, the Catholic missionaries made their entrance, most notably, Monsignor Alexander of Rhodes in 1636. Within two years, he converted 7,000 Vietnamese into Catholics. Vietnamese rulers saw the potential threat to their own ways of worship, and Rhodes was exiled.

A century later, in 1767, along came cleric Behaine. Only now, the Trinhs and Nguyens were involved in a war against a joint venture of peasants and merchants, called the Tay Son Rebellion. They wiped out the Nguyens first, except for a 15 year-old prince, Nguyen Phúc Áhn. Behaine, now a Bishop, gave Ahn sanctuary. After a year of hiding, Ahn formed an army of peasants and Chinese pirates, and under the tutelage of Behaine, retook several provinces, and Saigon. Ahn ruled as king of Cochinchina (Vietnam) for four years, but the Tay Son regrouped, came back and kicked his ass. Behaine went to France, and secured a treaty of alliance between the two countries. Cochinchina would get soldiers, arms and supplies; France would get territories and trading rights. But unbeknownst to Behaine, the French foreign minister rethought expansion into Asia, and didn't hold up his end of the bargain. So Behaine raised money from French merchants, supplied his troops with arms and was able to drive back the Tay Son. Ten years later, with complete victory still three years away, Behaine died, having never converted Ahn to Christianity, nor seen Cochinchina's first emperor, a Catholic. Ahn became the emperor, changed his name to "Gia Long," and gave his country back its ancient name, Vietnam.

During his reign, Ahn stayed friendly with the French, and put up with the Catholics. But his successor, Minh Mang, was not so nice a guy. Europe was getting much more aggressive, and the Catholics were the modern day version of Jehovah's Witnesses, knocking on way too many Vietnamese doors, looking for more converts. This brought conflict between Vietnam and France. In 1833, Mang executed his first Catholic missionary, and soon, more were to follow. The Opium War between England and China in 1839 didn't help France keep exclusivity of Vietnam. Other countries started eating up China like jackals on carrion. Minh Mang was keeping tabs, and didn't like what he was seeing. Now Vietnam was in danger of European colonization. Mang sent envoys to France to justify his years of missionary persecution, as fear rather than cruelty. But Catholics weren't ready to forgive – a very un-Christian-like stance – so negotiations didn't even get off the ground.

Ming Manh died in 1841. In the years to follow, other Vietnam rulers kept the anti-Catholic sentiment going. Finally, sixteen years later, after the Crimean War ended, Louis-Napoleon III was the ear that French Catholics and Vietnamese missionaries could bend. It was time to send the boys to Vietnam. Redemption was one thing, but everyone else on the planet seemed to have possessions in the East. And with no one to buy France's huge factory surpluses, it was just good business—something the United States merchants would realize 120 years later, in a horrible display of calloused greed. So the French navy, with the help of Spain, whose missionaries had also been persecuted by the Vietnamese, went in and bombed the hell out of The Bay of Tourane. And one day later, they moved in with ground forces, and France finally had a piece of the rock.[7]

However, acquiring something is one thing. Keeping it and acquiring more, is another ball game. And so the French found out. It was bad enough that the jungles, rugged terrain, bad weather, and disease—killed more soldiers than enemy fire. But there was hostility amongst the ranks. Who was in charge around here, anyway? The church or the state? The state won the argument, went in and took Saigon. Things looked good for a while, until French troops left back in Tourane started dying from Typhus and Cholera. Attempts to get reinforcements failed because Napoleon decided to declare war against Austria and couldn't spare a man. The French were now so busy defending the territory they already had, that they didn't have time to acquire new property. However, two years later, in 1861, like Phoenix rising from the ashes, France got it together and went back to Vietnam with massive troops and controlled all of Vietnam. But now they faced a new enemy: peasant guerilla, and another war on the home front.

With Otto Von Bismarck snookering Napoleon III into the Franco Prussian War in August of 1870 - then the siege on Paris in 1871-Paris surrendered. France had given Prussia their border region of Alsace-Lorraine, and they wanted it back. Who could blame them? That's premium wine country. The hell with Vietnam or any Asian colonization. Admiral Dupré, governor at the time in Vietnam, was on his own. And that was fine with him. He wanted control of the north. It took a quarter of a century, long after Dupre had resigned from his post, but France finally had all of Vietnam. They erased all of Vietnam's identity, renaming the country French Indochina. And though it looked real good on paper, governing "French Indochina" was almost impossible. The peasants and the mandarins combined their hatred, and guerilla resistance was on. The French burned villages and committed mass slaughtering. No matter what territory they controlled, they had no friends, no one they could trust. Sound familiar?

This went on for twelve years. The 20th century was three years away, and it was time to modernize this country from the ground up. This meant doing away with ancient customs, old Confucian teachings, social infrastructure—to a complete overhaul of old government. No more royal families. French schools were built. Vietnamese studied reading, writing, medicine, law, and science. Many learned to speak French so they could work for the French civil service. Those Vietnamese who went to France to study, learned about western civilization. But what these young kids were witnessing, was how "civilized" the French were in their own country compared to Vietnam. Seeing this liberty and equality was dangerous. They wanted to try it out in their own country. But not while the French were there. In spite of all the improvements they made—building roads, railroads, dams, and irrigation; making Indochina number three in the world in exporting rice; exportation of tea, coal, zinc—the Vietnamese still found themselves no more than second-class citizens. To compound matters, the Chinese were moving in and establishing themselves as merchants, traders, and bankers. The Mandarins cooperated with the French to gain whatever monetary foothold they could. And every time France needed capital for a new venture, who got hit the hardest with taxes? The peasants. And they were getting sick of it.So they worked for the French by day, while planting seeds for a new revolution at night.

We're now in the 1900's. Mini-revolts had been taking place all along by Vietnamese nationalists steeped in old traditions. Years later, in 1925, a new breed leader named Nguyen Thai Hoc formed the Nationalist Party of Vietnam - the VNQDD. It was divided up into a public unit and an underground unit. Most of the members were military men. Things were looking good until 1929, when a Frenchman was murdered and the VNQDD was suspected. Nguyen Thai Hoc panicked, thinking his secret underground unit would be busted. So he called for an uprising, which included his military garrison of Yen Bay, on the Chinese border. Originally scheduled to take place on February 10, 1930, Hoc called an audible and changed it to February 15. Well, horror of horrors, the Yen Bay Boys didn't pick up the signal, and attacked on the 10th. Guess what? They lost, and the VNQDD became history. So did Nguyen Thai Hoc. He and a dozen of his officers were introduced to the French Revolution's favorite toy, the guillotine. Whoever was left, fled to China, hoping to rebuild the party. It never happened, which proves the old adage that sometimes what you don't get can be a blessing. Because what happened instead was the birth of the Indo-Chinese Communist Party, and the emergence of a man who would lead them against France: Born Nguyen Sinh Cung, he took on several aliases: Nguyen Tat Thanh, Nguyen Ai Quoc, Bac Ho, or Bac for short. The world would soon come to know him forever as Ho Chi Minh.[8]

Chapter Ten
Ho Chi, communism, and Dienbienphu

The remainder of 1967 went by in a haze. I had moved just below Twin Peaks, to an area called Diamond Heights. I started graduate studies in September, and I hated it. Dr. Hough made me his research assistant, and in less than a month we both knew my heart wasn't in it. I wanted to pursue acting. There was only one reason I was even in school: that stinking war. I'd learned four very important facts in my Vietnam studies: The Viet Cong will never give up; Vietnam's landscape is comprised of rugged terrain, mountains and dense jungle; we were not nearly prepared to fight the Vietnamese style of guerilla warfare; a man is as likely to die from disease as a bullet; the Vietnamese were friends by day, and enemies by night. Now that all scared me. Graduate school, here I stay. As for Ho Chi Minh, our involvement with him began during World War II.

With Germany blitzkrieging all through France, French colonialism in Indochina was set to fall. Japan walked in and took over. France was allowed to keep their guns and fight off any rebellions. Ho Chi Minh found himself fighting two countries. He formed the League for Vietnamese Independence, or, Vietminh. That's when he gave himself the name that stuck... Ho Chi Minh. It means, "Ho, who enlightens." Cool, but he still needed help fighting France and Japan. First stop, China. Bad idea. Years earlier, he'd been imprisoned by the British in Hong Kong for forming the Indo-Chinese Communist Party. And this time it was Chiang Kai-shek and his Chinese Nationalists who didn't trust him. Mr. Enlightens was thrown in prison again. After one year of incarceration, America's OSS stepped in and convinced China they could all use this guy to fight Japan. Ho's Vietminh were assisting downed U.S. Pilots and gathering intelligence information. China complied, and Ho went back to Vietnam. Once home, he let America know he'd continue helping them against Japan, but it would cost them. He wanted arms and ammunition. After much letter writing to the White House, he got what he wanted. Ho's objective was ultimately to have enough firepower to continue his fight with France, hopefully with America's support, after the war with Japan was over. But for now, America and Ho Chi Minh were allies. What could possibly go wrong? Answer... The "C" word.[9]

World War II was over. America became the new power of the planet. We were smug, arrogant, proud, and we loved it. Not even a Robert Wise-directed movie, "The Day the Earth Stood Still," was able to drive the message home that we were now messing with a "rudimentary" form of atomic energy. Klato and his robot, Gort, traveled millions of miles and called the leaders of the world to meet in one place so he could address them. And with an eerie forecasting of things to come, an American politician spoke for the rest of the world and informed Klato that we were too screwed up to even travel a few thousand miles to hear his state-of-Earth address. So Klato addressed some world-renowned scientists, threatening to reduce our planet to a cinder if we threatened the rest of the universe.[10]And off they went, leaving us to destroy our own metaphor. Which we did. Though Klato's message was good, his timing was bad. America was the universe. And the threat was from a planet called Russia, Red China, or whatever other country harbored communism. But it wasn't communism abroad that hurt the American people. It was a no good scumbag who got tired of lobbying for Wisconsin's cheese industry, and wanted his name in lights. His name was Joseph Raymond "Joe" McCarthy. And with his communist witch hunts conducted in the early 1950's, Joe ruined more lives and careers than a corporate audit, and far more than Communism itself has done to this country in sixty-five years. The most famous were the "Hollywood Ten" - writers and directors who went from riches to rags. I was to meet one of those blacklisted writers seventeen years later, and his book would help change my life.

With Japan out of Vietnam, Ho Chi Minh became the new president. But France was like the guests in Edward Albee's "Delicate Balance." They just didn't want to leave. And with the help of the British, France declared martial law in South Vietnam. Fighting erupted in 1946 between the French and Ho Chi Minh's Vietminh. And with Mao Tse Tung and the Chinese Communists defeating

Chiang Kai-shek nationalist armies for ownership of China, the United States had no choice but to back the French in Vietnam. Communism.... remember? Too bad for Ho, who had been so valuable in assisting the U.S. against the Japanese. He was a communist, though he'd disbanded it in favor of nationalism. But with Mao on his border, America sent money and weapons to the French. Thus began our indirect involvement in Vietnam.

Despite our efforts to assist, America watched Vietminh General Vo Nguyen Giap take down one French fort after another. France then threw it's final bankroll on the table by bringing in their top General, Henri Navarre, who had a master plan: Build a fortress in the middle of a big valley, surrounded by mountains and jungle, but with a lot of wide open space below. This patch of space was called Dienbienphu. Navarre knew there was no way Ho and Vo could bring artillery through all the rough terrain. He wanted to lure them into attacking so he could mow them down. But while Navarre was amassing troops, Giap was doing the impossible. His troops were cutting and hacking their way through the mountains and jungles, creating a road for all their canons, food, and ammunition. Though Navarre knew Giap was on his way, he kept his eyes on the wide-open plain, twelve miles long, four miles wide. But Giap surrounded the fortress from high above and on March 13, 1954, let it all hang out. Day and night, for fifty-four days, he bombed Dienbienphu, until the noise of the explosions alone drove the French soldiers insane. At the same time, Giap sent wave after wave of infantry – 40,000 soldiers against 11,000 French. French planes couldn't penetrate all the anti-aircraft guns Giap had positioned. France asked America for air support, but "Mr. D-Day," Dwight Eisenhower, refused. We'd given France enough and watched them piss it away. Fifty-five days later, the bombing stopped, and France was history. Dienbienphu spelled the end of any hopes for an empire. Ho Chi, backed by Red China, sent France to the Geneva Convention in total humiliation. They so badly had wanted to come in a winner, their heads held high in victory. There were to be no terms of conditions for Vietminh surrender. It was a clear-cut victory.[11]Up next - the United States.

Ho Chi Minh

General Vo Nguyen Giap

Chapter Eleven
The dawning of Aquarius…and Michelangelo Antonioni

How I got through my first semester of Graduate Work is a mystery. I don't even remember what courses I took. But we were now into 1968 and the first quarter of the year got off to a miserable start. I was still working as Dr. Hough's assistant. But we both knew I wasn't happy. "You want to be an actor, Neckels. So get out of here. Go act." I didn't argue. I couldn't take college anymore and threw in the towel. I began studying with other acting teachers; started doing community theater; kept my graveyard shift at Wells Fargo; did a lot of extra work... and just... waited. In April, Martin Luther King was assassinated, taking away the most shining ray of hope in the history of civil rights, not to mention he spoke out against the Vietnam War. Riots ensued in major cities across the United States. It just all seemed so fucking hopeless - first John Kennedy, now Martin... What else could go wrong? But later that month, I thought I'd caught a ray of hope when I slammed my right arm against a basketball pole. I couldn't straighten it without feeling as though a pair of scissors were cutting through the tendons. Did I say "ray of hope?" Well... yeah.... This injury, which had me taking cortisone shots, just might reclassify me as 4-f and keep me out of the military. Within three months, I'd be able to straighten it and be mobile. But I was in constant pain. I couldn't even rest that elbow against a soft pillow.

By summer, I was all settled in my apartment on Capp Street in the Mission District - my fourth move in two years. The Mission had a personality all its own. And it was the warm belt of San Francisco. I was still working the graveyard shift at Wells Fargo and managed to save enough money to actually supplement a furnished apartment with two pieces of my own: a color TV set, and a Sears Silvertone console stereo. That was my version of "cool." I still wasn't hip enough for components. And the first record I played on my new stereo? Nothing by the Stones, Dylan, The Beatles, Airplane, or Steve Miller. No, I played "To Sir With Love," by Lulu. The current rock-psychedelic sounds were not leading me to any "hell no we won't go" attitude against my country just yet. But I was getting closer. And what really hit home happened in August.

I went to the Greyhound Bus Depot to pick up Terry, my new roommate and very best friend since elementary school in Merced. He had graduated from Fresno State College, did two years of graduate work, and was here to enter the Hastings School of Law. After we shook hands and said our hellos, these were the first words out of his mouth:

"John Martin died in Vietnam."

We had known John since elementary school. He was a very bright, popular guy. Senior Class President, varsity football, wrestling team, and class valedictorian—John seemed most likely to succeed. And now he was dead. He didn't die a hero. He died in a hospital bed in Vietnam, of malaria. The doctors gave him a penicillin shot, which he was allergic to, and he died. Never saw one second of combat. And the horrible tragedy of it all was that he was the only surviving son. His father was ex-military. That meant John didn't even have to enter the service. And he wasn't drafted. He joined! From what I understand, he felt it was his duty to serve.

I wasn't ready to question that yet. But from this, I could finally admit aloud, that I did not want to go to Vietnam. National sentiment was peaking, and I knew I wasn't alone. Very few people wanted to go, but they did. Likewise, many who were protesting against the war; would never have to go, and would never be tested with an ultimate decision. I was finally asking myself ... what would I do?

And poor Lyndon Johnson. Here's a guy who could have gone down as one of the greatest presidents in American history because of his stand on civil rights, but for that stinking war.

I was doing a lot of extra work and meeting new friends. A few were those hippy types, but I was getting used to them. In fact, I was starting to feel like the oddball, the one with the short hair, the straight-leg pants - especially when I started attending rock concerts at Bill Graham's Filmore West - perfect entertainment when you're living on a small budget. I mean, come on, where else could you see the Jefferson Airplane and Grateful Dead; Big Brother (Janis Joplin) and Pink Floyd; or Jimi Hendrix and John Mayall on the same billing for $3.50?

Still, I wasn't ready to get a pair of bell-bottoms just yet—although I did put on a navy uniform a month back when I was a film extra in a movie called "The Graduate." I hadn't reached the stage of refusing to wear a military uniform - even as a costume - because of what it stood for. But I remained on the sidelines hoping public sentiment would stop the war, or that Robert Kennedy would get us out of Vietnam. Richard Nixon had thrown his hat into the ring as the Republican presidential nominee. Johnson could've run again, but the war had taken its toll on him. And when Walter Cronkite went on the air one night and declared that the Vietnam War was hopeless and that we should get out, Johnson had lost an important news ally, which for all intent and purpose, lost him the war. But the most pathetic Johnson moment was a photo of him hunched over a table, head pressed against a tightened fist, as he listened to a tape recording of his son-in-law, a Captain in Vietnam, grieving over the losses of dead soldiers under his command. Johnson bowed out and Kennedy stepped in. Hallelujah! Little did we all know how quickly euphoria would nose-dive into a sea of tragedy in 1968. Bobby was assassinated, and with his death went the final breath of hope for peace.

But it was during the summer of that year when I experienced a tremendous growth spurt as an actor that opened my eyes to revolutionary times in America. It had to do with my very first movie. I'd been going out on a lot of commercial calls, but I still hadn't landed anything. Probably because I wasn't a Screen Actors Guild member, and my lack of on-camera experience was undoubtedly considered. It was frustrating because one day's work as a principle endorsing a product could result in thousands of dollars of residuals. A good national spot could run for one to three years. And so I got a call to audition for a beer commercial. It was to be a two-day location shoot at Pismo Beach. My first interview resulted in what's known as a "call-back." They were considering me. Then came a second callback. They were looking for ten principals and whittled it down to sixteen of us. And when they announced the ten, I wasn't one of them.

All of my best friends in the agency were. So as they headed out of town together having a ball and about to make thousands - I was sulking-mood pissed. But not getting that commercial changed my life.

While my friends were on their way to Pismo Beach, I was walking into my apartment carrying a bag of groceries. The phone was ringing. I answered. It was Ann Brebner, my agent. "You have an interview this afternoon at two o'clock. You'll meet the director. His name is Michelangelo Antonioni. He's doing his first American movie and right now is just looking at faces."

Antonioni!!?? He was one of the most famous directors on the planet! I'd studied him in my film class. Okay, so he put me to sleep with "L'Avventura" and "La Notte," but that was due in large part to working graveyard shift, then having my film class at 9:00 a.m. I was falling asleep anyway. And now I was going to meet him. And do you think I was the least bit nervous or impressed? No! Why? Because I was still sulking about not getting that fucking beer commercial! I looked at my watch. It was already close to two p.m. I didn't even have time to comb my hair so that it looked exactly perfect - And for me to not care how my hair looked for an interview, you know I was mad. I was wearing boots, jeans, a white t-shirt and a thin, red, zip-up jacket. Screw it. I didn't care anyway.

Ann called me from the waiting room and took me into the room where Mr. Antonioni, MGM's Executive Producer, Harrison Star, and his production assistant, Sally Dennison, were waiting. She introduced me and I sat down. I was still upset about that goddamn beer commercial. And it showed in the way I sat in my chair - not straight up - but almost leaning against it with my legs stretched out, and my arms folded. Antonioni was staring a hole right through me. Finally, in very broken English, he spoke.

"Tell me about yourself, Bruce."

Okay... well, I told him I'd just graduated from college with a degree in R-TV broadcasting and a minor in drama, but that I wanted a career as an actor.

"Have you been in any films?"

Only as an extra... and I wanted to say, "And I just missed out getting a beer commercial!" But I didn't.

"What kind of actor do you want to be, Bruce?"

"Well," I replied, "I don't want to be pigeon-holed into any one style or similar character. I want to do a variety of characters. I want to work with accents; play characters from other parts of the world... I don't want to be John Wayne."

And that was it. That was my interview. Antonioni thanked me - said he was just looking at faces. I wished him luck with his movie, said good-bye to the others, and went home. By the end of the day, Ann called me. "Antonioni is very interested in you. He's going back to L.A. tonight, but he wants to see you again in August."

I was stunned. Why was he interested? Because in that brief time, he saw who I really was at that moment - a young guy on the edge, who didn't want to be labeled. He saw a rebel in me. I wasn't some smiling, glad-handing-wanting-to-please actor ready to say anything to get a role. I was mad, and I didn't give a shit. And my attitude was what he was looking for. And all because of that beer commercial I didn't get.

Michelangelo Antonioni

Chapter Twelve
Comedy of Errors - A Shakespearian Tragedy

Augustus was two months away. I passed my time in San Rafael, rehearsing for the upcoming Marin Shakespeare Festival. Ann was the executive producer, and it was important to me that she see me as a serious actor, not just somebody out to get his face on screen. Truth be told, I didn't even have the balls to audition that spring because the quality of the auditions were so outstanding that, being a novice, I didn't want to embarrass myself. So after I watched a wonderful actor named Gail Chugg, do the "Gatekeeper" scene from Macbeth as his audition, I went home. I wasn't ready. But later that night, I received a phone call from the festival's artistic director, Dan Caldwell. I'd been studying with Dan at the California Actor's Lab for the past several months. In fact, it was Dan who had told me to come audition, and now he wanted to know why the hell I didn't show up. I told him why, but he refused to let me off the hook. He gave me a small role as the "Comic Servant" in Comedy of Errors. Yes, it was a comedy, but the play was filled with the most overwhelming tragedy that no one in the cast could have imagined.

The play is about two masters; twins named Antipholus, separated at birth, along with two attendants named Dromio, also twins: One master with one attendant. Antipholus of Syracuse sets off in search of his brother and mother, taking Dromio with him. They end up in Ephesus, unaware that his twin brother and twin attendant are living there. And all hell breaks loose- the wrong master with the wrong slave; the wrong mistress with the wrong master; etc. Playing the role of the Antipholus twins was a wonderful actor named Bob Feero. In the role of the Dromios, were actual identical twins, Richard and Paul Willis.

Everything was going smoothly. I created a hell of a scene with my comic servant role. And I was getting used to being around actors who were... "hippies." Crazy clothes, long hair, free-spirited, pot-smoking, psychedelic music - everything I had once scorned.

One Saturday morning about 7 a.m. - a week before opening night - my phone rang. There was an angry voice at the other end. It was Bob Feero. Mind you, at this time, I hadn't really spoken with him that much. In fact, I don't think he really liked me.

"Neckels, this is Bob Feero. Richard Willis was killed in a car wreck last night. Danny wants you to start learning both Dromio roles, because Paul may leave the show. "He hung up.

I stood there in absolute shock. My guts were churning; the adrenaline was pumping so fast, I couldn't even think. I don't even remember how I made that 17-mile drive to the Forest Meadows outdoor theatre in San Rafael. But when I got there, actors were sitting in the bench rows in front of the moat and stage. The morning was overcast. It was so quiet. All I could hear was the sound of the wind cutting through the high branches of the pine and Eucalyptus trees that filled the park. Ann Brebner was there huddled with Dan, deciding whether or not to cancel the show. Do we open and have it all fall on my shoulders? Dan then made the announcement that the show would open, "and Bruce Neckels will play both Dromios." Dan had so much confidence in me. He'd worked with me in the lab; he knew I had a good imagination; and he knew I was a quick study. But two roles in Shakespeare, with one week to prepare? This was insane.

And I felt like such an intruder - like I was invading someone's space. An unwanted guest who couldn't be asked to leave the party. Nobody said anything. We just went to work, people crying on stage. I'll always remember my very first entrance at that rehearsal. Hope Alexander, one of the greatest actresses I've ever worked with, was on stage as "Adriana. "She had just finished her first scene with "Luciana," sister to Adriana. Next entrance, Dromio, of Ephesus, the role Richard had played.

Adriana: Say, is your tardy master now at hand?

Dromio E.: Nay he is at two hands with me, and that my two ears can witness. " (Shakespeare. Act II, Sc. I)

That's all I needed to say. I looked at Hope and tears were rolling down her cheeks. And that's how it was for the rest of the day - doing scenes with Bob and feeling his anger at the loss of his friend, having to face me.

But it came together. Paul returned, and the two of us did the roles together. My back was to the audience whenever both Dromios were on stage at the same time. I even learned to imitate the pitch of Paul's voice so that we sounded the same. I gained the respect of Ann Brebner, who saw how serious I was about wanting to be an actor. And I gained many friendships and respect from my fellow actors. In fact, I even started to dress like them. My first pair of bell-bottoms were a deep burgundy corduroy; my first "hippie" style shirt was a light purple with tiny print flowers; and I bought a pair of Frye square-toed boots. My hair was short by comparison, but longer than I had ever dared let it grow. I bought a pair of rose-colored glasses. Glasses that in one more year, would prompt an FBI agent to think he was being real clever by saying, "You're looking at the world through rose-colored glasses, Neckels." I can say that my transformation from being straight to "conservative" hippie, changed in the summer of 1968. And during the final weeks of the play, Ann Brebner received another call from Michelangelo Antonioni. He wanted to see me in Los Angeles... At MGM. Through a fictional movie, based on the realities of what was happening in America with civil unrest and the anti-war movement, I was one step closer to changing my whole philosophy about the meaning of patriotism, which I had previously defined as "My country, right or wrong."

Chapter Thirteen
MGM - My Golden Moment

I'd only been on an airplane once in my life, and that was a PSA flight to Burbank from San Francisco a year earlier when I went to Disneyland with two of my work associates from Wells Fargo. But that trip to Los Angeles and MGM was the most exciting flight I've ever taken to this day. According to Ann, Michelangelo was considering me for a small role as a uniformed cop. I didn't care. I had a chance to work with one of the world's greatest directors.

Walking into the foyer of MGM gave me goose bumps. Seeing the Oscar of "Ben Hur" showcased on a revolving pedestal, pictures of Charleton Heston, William Boyd and I don't remember who else. It all sent my expectations soaring, and I was nervous as hell. The man at the info desk directed me to the building where "Zabriskie Point" had their production offices. I walked in, introduced myself to the receptionist and was told to have a seat. It was just me. No other actors hoping to get a job were in that room. After a few minutes, the production assistant, Sally Dennison, came out. Sweet lady. She told me Michelangelo would talk to me soon. He was in a meeting with Kodak reps discussing color. I asked if there was a script I could read, and she said Mr. Antonioni would have something for me once I got inside, but as far as she knew, he just wanted to take another look at me.

So I waited... And I waited... And I waited some more. For an hour and a half I waited, interspersed by Sally coming out every 20 minutes and apologizing. Finally, the door to Mr. Antonioni's office opened and out he came with Sally, Harrison Star, and two guys from Kodak. He looked at me and came right over.

"Bruce..." he said in broken English, "I'm so sorry... the meeting was long."

Sally stepped in.

"Michelangelo, do you want to see Bruce in your office now?"

He looked at me for all of two seconds.

"No, he's fine."

"You don't need him to read for you?" Sally asked.

"No, he's fine."

Sally seemed as taken aback as I was.

"Which role? The cop?" She asked.

"No... For Bill."

Michelangelo then shook hands with me and told me again he was sorry he couldn't talk longer but that he had to catch a flight to Italy. He instructed Sally to give me a script, then left. I looked at Sally.

"Who's Bill?" I asked.

"The lead's roommate."

My stomach was turning cartwheels. Sally handed me the script, congratulated me, and told me my agent   contacted. The receptionist called a cab for me, and I was on my way back to the airport, script in hand. I barely sat down in the cab and opened the script. Some guy named Mark Fretchett was the lead; Daria Halprin, his girlfriend; then Rod Taylor ("Time Machine," Hitchcock's "The Birds"); and I was either fourth or fifth lead. I couldn't believe it. Thumbing through the script, I saw that I was in the first quarter of the film. The rest of the movie was in Arizona with Mark, Daria, and Rod. But I had several lines. I felt like an upcoming star!

I arrived at LAX early, so went to the cafe counter to grab a coke. There, slouched over a cup of coffee, wearing a long trench coat, was Jimmy Durante. Feeling like one of the gang, I walked up to him and introduced myself. I told him how much I'd enjoyed his work over the years.

"Thanks," he said, without looking up.

"I'm Bruce Neckels, sir. I just had an interview at MGM. I got a nice role in Michelangelo Antonioni's movie. It's called "Zabriskie Point.""

"Good luck, kid," said Mr. Durante, showing very little enthusiasm. I was now feeling like a fly buzzing around his coffee cup. So I left. (Durante, personal communication, August, 1968)

Once on the plane, I broke open the script and started reading. Again, the irony of who I was; how I felt about student protestors; civil unrest, and the Vietnam War - would force me to reconsider my way of thinking from a fictional, cinematic point of view. Little did I realize that this script in its' current form would only become a shell of itself ... that my favorite line in the film was a line I would give... But would never see the light of day.

Chapter Fourteen
"We've gotta find out what's happening."

That was my opening line on the first day of shooting—but not that "favorite" line I mentioned. Mark, Bill (me),and Morty (Bill Garaway), are in our apartment, listening to the radio. We're hearing about the demonstration taking place out on the streets. We want to be a part of it. I put on my watch, as I said:

"We've gotta find out what's happening."

Then the three of us hurry out of the room, and "Cut!" And that was it. We shot that scene at least a dozen times... and the line was cut out of the film! I'd been flown into Los Angeles the night before, put up in a motel somewhere in Culver City. The next day, I took a cab to MGM and from there taken to a location in a not-so-great part of East L.A. That's where I met the lead, Mark Frechette. He was tall, thin, and had piercing blue eyes. Looking very much the rebel, he played that role both behind and in front of the camera. The first thing Mark did when we met was invite me to his trailer where he offered me a hit off a joint. I had started smoking grass a year before, but I wasn't into "buying lids" or "twisting one up" just yet. And damned if I was going to get stoned before my first film job ever. I was nervous enough, but getting ripped wasn't the answer. I wanted to have a clear mind. But I figured it was probably a bonding thing with Mark, so I took a hit, pretending to inhale. Our bonding continued as Mark then picked up an 8x10 glossy photo of a young man, I'd say in his late 20's, early 30's. He handed it to me.

"Look at this and tell me what you see in his eyes."

I studied the photo for a few seconds. I saw megalomania. His expression was stoic; his eyes piercing, rather scary. I didn't have a good feeling about him, but given Mark's apparent reverie for this guy, I didn't want to rub him the wrong way before we shot our first scene together. I took the diplomatic route.

"Well, I see inner-peace, confidence" –

"Love... that's pure love." Said Mark, cutting me off.

Ohhhh-kayyyy... Love it is. Good thing I said "inner peace," and not "inner rage." Mark told me his name was Mel Lyman, but didn't give me any distinct selling points, other than to say he was a spiritual leader. Years later, I learned that Mel and his family of acolytes, appropriately named "The Mel Lyman Family," had their commune headquarters in the Fort Hill section of Roxbury, in Boston. Mel was a devotee of Timothy Leary and attended many a Boston LSD Party; ran a Boston underground newspaper called The Avatar; created a spin-off paper called American Avatar, in which Mel proclaimed himself to be what most self-styled gurus, cult leaders, and "avatars" of spiritual adolescence, claim to be: the embodiment of truth; the greatest man in the world, and the current Jesus Christ. But Mel added one more entity to his resume: an alien sent to Earth in human form by extraterrestrials. Before gurudom, Mel had also been a member of a Boston-based jug band. He was a great banjo player and a virtuoso harmonica player, having once performed a 10-minute impromptu version of Rock of Ages at the 1965 Newport Folk Festival. Apparently, when Mark first showed me Mel's picture, he had just become a member of "the Family." He'd been previously denied membership, but once he was selected as Antonioni's new star, and handed over nearly all his Zabriskie Point earnings, Mel welcomed him in with open arms. [12]

Stories vary as to how Mark was discovered for the lead in "Zabriskie Point". He had never acted before and worked as a carpenter in the Boston area. During a nationwide hunt for the role, a talent scout saw him screaming at a lady, then throwing a flowerpot at her. Another story has it that Mark was watching a sailor and a woman arguing, and intervened. Pushing and shoving ensued when the talent scout pulled Mark away and asked him how old he was. Mark answered; the scout dragged him into a limo, and yelled to a fellow companion, "He's 20 and he hates."[13]And finally, Mark claimed that while at a bus stop waiting for a bus, he was seen by two talent scouts, screaming at some guy looking out a third floor window of a building. Whichever story is true, that angry rebelliousness was what Antonioni had been seeking.

It took me a few hours on the set with Mark to see that I wasn't going to like him very much. He seemed to be more intent on causing trouble and being difficult. I remember a wardrobe lady handing him the shirt he was supposed to wear for the shoot, cautioning him to be careful because wardrobe didn't have a similar backup shirt.. So what did he do? He laid down in a driveway and got oil stains all over the shirt. It caused a delay while they had to find something else. Another time he left for ten days during filming because of script conflict and refused to come back until dialogue was re-written. I never felt he realized what an incredible thing had fallen in his lap – working with one of the world's most famous directors - and I disliked him for abusing the privilege. But this was only my take on him. I'm sure others liked him. I know Daria Halprin, the female lead, certainly did.

My first day of shooting was complete, and so I flew back to San Francisco. It was October, and I wouldn't work again until January or February—when all my major scenes would take place. So while Antonioni and crew headed off to film scenes at Zabriskie Point in Death Valley, California, and then on to Arizona – I went back to my graveyard shift job at Wells Fargo Bank. The supervisor wasn't very pleased that I'd been gone for three days. But a few days later, I got a call from my agent. The weather in Arizona had taken a turn for the worst, so cast and crew were back in Los Angeles. They wanted to do two scenes that included me. When I broke the news to Wells Fargo that I had to leave again, I was fired. They weren't even interested in my willingness to train someone else in my position for a couple of weeks. They wanted me out that night! I didn't care. I was starting a whole new life. Back I went to L.A.

The two scenes were with Mark and I walking into gun shops to arm ourselves with weapons... "for self- defense" We were a good half hour from filming, but I was over-anxious and couldn't just sit in my trailer. So I walked into the gun shop, just to watch Mr. Antonioni at work. He and his cinematographer, Alfio Contini, spoke in Italian, so I didn't know what they were talking about, but I hung out anyway. After the shop was lit, Mr. Antonioni walked up to the glass counter, and carefully studied all the pistols on display. I walked up to him, said hello, and stood quietly as he instructed his prop man, standing on the other side, to bring out two pistols. They were ugly, and I knew immediately what he was going for. He didn't want the audience to see the beauty in these weapons at all - no smooth shiny 357-Magnums, Beretta's, or silver Colt 45's. These were black, short and long-nosed 38's.

The actor playing the gun shop owner walked in and Mr. Antonioni had him take position and told him the two guns he wanted. The actor understood and put the guns back inside the display case. Moments later, Mark arrived, and while Mr. Antonioni was quietly conversing with Mr. Contini, we decided to rehearse. Mark and I walked up to the gun shop owner and:

Bill (me): "We need some guns, right away... for self-defense."

The owner gave his line, I gave another one; Mark gave his line, then the gun shop owner brought out the two pistols Mr. Antonioni had selected. Mark and I examine the guns and buy them. But Mark looked at his ugly 38 and said to the actor behind the counter:

"I don't want this gun."

He stared scanning the display, and sure enough, pointed to another pistol.

"Give me that one."

The actor playing the gun shop owner gave me a look of quiet desperation. Mark was the star and the other actor was too afraid to say anything. So, I stepped in.

"Mark, I watched Michelangelo take a lot of time selecting the two guns he wants to use in this shot. I don't think you should change."

Mark looked at me like I knew absolutely nothing about acting.

"I don't care. It's not the gun my character would use."

He looked back at the gun shop owner.

"When we shoot the scene, hand me this gun," indicating the gun of his choice.

Fine, I thought. Michelangelo will notice and change it back. But he didn't. We shot the scene a half dozen times, and because Michelangelo just assumed things were as he wanted them, his attention was not on the guns.

This was the last shot of the day, and when the Assistant Director yelled wrap, we were finished. Mark and I put our guns on the display case, and were milling around. The gun shop owner/actor was still behind the counter. Michelangelo walked slowly up to the counter, talking to either the producer, Harrison Star, or Mr.Contini. As he was talking, he happened to glance down at the pistols on the display case. He looked away, and I swear to God, within a second, it hit him the way the shit was about to hit the fan. He did a double take on the guns. He picked up the gun Mark had used.

"What's this?" He asked, looking around.

"Those are the guns we used for the shot, Michelangelo," said the prop man.

"No!(waving the pistol)I did not choose this gun!" He looked at the actor behind the counter.

"Why you change this gun?"

That poor actor was speechless, red as a beet. I glanced at Mark, who tried to be calm. He knew he had to, uh... bite the bullet on this one.

"I changed the gun, Michelangelo. The one you picked isn't the one I would've used."

Wrong Answer.

"You!?"screamed Antonioni, in broken English. "Who the hell are you? You're a goddamn actor! I have my reasons for wanting the gun I choose."

Then he slammed the gun so hard on the glass case, I thought his hand and the gun were going to go through the glass. Miraculously, the glass didn't break.

"Now we have to do the scene all over again!" And with that, he draped his long coat over his shoulders, stormed into his limo and drove off. Mark looked at me. There was egg all over his face. I did my best to avoid giving him an I-told-you-so look. So what did Mark say to retrieve some sense of dignity and control?

"Yeah, well fuck him," he said, referring to Mr. Antonioni.

Then he left. I stood there with one thought in my head: Thank God I happened to have read a Playboy magazine interview with Antonioni a couple of years earlier:

Playboy: So you want your actors to do what you tell them without asking questions and without trying to understand why?

Antonioni: Yes. I want an actor to try to give me what I ask in the best and most exact way possible. He mustn't try to find out more, because then there's the danger that he'll become his own director. It's only human and natural that he should see the film in terms of his own part, but I have to see the film as a whole. He must therefore collaborate selflessly, totally.[14] Had I not seen Michelangelo meticulously select the guns, I probably would've gone for the Beretta.

The next day, we shot a quick scene at another gun shop. We're walking out the door carrying our guns in a bag, as the owner tells us to be sure and drag our victims indoors if we shoot them outside.

It was an easy day, and once again, I was finished for a few months. So while cast and crew were headed back to Arizona, I returned home to San Francisco, where waiting for me in my mailbox... A report for induction letter.

Bill, me, Mark in our no frills, sleazy apartment...

Buying guns...
Bruce Neckels, Mark Frechette, gun shop owner

Chapter Fifteen
"Hell no, I can't go!"

There was no way I was going in for a pre-induction physical. I called the draft board in Merced and arranged a personal interview. I then called Harrison Star at MGM, told him my situation and asked him to write a letter on my behalf, stating that I was working on a film, and had scenes yet to shoot. Within two days, I had my letter in hand. I drove to Merced on the scheduled day of my appointment, sat with the draft board staff, and presented my case. I thought for sure they'd balk at the fact that the movie wouldn't wrap until March of 1969, five months away. Janet Leigh was the biggest star to ever come out of there; and not since Natalie Wood and James Stewart came to Merced in 1955 to film "Strategic Air Command," had anyone even come close to "Hollywood." I was granted a deferment until completion of the movie.

So because I hadn't been signed to a weekly contract, in which I would have been paid every week while on "hold," I was soon out of money and collecting unemployment. I couldn't audition for another film in case I was suddenly needed back on ZP. To bide my time, I went back to studying and keeping an eye on the Vietnam War. The election was a month away, and it just didn't look good for the Vice-President Hubert Humphrey, who would be filling in for Robert Kennedy, who had been assassinated earlier that June. The Democratic National convention in Chicago two months later, proved that. Humphrey had a record of being a hawk, so the antiwar movement paid a visit to Chicago - SDS, hippies, yippies, and anti-Johnson activists - and all hell broke loose. While Humphrey was inside the convention center, droning on about a "Great Society," Mayor Daley gave the green light to his police force to beat the living hell out of the demonstrators. They were clubbed, bloodied, tear-gassed and arrested. And even though Humphrey later blamed the Chicago convention for his defeat, the fact is he gave a speech in October about how he'd always been a peacenik and was going to approach Vietnam differently than Johnson. This kind of threw the Democrats. In their minds, Humphrey had always backed Johnson. So now they didn't know who he was. Coupled with Richard Nixon, who claimed to have a "secret plan" to end the Vietnam War, enough democrats and antiwar activists swung their votes to Nixon, and he ended up winning the election by less than one per cent[15] -the closest election in history, until Gore defeated Bush... and Bush took office.

But Nixon didn't have shit. There was no "secret plan." Instead, Nixon's private tutor, Henry Kissinger stepped up with a plan of his own. As much as Nixon wanted to bring the boys home, Kissinger informed him it would be a bad moon rising. The U.S. would look like a fair weather friend, running out on South Vietnam. Japan, South Korea, Taiwan and other allies, would disavow knowing us and ask us to get our military bases out of their countries, and establish their own policies. Vietnam would surely fall to the communists, but in the eyes of the world, it would be a defeat for the United States. So Kissinger pitched an alternative called "Vietnamization." We had about 700,000 troops in Vietnam at the time. To appease the antiwar movement, Nixon would pull out 25,000 men at a time over the course of a dozen years - into the early 1980's- Enough time for South Vietnam and the ARVN to take care of itself.[16]

Twelve years - even ten - That was long enough to lose a quarter of a million of our young men. By 1969, we had already sent home 48,000 in body bags. And just because we were pulling men out, the ones still there would have to be replaced by new recruits - young men yet to be drafted. Like me.

I was losing hope. There was no way South Vietnam could go it alone. They couldn't even hang on to a leader. Ngo Dinh Diem had been assassinated in 1964. Once heralded as Churchill and George Washington rolled up into one, this guy was corrupt, oppressive, and brutal. He established a secret police force, which was run by his brother, Ngo Dinh Nhu. His whole regime was run by members of his family. It was Ngo who came up with the name, "Vietcong." It meant anyone who was in favor of killing him and his family. And before 1960 he had imprisoned 50,000 Vietnamese people and executed thousands more. Diem himself was causing the collapse of South

Vietnam. So in November 1963, with the alleged blessing of John Kennedy, who sat in the Oval office in deep depression afterward, Diem and brother Nhu were shot to death. A twelve-man Military Revolutionary Council was formed, headed by Nguyen Ngoc Tho, Diem's VP. But the real leader behind him was one of Diem's former generals, Duong Van Minh, one of the ringleaders who plotted to kill Diem. He stunk as a politician and within months—Vietnam was in total disarray.

Diem was replaced by General Nguyen Kahn. This guy was a joke. He'd quit, then come back; get forced out, come back - like someone with a bad case of diarrhea afraid to walk too far away from the toilet. I don't know how many times it happened. And in between, a few civilians took a shot at the title. But America kept supporting them and lying that we were winning. Kahn took his final walk through the turn-style in February of 1965, and was ousted for good. Dr. Phan Huy Quat took over—the ninth regime since Diem's assassination fourteen months earlier. And we were fighting for this? He lasted three months, then Air Force Commander, Nguyen Cao Ky, 34-years old, became premier in 1965. He was the golden boy - flashy, playboy, with a beautiful wife at his side. But he knew zilch about running a country. And now was not the time to try his chops. The communists were crossing the lines with regiments of guns blazing. Within two years, he was hated. President Johnson made sure of that by taking a meeting with Ky in Honolulu. LBJ thought if the Vietnamese people saw Ky standing next to the President of these here United States, that they'd feel more secure. But why should Johnson study the Vietnamese people, their folkways, mores, customs, when no one else did? The Vietnamese hatred for America was growing. They felt Ky was getting too cozy with a foreigner—especially after Johnson gave him a big ol' Texas bear hug - Johnson's exclamation point for his "pacification program." Anti-Ky demonstrations took place; Buddhist monks started roasting themselves in suicide. Ky was gone by September of 1967, and Nguyen Van Thieu was in. [17]

North Vietnam celebrated his arrival several months later with a little surprise called Tet Offensive. Tet was their lunar new year holiday, a time to lay back and observe its' importance. LBJ and

General William Westmoreland - Waste-more-land - as we used to call him - knew something was happening at Key Sanh. Westmoreland was licking his lips—well, wait... He was always licking his lips. That's how we knew he was either apprehensive or lying. Anyway, the General felt this would be his history-making D-Day - the great battle that would bring peace and victory for the United States. As for Lyndon Johnson? He'd be able to play this card in all the upcoming primaries and assure himself a second term in office.

Now mind you, the general public didn't know about this Tet offensive until it happened. And while Westmoreland readied for a major ground attack at Khe Sanh, what he got instead was a major dose of Dien Bien Phu: A constant barrage of shelling. Meanwhile, the ground forces of the North Vietnamese Army (NVA) were attacking major provincial capitals of the Mekong Delta, and the results were devastating. General Vo Nguyen Giap, hoping for back-to-back championships against two major powers, was the mastermind of the Tet offensive. He killed anything that walked, including 12,000 civilians. But after we got over the initial surprise of the attack, the Vietcong lost an estimated 15,000 killed in the Khe Sanh area - that was according to the famous American "body count." Less than half of the bodies were accounted for. Total enemy losses for the enemy in the Tet offensive were estimated to be 40,000.[18]Westmoreland held his head up high, licked his lips, claimed victory, and that the end was near. But to get that "victory" he licked his lips and requested more troops – about 200,000 more. That's a whole new army and that meant stepping up the draft. The American people and Johnson had had it with this guy. Johnson ponied up 13,000 more troops and brought Westmoreland home, replacing him with General Creighton Abrahms.

And that's where I was in my Vietnam studies. It was February 1969. Nixon was in office; Thieu was still premier. And nothing had improved.

Chapter Sixteen
"They're only pretending we're tough."

A line I never got to deliver when "Zabriskie Point" returned from Arizona.

Mr. Antonioni finished up in Arizona, and was now in Northern California, not Los Angeles. In the few months I waited, the script had changed. No longer were Mark and Bill (me) going to participate in a street riot, in which our oxidized-red pickup truck would crash amidst tanks and National Guard. Instead, he, Sam Shepard, Fred Garner, Tonino Guerra, and Clare Peploe followed the current movement of the anti-war/civil rights demonstrations from the streets to the college campus. Instead of a group of protestors meeting in a small church somewhere in L.A. discussing the current flow of protest, we were now in a sleazy section of Berkeley, in a free church, planning the shut-down of our college campus. And running the meeting was pretty, Afro-haired Kathleen Cleaver, book-ended by several members of the Black Panther Party.

For five days, we convened at that church, and improvised our way, interspersed with a few lines of actual written dialogue. We shot five miles worth of film, then used five minutes of it to overlay credits and another five to start the show. But it was an interesting experience from the standpoint of acting. We all forgot about the movie and began integrating our own personal feelings. I wanted to know as Bruce Neckels, that once the black revolutionists won their victory, would they remember me, or would I just be filtered back into the mainstream of white oppressive America? It was a stupid hypothetical question, and Mark started an argument with me after the cameras stopped rolling. I was feeling what Mark's character said when the final day the free church scenes mercifully concluded: "Well I'm willing to die, too... but not out of boredom."

The next day, I was standing outside the free church, when suddenly I felt these arms come across my chest. It was Mark. He gave me a smile.

"Bruce, I'm really sorry about that argument yesterday. I was just in a pissed-off mood. I hate the script now and where this film's going." I turned around.

"I know what you mean," I said. "I lost all of my dialogue for this shit."

We shared a laugh and everything was cool.

What Antonioni showed, whether he meant to or not, was the boredom of students debating the definition of a revolutionist discussing war tactics against the establishment. Give me a break! The Black Panther Party wasn't going to win any war having to do with violence. Our military and law enforcement complex was just too powerful. All they could hope to do was wake people up and ask them to pay a little attention to what was going on in the country. And the line I never got to give said it in the shortest time and space, in reference to our nation's front line defense: "They're only pretending we're tough." Yes, we may have been living in the "Free Love, Flower Child" capitol of the world, but the two city governments of Oakland and San Francisco were conservative, and the cops were mean. They loved being called "pigs." They wore pins on their uniform shirts that said "OINK."

But dialogue didn't matter, as Mr. Antonioni slowly drifted away from the narrative and let his cameras tell the story through the abstraction of objects and the viewer's imagination.

"Zabriskie Point" was Antonioni's interpretation of commercial, corporate America - the establishment - the destroyer of everything pure and natural. Mark and Daria are at opposite ends of the spectrum as the show opens. He's a college student who takes part in a campus riot between police and students. A policeman is shot to death and Mark, thinking he may have done it, steals a small plane and flies away from the madness and heads for the Arizona desert. After buzzing closely over a car driven by Daria, on her way to Phoenix to meet her boss, who is planning a huge home development project, Mark's plane runs out of fuel and he's forced to land. She goes to him and together, they venture off into the desert... To Zabriskie Point. And here Antonioni finds his reality... his utopia. Daria and Mark get naked and make love, blending and morphing with the dunes and valleys, becoming one with millions of years of geological transformation.

Their lovemaking brings an end to anything that ever resembled realistic narrative and the rest of the film is symbolic. Suddenly, ensembles of naked couples appear out of nowhere, making love, releasing the natural force of life... or was it a vision of the new free love world order?

Mark refuels his plane, and with a few cans of paint, turns it into something psychedelic. He says goodbye to Daria, leaving this once fairly conservative-but-pot-smoking corporate secretary, a changed woman. She hops in her car and continues on her way to the development site where yet another part of pure, raw nature is about to be replaced by a resort community. Over the radio, she hears that a young man, who hijacked a plane, has been shot to death upon landing in L.A. Knowing that it's Mark, she arrives very distraught at a full scale, totally maxed out furnished tri-level home—complete with all the bells and whistles symbolic of modern day mass consumption America. She can no longer look at her boss (Rod Taylor) and his capitalist cronies in the same light any more. So she hops in her car and drives off, stopping far enough away to keep from being sprayed with household shrapnel. Via her subjective mind and Mr. Antonioni's 17 cameras strategically placed, Daria detonates the building from two-dozen different angles, in a series of surreal explosions. We see the objects of mass consumption - food from a refrigerator (including a lobster), toys, clothes, and television - gracefully implode in slow motion. American capitalism has brought a poetic end to itself, as a bright red sunset tells us that everything is right with the world once again. Daria smiles, leaving with a sense of satisfaction. [19/20]

At least... that's what I got out of it.

Which was a hell of lot more than I left with when filming ended. That free-church experience assured me that I wasn't ready to become part of any counter culture group. Kathy Cleaver's entrance in the film wiped out most of my scenes, and earned her billing credit. But "Zabriskie Point" had bought me a little more time. And time was up. Two months later, I received notice to report for my pre-induction physical. Whatever was about to happen to me, I would be going it alone.

Me, Mark, Bill at "revolution" meeting

Chapter Seventeen
An unfriendly visit to my local draft board.

I didn't let the draft board know I was finished filming just yet. After all, there could be retakes, dubbing - and I needed to be available. My roommate was still in law school, but the way the draft had stepped up, he knew there would be no more deferments after his first year. I never let him know that I had been studying up on the history of Vietnam. The one time I even mentioned that I was considering refusing induction, he very stoically replied, "Neckels, when we get drafted, we're both going." End of discussion.

For months, my right arm had been giving me fits. I hated those cortisone shots, but I figured I'd better keep building up a case, so I kept up with the injections. If I could get out on a medical, I wouldn't need to worry about making a moral decision. Hope Alexander, the aforementioned actress I'd worked with at the Marin Shakespeare Festival, had a stepfather who was a doctor - and very sympathetic to anti-war activists. She told me to go see him, so I set up an appointment. He took X-rays of my elbow, which showed I'd been walking around with a bone chip all this time. I also had a bad case of bursitis. Without hesitation, he wrote a letter stating that I was not fit for military duty.

I felt safe to contact the draft board and file a motion to appeal my I-A status. I also got a letter from my very first doctor who was not nearly as sympathetic, stating, and I paraphrase, that I "did seem to have a case of bursitis, and was experiencing some soreness there..." I should have just thrown that one away, but I needed more than one letter.

I don't have the exact month and day I took a Greyhound Bus to Merced, and met with the draft appeal board - I'm guessing early May of 1969. I didn't own a car. You really didn't need one in San Francisco. My father picked me up. We went to his house and I visited with him and my stepmother, Lavon - his next wife after Opal. I loved Lavon. I can only imagine what a great childhood my sister and I would've had if Dad had met her first. I'm sure Bonnie would be alive today. As a result of her moving away from a lady she hated, she met someone who caused her death in an auto accident.

I expressed my feelings about Vietnam; that I was going to try and get out on a medical. Dad hoped I could get a IV-F. But if that failed, felt that after basic training, because of my education, I'd probably not see combat. In his mind, I would just accept my fate and go in. We caught up on what was going on in the family; then I borrowed his car and went to the Selective Service office. It was an awkward meeting. They looked at the letters and didn't seem all that impressed, telling me they'd review the material and if I did receive my pre-induction physical notice, to take the letters with me for further review. My heart sank. I had no trouble reading the subtext on that one. The people I was facing were going to leave the decision to someone else. And with the way things were going in Vietnam, unless I was gay, a drug addict, or blind... I would be getting on a bus heading for Fort Ord, California. And so I said it.

"The problem with my arm is very legitimate. But I want to say that I'm having moral issues about this war. I think it's wrong."

"Are you against all wars, Bruce? Or just against this one?"

I was stuck for an answer. What kind of stupid, hypothetical question was that? World War II was a declared war. Young men wanted to serve. My father was totally depressed when he wasn't found physically fit because of his knee. Most men, who failed their physical exam, didn't do it on purpose. How can anybody ask a question like that?

"Well, I only can only relate to Vietnam. Had I been 18 years old in 1943, I might have joined up to fight WWII. I don't know."

Really not much of an answer. Jesse Hopkins, head of the draft board, and the others seated were no help. They had a monthly quota to fill. Unless I was a religious conscientious objector with letters from my priest, rabbi, or minister, I was wasting their time. I walked out of that 18th Street building knowing that I'd be on June's draft manifest. I took the car back to my Dad and told him what happened. I was very depressed and even though we never shared our deepest thoughts in the past, it was time he knew my feelings about this war, and where I was headed with it.

Dad was very unemotional about it all. I know it bothered him that I would even consider refusing induction, but he said I had to do what I felt was right. I didn't bother asking him how he would handle it in the eyes of his friends in Merced—the negative comments forthcoming - because I wasn't about to start living for him. Knowing my Dad, had I gone to Vietnam and been killed, he would have cursed that war until the day he died—like so many are still doing today. My bus ride back to San Francisco was filled with angst and confusion. I was closing in on the heaviest decision of my life, and it was time to weigh my options.

Chapter Eighteen
Draft Evasion 101

There were four different types of draft evasion: first, was the "Ethical deferment." If you stayed in college (II-S); became a minister (IV-D); hardship case (III-A) - having a child or being the sole support of your invalid parents. I'd used up my II-S, wasn't a minister, didn't have child or an ailing parent.

Second, is the "Unethical deferment" - A Heinz 57 Variety of cheating: failing to register and obtaining fake draft cards; bribing a doctor to write a phony medical report (mine was legitimate); committing a felony - or just being convicted of a felony - like three UC Berkeley guys who "hunted" an American Bald Eagle in Colorado, allowing themselves to be caught. This felony conviction declared them ineligible from the draft. Or, you could walk into your induction physical wearing a woman's bra and panties; fail a literacy test; become a mail-order minister; not eat for a month and come in with malnutrition; puncture your arm with a needle to look like a heroin addict. Even being an acid-head would get you out.

But damn my conscience. I just couldn't do that. As an actor, I could have pulled off any of the above. But in my selection of moral do's and don'ts, I just couldn't lie to, or dishonor all the guys who had died and were about to die in that war. I was looking to the future. And in the future I saw myself talking to a Vietnam vet in a wheelchair who would ask if I'd fought in Vietnam. I wanted to look him in the eye and say, "No I went to prison for my beliefs," rather than tell him I went into my pre-induction physical dressed up in women's clothing. That's just how it was for me. But in the big picture, it all served to show the government how far young men were willing to go to avoid an undeclared, senseless war in Vietnam.

Third, was the "Conscientious Objection" deferment. That consisted of men who were opposed to killing but willing to serve in a non-combatant, government, and bureaucratic capacity. But that was under three conditions: you had to be religious; opposed to all wars; and, be sincere in your application to life.[21]Right off, "religious" eliminated me. I believed in God, in some higher power, but was it all consuming? Did I feel God was guiding my every move? No. In fact, the only time I'd gone to church in the last twelve years was during my senior year in high school. My girlfriend went to church every Sunday, and it was a way to be with her. In the movie, "The Majestic," Peter Appleton goes to a communist meeting in 1945, because his girlfriend wanted him to go along. He had no idea where he was going - he just wanted to be with her. When asked by a witch hunt sub-committee if he wasn't a communist, then what did he attend a communist meeting as, he replies he went as a horny, young man. That's how I went to church. But for the record, I truly did love the girl.

I fell off the religious grid when I was seven years old, while still living with my grandmother in North Dakota. She was deeply religious; prayed every day and every night. We attended St. Peter and Paul's Greek Orthodox Church and never missed a Sunday. I learned to sing and pray in Ukrainian. To this day, my sense memory can still smell the overpowering stench of that incense the priest waved back and forth as he slowly walked past our pew. But religious as Grandma was, she didn't miss too many nights at Mike's Bar, or John & Joe's Bar. As I mentioned earlier, she loved those straight shots of Four Roses Whisky. She would leave me alone at home quite frequently at night - - (you could do that way back then, in a little town like Belfield) to join her Ukrainian friends. I didn't mind. I loved sitting home in my little red leather rocker, listening to country music on the radio: Hank Williams, Hank Thompson, Lefty Frizzell, Little Jimmy Dickens, T-Texas Tyler, Roy Acuff. But on occasion, if I got scared or lonely, I'd go out and find Grandma in one of those bars in town. I wasn't allowed into bars - that silly age rule, you know - but since we had one sheriff in town, and with not much to do for a sheriff in Belfield, population 900, we rarely saw him. So, Grandma and her buddies would let me hide under their table. They'd buy me a bottle of Ni-Hi orange pop, put a straw in it, and hand it to me. And there I would quietly sip my drink, eyes transfixed on a Wurlitzer Bubbler jukebox blasting away my favorite country songs. Now what I learned by attending a few of these nights out, was that Grandma and her buddies weren't just drinking, they played a little Canasta or penny-ante poker. On a good night, Grandma would come home with a coat pocket loaded with change. With visions of penny candy dancing in my head, I would wait until she thought I was asleep, then sneak into her closet and steal some of that change, thinking she never noticed. But we were so poor, that Grandma counted every penny. And I'm sure she either let me slide or thought she miscounted when she came home inebriated.

It was around this time I broke away from religion. To wit: One night Grandma came home with two dimes in her pocket. I took them both. The next morning I was off to school before she awakened, stopping by the Red Owl Store to pick up twenty cents worth of candy - and you could get a hell of a lot of candy back then for twenty cents. That afternoon, I walked in the door, and there she was, glaring at me.

"Brucie," she asked in her thick Ukrainian accent with those trilled r's. "Did you take twenty cents out of Grandma's coat pocket?"

I lied and said no - I think I tried to even accuse my neighbor across the street of stealing it. But when she told me I'd just written my own ticket to hell, I confessed that I'd done it. Fully expecting her to come at me with fists flying, she instead said something that put more fear in me than I'd ever experienced at my young age.

"Sunday, we go to church, and you confess to priest."

Oh, Jesus H... not that! Beat me instead! I begged Grandma not to make me do that. I was terrified. I screamed in fear. I cried. But she wouldn't budge. For the entire week, I couldn't eat, sleep, or think about anything except having to confess I stole money from my Grandma.

"Why do I have to confess to the priest, Grandma? Doesn't God already know what I did?" That wasn't the point, Grandma explained. In order for God to forgive me, I first had to confess. Fine, I will. But can't I just talk to God on my own? Can't we cut out the middle man?

The closer we came to Sunday, the more terrified I got. In the first place, I was already intimidated by the priest in his long robes and pointed hat. And that incense! Was I going to have to inhale that vile shit stench in his chamber while confessing? I didn't sleep Saturday night. Sunday morning, and I was groveling at my Grandma's feet again, begging her to reconsider. Forget it. We were out the door and on our way.

Now what always happened after the church service was a potluck lunch. Everyone would bring a dish and we'd go down into the basement and sit at this long table. The priest always sat in the same chair, not at the head or end, but dead center - kind of where Christ sat during the Last Supper. So what Grandma did was grab me about five minutes before service ended, and drag me down to the basement so we could get both seats on either side of the priest. And there we waited. I could hear the distant singing of the final hymn. I was shaking in anticipation, surprised I didn't piss my pants. Minutes later, people started trickling down. Finally, the priest appeared and took his seat between Grandma and me. He said a blessing and food was passed around. Grandma gave him a few minutes to fill his plate, then in Ukrainian, every word of which I understood:

"Father, my Grandson has a confession he'd like to make."

The priest turned to me and looked down. In his throne-of-a-chair bigger than the rest, and me being so little, this guy looked eight feet tall sitting down.

"Brucie," he said in an accent equally as thick as Grandma's. "You k-have sometink you vant to tell me?"

I felt as though everyone had stopped eating and all eyes were on me. I looked up at him, trying to keep from fainting, and said:

"Father... I stole two dimes out of my Grandma's coat pocket and bought candy. I'm sorry..."

And may God strike me dead on the spot if I'm lying as I write these words:

Without looking at me, the priest picked up his spoon with his right hand, filled it full of red and green Jell-O, and stuffed it in his mouth. Simultaneously, he put his left hand in front of my face, made the sign of the cross, and with a mouth full of red and green Jell-O, some of it dribbling off his lower lip, he said in words barely understandable:

"You're forgiven............."

That's it? That's fucking it? I went through a week of emotional torture for that!!? Then it hit me .Lose that long robe and pointed hat, and he was probably one of my Grandma's drinking buddies at John and Joe's Bar! I stopped taking religion seriously right on the spot. Oh, I prayed and talked to God - swore at Him a lot when things didn't go my way - but never would I allow myself to be intimidated by God again. In fact, the following Sunday, I even brought my bean shooter to church. I do confess, however, that today I have great conversations with God. I always let Him know that I'm a wretch, bless me and please, take me before you even consider taking my daughter or wife first.

So religion was out. So was being a Conscientious Objector.

The Fourth and final deferment was totally out of the question. I couldn't even discuss it. And that was the "Full Draft Resistance," which included the following: Burning your draft card, going underground, bolting for Canada, or going to prison.[22]I was not prepared to go that far. What good was burning my draft card at this point? It was strictly ceremonial anyway. Going underground? Hiding and looking over my shoulder until I would eventually be caught; I couldn't do that to my parents. Besides, I'd just auditioned for the Marin Shakespeare Festival, and was set to play Tranio in "Taming of the Shrew;" and in "Henry V," I was cast as Captain Gower and understudying Henry V. Plus I was working on a film career. Leaving the country? No, I love America. I'd rather face prison than leave my country. This brings up my final choice... prison. Just the thought was terrifying. However, the word was out that San Francisco was the Mecca for draft resistors. At most, I'd get probation. It was still a felony. I'd lose my right to vote, hold public office, or buy a gun. I could live with that. I wasn't planning on running for office. The only gun I'd ever owned was a Red Ryder BB gun, which my stepmother, Opal, destroyed. My next-door neighbor shot at her underwear that was hanging on the clothesline. When Opal saw all these BB marks on her bras and panties, she assumed I did it. I actually watched her put my gun in a vise and with a wrench, bend the barrel to a 90-degree angle, in spite of my pleas of innocence. And the only time I fired a "real" gun, was when I went rabbit hunting with some of my high school buddies. I wounded a rabbit with a 16-gauge shotgun, and then listened to it cry out as it frantically attempted to burrow a hole in the

97

ground to hide. I felt like the lowest form of life on the planet. I put it out of its' misery and never fired a gun again, except as a movie prop. Maybe that's what I should have said to the draft board. "I'm terrified of guns; never owned a gun and couldn't even shoot a rabbit. "But then, no... How many other guys going into the service could say the same thing? That's why it's called "basic" training. You learn to shoot a rifle. You learn to kill people. So that wouldn't have worked. Not emotional enough. Damn! Why didn't I hit 'em with my story about Pudgy. Pudgy was my dog—actually, my Uncle Steve's dog. But he was in the Navy, so Grandma and I had Pudgy. I was four at the time. Two brothers lived next door to us - Frank and Nick. They owned a pool hall/bowling alley, along with a junk yard-scrap metal business. The latter was located in their front yard. Place looked like a garbage dump. Frank, I remember, was a pretty decent guy. Soft spoken, quiet. Don't remember Nick. But there was this guy – let's call him Pete – who used to come around all the time, either selling or buying whatever. Burly guy, a real asshole, loud and mean. Pudgy didn't like him either. Whenever Pete came by, Pudgy would bark at him, and Pete would either yell back or throw rocks at Pudgy. And I'd yell at Pete to leave my dog alone. Well, one day Pete was outside in the junkyard, and Pudgy started barking at him. Only this time, Pete didn't say a word. Instead, he went back to his truck. A few minutes later, he came back carrying a rifle. To my horror, he stuck the barrel between the chain-linked fence that separated our property, pointed it at Pudgy, and shot him to death. Right in front of my eyes. Pudgy dropped to the ground without even a whimper. I remember screaming and crying at what I'd just seen. I ran as fast as I could into the house, terrified that Pete was going to shoot me, too. I hugged my grandma, crying beyond control. She peeled my arms off of her and headed for the door. I followed behind, begging her not to go out there. But Grandma was a tough lady. She went outside, looked at Pudgy, then screamed at the guy, calling him every filthy name she could, in Ukrainian. The guy yelled back at her, then walked away. I ran up to Anna, still crying. She knelt down and hugged me as we both cried over our dog. Grandma put Pudgy in a burlap potato sack, and we buried him in the back yard, underneath a lilac bush. We made a little wooden cross that marked his grave. It lasted throughout the summer, until the first winter blizzard.

We really had no recourse. Grandma could barely speak English; Mom was in Grand Forks, teaching, distanced by the grief. I doubt that the sheriff would've done anything - probably drunk anyway. So in a pure case of misplaced aggression, Grandma blamed Nick and Frank for Pudgy's death. However way the brothers handled it, we never saw Pete again. Nevertheless, we got even over the next few years the best way we could. Frank had a shed in his back yard where he kept a cow. Whenever he and Nick weren't around, Grandma and I would sneak over there with a bucket, and milk his cow. And me? In Frank's pool hall/bowling ally/cafe, was a comic book stand alongside the wall across from the food counter area. For the next five years, I stole every comic book I could get my hands on. I had quite a collection: *G.I. Joe, Red Ryder and Little Beaver, Lash Larue, Roy Rogers, Donald Duck, Beetle Bailey, Little Lulu, Mr. Magoo, Crime Busters, Superman, Plastic Man* - I had them all. And I kept stealing them until the day Frank caught me. He picked me up by my ears and carried me behind the counter and dropped me on the floor. He took the comic book away from me, and threatened to call the sheriff. I remember kicking him real hard and yelling. "Go ahead. I'll tell him you shot my dog!" He then told me to get out of his place and I did. One week later, Grandma and I took the train to California. Thinking I would be coming back with her, I left my entire collection behind. Once she got home, it was too expensive to send them to me, along with three coffee cans filled with marbles. So she threw them all away. All that work for nothing. Pudgy's death was in vain. But after second thought, I doubt if that story would have had any effect on those people at the draft board. Pudgy had nothing to do with the Communist "threat" in Vietnam.

St. Peter&Paul Ukrainian Orthodox Church

Uncle Steve and Pudgy

Chapter Nineteen
D-Day....

F or the remainder of May, I approached my mailbox with trepidation. Then it came in the first week of June. Terry and I both received our letters on the same day. *"Greetings... You are hereby directed to present yourself for Armed Forces Physical Examination by reporting at...."*[23]In two weeks - Army Induction Center - Fresno, California. I didn't record whether or not our draft notices actually came on June 6 - the day U.S. forces landed on the beaches of Normandy in 1944 - but the irony was close enough. This was our D-raft day.

While Terry was packing to leave San Francisco, I wrote a letter to the Merced draft board requesting transfer of my induction location to the Army center in Oakland - explaining that since San Francisco was my home, it would be easier to leave from here. The truth? If I decided to refuse induction, my chances were better of getting a break here, given the reputation for leniency. Most draft resistors here went to court, were given probation and/or alternative service. I didn't see that happening in Fresno. And I figured I could prolong the inevitable. According to reports, after a draft resistor refused induction, it could take a year, maybe longer, before he was finally brought to court. Who knows what could happen in Vietnam in that time? The negative publicity there had been escalating since early 1967, when atrocities began filtering in. By the end of 1967, almost 200,000 civilians had been made homeless in the Quang Ngai Province. 70% of their dwellings were bombed, burned and destroyed. Obviously the importance of the Vietnamese peoples' religious beliefs didn't matter: In order to re-unite with their dearly departed ancestors, those left behind had to remain on their land until they died. Then it was a direct flight to heaven, and those awaiting them. But when their villages were destroyed, they were forced to live in Saigon. There would be no grand heavenly reunion for these homeless victims. No wonder the people we were supposed to be helping, hated us so much. We destroyed their afterlife by driving them from their homes in this life.[24]

So follow that with the Tet Offensive in 1968 and the assassinations of King, RFK, and the aforementioned, shameful, Democratic National Convention in Chicago late August 1968, when the Chicago Police decided to riot in the streets and just start swinging clubs; then Nixon's new plan of "Vietnamization," a publicity gimmick, at best. Add it all up and Vietnam was chipping away at even the most buoyant spirits of those supporting that undeclared war.

I said good-bye to my roommate, telling him to not be surprised if I refused induction. He wanted to become a lawyer. There was no way he could refuse or go to Canada. So while he was off to become a 90-day wonder at Fort Ord, I gave 30-day notice at our Capp Street apartment. I had no idea where I was going. Since the apartment was furnished, all I'd be looking for was storage for clothes, books, dishes, a TV and a Stereo. Nothing to do but wait for my notice of transfer to the Oakland Induction center. I figured it would take a month. It came in one week. I was to report to the Oakland Army Induction Center for my pre-induction physical ... in one week. They were not going to screw with me any longer than necessary. I was about out of room. My arm and doctors' letters were the only hope I had at not having to admit I was a draft resistor - a moral conscientious objector. If that failed, then I'd find out just who the hell I was. I knew this much: The idea of showing up on induction day and not stepping forward to take the oath, was more terrifying to me than Vietnam.

So, on a day in June, 1969, while driving across the Bay Bridge to the Oakland induction center, a young man was being flown to the United States from Vietnam, to face a line-up and criminal charges of premeditated murder. His name was William Calley. Of course, I didn't know it at the time because the Army had done a secret massive cover-up. But by November, Calley's sickening story would become part of a barrage of anti-war messages I would be receiving.

Chapter Twenty
The Pre-induction blues and the Presidio show-and-tell.

I arrived at the Oakland Army Center amidst chaos. Anti-war student protestors, were lined along the sidewalk in front of the building, screaming at inductees - "Stay out," "Turn around and go home," "We support you." Many were holding up anti-war signs. But I walked passed them, clutching my doctors letters, hoping to be walking back out with a big smile on my face.

Never happened. I handed the letters over to some doctor, then was told to go through the line for hearing, eye, and movement tests. The hearing test was a high frequency sound they ran through your ears over headphones. You didn't want to fake that, or you'd go out of there deaf. The eyesight test was a joke - especially the color-blind segment. For that, all you needed was good hearing. The inductees ahead of me taking the test were two feet away going through the book of dots.

"Six,""Twelve,""Four,""Seven."

"Next!"

"Six," "Twelve," "Four," "Seven."

"Next!"

I walked up to the officer administering the test, and said, "Six, twelve, four, seven." He glared at me for a second, and then opened another book, getting the message. I answered correctly and moved on. Somewhere along the line I had to meet with a doctor who had read my letters about my arm. He ordered me to raise my arms. Not trying to fake anything, I did so. "You're fine," he said.

"No, I'm not," I replied. "I can straighten my arm - But my elbow is so painful, I can't even touch it against anything. And there are times when it actually locks on me" He backed off and told me to contact Letterman Hospital at the Presidio Army Base in San Francisco, as soon as I got home. They would be anxiously waiting to give me my appointment date for X-rays. I thanked him, and left. My hopes were at an all-time low. And they would get even lower after I was given Letterman Hospital's designed grand tour.

Within a week, I was at the Presidio, getting X-rays. I'd always liked that place. It was nestled in between Cow Hollow, the Marina, and Pacific Heights. Two winding, scenic roads provided shortcuts between the Heights and the Avenues, with the Marina. I loved driving through there. If you had to be in the Army, this was the place to be. However, during the Vietnam War, it was where they brought many returning soldiers - the ones missing arms and legs. So when my name was called to go have X-rays, the attendant said, "So you got a sore elbow, huh?"

I replied that it was a little worse than that. He then marched me through the ward filled with G.I.'s in wheelchairs and in beds, all of them missing some part of their bodies. Wrong psychology. Obviously, they wanted me to see what a real arm and leg injury looked like. That this was the price these guys paid, and who the hell did I think I was, trying to get out of the draft because I had a "sore" elbow?

After my X-rays were taken, the doctor told me he'd report his findings to the draft board, and I'd be hearing from them soon. But before he let me go home, he told the orderly to take me to the cafeteria and have lunch. I knew what was coming. They now wanted me to see limbless soldiers being spoon-fed by nurses and orderlies; soldiers with head bandages sucking their food through a straw. I was right. As I walked down between rows of beds filled with wounded soldiers, a black kid propped up by two stubs that were once legs asked if I was being drafted. I nodded.

"Don't go," he said." Wish I hadn't!"

We reached the mess hall. It was lunchtime, and there were quite a few G.I.'s in there. It wasn't a pretty sight. The orderly told me the beef stew was real good.

"You don't have to stay if you don't want to," he said.

Gee... you couldn't have told me that before bringing me in here? But I didn't fall for it.

"No, I'll stay. I'll have lunch with these guys. I want to find out if it was all worth it."

The orderly gave me a dirty look and left. I had no intention of asking that question. I got a tray, ordered a hamburger and Coke, and found a table where one young vet was sitting in a wheelchair. I asked if I could join him and he said yes. Wearing my bell-bottom jeans, light blue denim shirt, red leather vest - and having all my body parts, he wanted to know who I was and what I was doing here. I told him, adding that after seeing the conditions of all the returning vets, that my medical would be considered quite frivolous, and that I'd probably be inducted next month.

"You're crazy if you go," he said. "I'd run for Canada."

It wouldn't be the last time I heard someone say that. This poor guy was sitting there with no legs, and an arm missing. He wouldn't be running anywhere again. I ate half my burger, shook his hand and said something dumb, like, "God Bless You." But I walked out of there hating God. Of course, it was misplaced anger. I hated the people who sent these boys to Vietnam to be butchered; I hated them for using God's name to seal the deal as these young men took the patriotic oath.

That night, I had dinner with my friend, Susan. Years later, we both recalled sitting in the crowded Spaghetti Factory, having a very boisterous argument. I had told her about my day at the Presidio, and that I would undoubtedly be getting an induction notice. She questioned why I would go, given my growing anti-war sentiments. I tried to rationalize that it all came down to it being my duty, and I didn't want to have to face prison. She looked me dead in the eyes, and very loudly:

"Brusso, your feelings are so incongruous with your plan of action. You're not making sense." She was right. I was pissed. I had no argument, so I just exploded on her.

"Look, god-dammit, you can sit there all night long and tell me what I should be doing. But for as long as you live, you will never have to make this choice! You can protest, march in demonstrations, talk against the war—but then you'll be able to go home. You will never have to decide whether to get on a bus for basic training or go to prison. You've got nothing to say about it!" We didn't talk much the rest of the night. She knew I was right. I knew she was right. What was

I going to do? I answered that a question a couple of nights later, in a very strange way:

I had dinner with Susan at her house. She lived in the Marina District, just a couple of blocks away from the Palace of Fine Arts. After dinner we went for a walk. It was around 6:00 p.m., still light out. We passed the home next to the Palace where Marilyn Monroe and Joe DiMaggio had once lived; then walked down Francisco Street, DiMaggio's current place of residence. He was doing Mr. Coffee commercials these days. Even though Marilyn had been dead for seven years, he still loved her, and wanted to be within walking distance of where they once lived. As we got to the corner of Francisco and Scott, I looked to my left, and there was Marina Boulevard. Across from there, Marina Green, running next to the Bay, with Alcatraz Island directly ahead of me. To the left of Alcatraz, was the Golden Gate Bridge. And with the sound of a distant foghorn blaring off the Bay, I didn't think it could be more beautiful, more enchanting.

But it could. There it was. A quaint, four-unit apartment building with a "For Rent" sign by the rose bushes. A man and woman, both Asian, were standing out front. He was watering plants. She was standing there holding a binder. Without saying anything to Susan, I quickly walked across the street and approached her.

"Is this your apartment building?" I asked. She said yes, and I asked how much the rent was.

"$165.00 a month (no, that's not a typo. $165.00 A month... In the Marina!!!), but I'm waiting to show it to someone."

"Well, could I see it while you're waiting? I mean, obviously if she shows up and likes it, she has first priority. But since I'm here, why not show it to me?"

I charmed her into taking me inside. By that time, Susan was standing next to me. It was one-bedroom, tiny bathroom, tiny kitchen, hall closet had been converted into a sort of, Japanese-style sit-on-throw-pillows-dining room. The living room was good size with a fireplace. I was in love with it.

"I want this apartment." I said.

"Brusso...." Susan was dumbfounded. She obviously couldn't say what she wanted to say.

106

"Well, I need to show it to the other lady," said the landlady.

"Fine. Do you have an application I can fill out while we're waiting?"

"First tell me... What do you do?"

"I'm an actor."

(Long Pause) "Oh... I see. Well, can you afford this place?"

See! Even an Asian landlord has a preconceived notion about the acting business! And I at once became... the actor.

"Yes. I'll pay you six months in advance, if you like." Susan was biting her tongue.

"That won't be necessary," replied the landlady. "First and last month's rent and a hundred-dollar security deposit, will be fine. "$430.00. No problem," I said.

No problem, my ass. I had one quarter in my pocket, and that was for my bus back to Capp Street. Maybe I had thirty dollars in my bank account. I filled out the application and handed it back to her just as the other party showed up for her appointment. We all went outside and waited, giving her a chance to look at the apartment on her own. Susan was beside herself. Given my current situation, which she couldn't bring up at the moment, what the hell was I doing?!A few minutes later, the lady came out.

"Too small," she said. My heart leaped from my throat.

"It's yours," said the landlady. I was believing in God once again. This was meant to be. I told the landlady I didn't have my checkbook, but that I'd meet her tomorrow evening. I told her I was working on a film during the day. Lies, all lies - but I had to let her think I was working. To give her a bum check in the morning meant if she made an immediate deposit, she'd see it was bad. And I actually was waiting to be paid for an industrial film I'd done a week earlier. Maybe I'd get it in the mail tomorrow. Of course, the landlady had to do a check of her own - a reference check. I gave my agent's name, and Susan's; went into my new home one more time, just to look at it again. Susan followed me in. Her face registered shock and bewilderment. And making sure we were alone:

"Brusso... do you realize what you've just done?" I knew exactly what she meant.

"Yeah. I've just refused induction into the service."

She cupped my face in her hands.

"Are you sure this is what you want to do - that it's not because of the fight we had last night? You were right. I'll never have to make that choice."

I was honest with her. She made me realize that, yes, my feelings about Vietnam were incongruous with my plan of action. But it was also that soldier at the Presidio; the callousness of the doctor at the induction center; the reading up on Vietnam I'd been doing; and of course, just seeing what was coming out of Nam on a daily basis through the news media. And in the next four months, my anti-war dosage of horror would be increased, and no anti-war-biotic would turn me around.

My check didn't arrive the next day, but I still met the landlady that night and handed her a bum check for $430.00. I then headed up to Twin Peaks to visit my friend Sig Vandenburg, who'd been my former roommate. Yes... God was back. He had a friend there, Ron, who worked in San Jose, but had to be in San Francisco two nights out of the week. He was looking for a place to stay. I told him about my Marina Apartment - only one bedroom. He didn't care. He'd sleep on the couch. And for that he was willing to split the rent. He handed me a check for $215.00 to cover first and last, and half the security deposit. I couldn't believe my luck. And the next day, my check for about $700.00 arrived at the agency. It couldn't be issued until the following day because it needed to be processed. I quickly called my landlady, told her not to cash the check, because it would bounce. This is pathetic, I know. I told her I was at my bank the other day "making a deposit" and left my checkbook on the counter.

"Someone stole it and has been cashing checks," I told her. "I've put a stop payment on that account."

The landlady felt terrible for me. I assured her that because I reported it immediately, the bank would enter it back into my account.

"I've opened a new account. May I bring you cash tomorrow?" She didn't care - Cash, cashier's check, new check - didn't matter. The next day, I handed her $430.00 in cash, and I never missed a rent check again. One week later, I was living in my little apartment in the

Marina. I had a Mediterranean style couch I bought from Susan, an orange shag rug, one palm tree, a twin bed, a two-foot high dining table, my TV, and stereo... Remember that Sears Silvertone? The first song I played in my new home, was from Buffy Saint-Maire's *Illuminations* album:

"God is alive, magic is afoot."

Yup - that was my wardrobe when I walked
into Letterman Hospital at the Presidio.

109

Chapter Twenty-one
Moment of Truth...

"*G reetings - You are hereby ordered to report for induction into the armed forces of the United States, and report to....*"

I was told to report back to the Oakland Army Induction Center where I'd be boarding a bus to the Fort Ord training camp... Bring Social Security number, life insurance information and three days worth of clean clothes.[25]

I'd started rehearsals for the Shakespeare festival, and the word was out amongst the cast that I had received induction papers but would not be stepping forward. I felt like a pitcher who had a no-hitter going into the eighth inning. Nobody wanted to jinx me by talking about it. Which was fine. The more I thought about my big day, the more scared I got. Rehearsing at the beautiful Forest Meadows outdoor theatre, with a moat in front of the stage; a huge oak tree in the back center of the seating area, and oak trees on both sides of the stage; a stream which wound its' way up to the moat, and a wooden bridge crossing over the stream about twenty yards from the stage - gave me a wonderful sense of calm before the certain storm.

I barely slept the night before induction day. I couldn't even imagine what the experience would be like. Would I be the only one not stepping forward? Would there be many? And would we be jeered and spit at by those new recruits headed for the bus? Would several try to beat the hell out me while army officers stood by and smugly watched? And maybe I'd been given the wrong information by those familiar with draft refusal procedure. What if it's changed, and the FBI hauled me to jail right on the spot instead of catching up to me a year later? The final question of course was, would I turn coward and get on that bus? Would I submit to a war that was illegal and morally wrong?

Obviously not. The next day I borrowed a friend's car and drove to the Oakland Induction Center. I certainly had every intention of returning it. Second, I didn't bring any extra clothes or life insurance policy information. I planned on coming home.

It was an overcast day. When I arrived at the parking lot of induction center, I could see that it was a circus atmosphere. Dozens of war protestors once again lined the sidewalk leading up to the entrance, many carrying anti-war protest signs. As I got closer, I heard chanting from people who had formed a huge circle around one man, in an open space, off to right of the sidewalk. I had trouble making him out, but he had long, stringy hair, wearing a tie-dyed undershirt, and was standing next to a minister dressed in a colorful robe. It was scene right out of the musical, "Hair." I was already feeling better. He was obviously going to refuse induction. I wouldn't be alone. And with all the shouting demonstrators, I was gaining confidence that there would be many of us not stepping forward today. As I walked down the sidewalk, one of protestors yelled to me:

"You being inducted today, brother?"

"Yes."

"Are you going?" Someone else chimed in.

"You don't see me carrying a suitcase, do you?" I hollered back.

The demonstrators erupted in cheers.

"Right on, brother!" "Far out, man!" "Peace, brother!"

Once inside the door, I checked in at the first station. The officer looked up at me and asked:

"Where's your gear, draftee?"

"I left it home, sir. I won't be stepping forward today."

"You understand you're committing a felony crime punishable by imprisonment?"

"Yes."

The officer stared a hole through me for a few seconds and told me to move ahead to the next station. Again, I informed the next assembly-line officer I wouldn't be stepping forward today. To my amazement, he didn't try to humiliate me by yelling out to all the other draftees that there was a "chicken shit coward" in the room. Instead he told me to move into the next room.

It was a huge room packed with draftees standing in several rows. I took my place in the back row. No one was talking. After a few minutes, a young lieutenant with short, blond hair, walked in briskly and up to a podium in front of the room. To his right of the podium was the American flag.

"Attention! Listen up. I will read the loyalty oath after which you will step forward, across the line. You will then board the buses waiting to transfer you to Ford Ord, California where you will begin military training."

I couldn't have been more nervous. The lieutenant read the oath, punctuated with:

"... So help me God. Step forward."

It felt like a four-point earthquake. The entire room stepped forward. And there I stood... in all my revolutionary fervor, sandwiched between two sleaze ball, grunged-out looking hippies. On my right was the guy who'd been standing next to the minister in that circle outside; and now I got a real good look at him. He was about 5'6" tall; weighed all of 120 lbs. -Skinny as a rail, arms the size of toothpicks. I looked at his face. His mouth was half open; his glazed eyes looking up toward the ceiling. This dude was in psychedelic la-la land. His upper torso slowly revolving around and around. Why was he resisting? The Army would have never let him on the bus!

And on the other side of me was a guy about 5'10"; 160 lbs.; long, black hair, mustache and beard... And shit for brains! He was a true conscientious objector. He yelled at all the draftees who stepped forward:

"You guys are fuckin' crazy, man! You're gonna die!"

I couldn't believe it.

"Shut... the... fuck... up!" I was thinking to myself. There were over a hundred new draftees about to board a bus, and none of them looked happy about it. I could just imagine a dozen of them totally losing control and coming at us. But they didn't.

"Fuck you, chicken shit!" yelled one of the draftees walking out the door. Others turned and shot dirty looks at us - except for one kid, who stopped, turned and looked at us, not with anger or hatred, but I swear I felt as if he was considering joining us. But he didn't, fortunately for him; otherwise, since he'd stepped forward, he might have been arrested for desertion. In a few minutes they were all out the door, leaving the three of us and the young lieutenant - alone. The lieutenant gestured to a door on our right.

"Go in that room and have a seat. The FBI will be with you in a few minutes."

He followed behind as we went into a small office and sat down. He closed the door behind us. Psychedelic Sam sat down and continued tripping out. The other guy extended his hand in a "power" shake.

"Power to the people, man... Way to go."

I shook his hand and sat down. Yeah... power to the people, my ass. Like I really felt in control. But it was over. I had done it. I was drained. Empty.

As I sat there quietly waiting for an FBI agent to interview me, I thought about the amputees I met at Letterman Hospital, wondering if they'd stand and applaud... if they had arms and legs.

Entrance to the Oakland Army Induction Center.
No police the day I arrived. Just lines of protestors.

Chapter Twenty-two
Up next... The FBI

I can't imagine a more cushy, stress-free job than an FBI agent assigned to busting conscientious objectors at an induction center. Since we're against killing, he doesn't need to fear for his life. Hell, he doesn't even need to pack heat. And he doesn't have to worry about hunting us down. After all, the reason we're here is because we didn't run. Such was the very easy-going, painless interview with my FBI agent - let's call him Special Agent Jones. Though we met in another sparse office, we might as well have been having coffee at Enrico's on Broadway Street in San Francisco.

Agent Jones politely introduced himself and we sat down. He rifled through a folder containing information about me, heaved a big sigh, then slowly, sadly shook his head, which he then buried in his hand, really putting on an act.

"Bruce, what are you doing to your life, son?" He asked.

"Trying to stay out of a war I think is wrong, sir." I replied.

He ignored my response and pushed on.

"I've gone over your records here, and you're a fine young man. Student Body President of your high school, varsity athlete; graduated from junior college - AA degree; graduated from San Francisco State with a BA degree. Not even a parking ticket. And now you've committed a felony, son."

"Sir, I came in here with a legitimate medical problem, which went ignored because my draft board made no effort to make a decision on it themselves. I was ignored by army doctors, and I just finally decided after studying this war and talking to ex-vets, that I don't even care about my arm. I am a moral conscientious objector against this war."

Agent Jones had an answer.

"So then, why not get on that bus, go to basic training, show them that your arm is bad, or if you feel strongly, tell them you're a CO? They'll put you in a special unit, away from the other trainees."

Yeah.... right. I believe that special unit was called "The Brig" where CO's got the shit beaten out of them. But I played ignorant.

"I didn't know that, but it doesn't matter. I'd just as soon go to court and ask for alternative service."

"You may not get it. You could go to prison. You'll have a felony on your record forever. Please, Bruce... The bus is still out there. Go get on it."

"I can't. See, I borrowed a friend's car, and I've got to get it back to her."

And then I just had to be a smart ass.

"Besides, I looked at the Army menu, and I just don't like your wine list."

It felt as though a blast of cold, Antarctic wind blew through the room.

"Still living on Capp Street?"

"No, sir - I'm in the Marina."

I gave him my new address. He quickly made a note in his folder, closed it shut, and very curtly said:

"Enjoy it while you can, Neckels. You'll be notified within the next six months to appear in court. You can go."

Ouch! Dude, what happened to the warmth?

By the time I walked out the front door, the protestors had all gone. No one around to cheer me on or congratulate me. It was a lonely walk back to my car. I felt such relief, even though I knew I had just written myself another uncertain ending. Agent Jones was right. I'd better enjoy it while I could. But he was wrong about one thing: It took longer than six months to notify me. It took a year to indict me, and another year before I would finally have my day in court. And what happened in those two years, not only in Vietnam, but in this country, with two books I would read, and a man I would meet... would firm my resolve about the war and being a moral CO against it. It would redefine my meaning of patriotism.

My drive back over the Bay Bridge was not nearly as exciting as four years ago, with Petula Clark singing "Downtown" on the radio. But at least I was going home. As soon as I got in the door, I called Susan to let her know I was home. But she was in a hurry - on her way to an interview. I hung up and called Frances. She, too, was in a hurry. "Good for you, love. I'll call you later." I hung up the phone at just sat on the edge of my bed feeling very, very alone. How dare you go on with your lives! What was I expecting? That everyone I called would drop what they're doing and come see me? It was a tough day, but from that point on, things got a whole lot better. Within days I got a small role in a movie called "Strawberry Statement," starring Bruce Davidson. During my audition, I told the director, Stu Hagman, about the recent events of my life. So what did I play? A campus revolutionist at Columbia University - standing on a platform, railing against the Vietnam War. Stu even let me write the speech. Interesting footnote: After my scene, I was sitting off by myself when this strange, quirky guy, with a black top hat and long beard came and sat next to me.

"Hey, man - I like what you said." I thanked him. "Listen, man - I wrote something that I'd like you to take a look at. Would you mind?"

"No, give it here. I'll read it," I replied.

He gave me this piece of white paper with a poem running all the way down the center of it. It was a re-write of the Star-Spangled Banner - only related to modern times and the war. It was fairly clever, I thought.

"Keep it. It's yours."

Then he walked away. I noticed one of the other actors off to one side staring at us. I walked up to him.

"You know that guy I was talking to?" I asked.

"Yeah!" He said.

"Who is he?" I asked.

"That was Lawrence Ferlinghetti."

One of San Francisco's top poets! And just like that, he was in and out of my life. I turned to go after him, but he was gone. I don't know whatever happened to that poem he gave me. I lost a lot of things during the next two years.

The next day I went over to City Lights Bookstore near Columbus and Broadway. I wanted to find some of Lawrence's work. Instead, I came across a book by William Lederer, author of "The Ugly American." The book was called "Our Own Worst Enemy." It was based on Lederer's personal observation of what was going on in

Vietnam. And what I read made my blood boil. Lederer uncovers the deception handed the American people by our own officials; the corruption that South Vietnam was pulling on us and how we were allowing them to do it because "we are guests in their country and must accept their demands." Bilking us to the tune of billions of dollars of black market products, that not only made South Vietnam leaders wealthy, but also helped North Vietnam. In an interview with Vietcong logistics officer Major Pham Van Linh in 1967, "Without American money, guns, food, medicine and supplies, we of the National Liberation Front would have a hard time surviving." I was absolutely appalled at the way America allowed themselves to be first humiliated by the very people we were fighting for, then beaten by an enemy we were supplying. And it sickened me how American merchants came to Vietnam by the droves with their shiploads of goods - having to pay South Vietnam money not only to dock our ships, but to unload the cargo onto trucks we had to pay for, and then pay South Vietnamese soldiers - not our own - to drive those trucks. And where do you think a lot of those trucks ended up? Cambodia, Laos, and North Vietnam. The South Vietnam black market made ten billion dollars a year in American products and money. Payoffs were made to Saigon embassy officials by American pharmaceutical companies. Marines raided a Viet Cong village and found American record players and refrigerators, filled with U.S. antibiotics. And even when everything one could buy at shopping malls in America - made it to the PX and commissary, it was usually scooped up by the Koreans and Filipinos before our own soldiers could purchase them - and sold on the black market. And I'm talking diamonds, fur coats, liquor, Edgeworth tobacco, alarm clocks, gourmet foods, and major appliances. Saigon had been turned into a fucking Walmart. And I'll be damned if I'm going to fight for two countries allowing their boys to get slaughtered in the jungles of Vietnam while corrupt officials, officers, and merchants made billions of dollars. You can stick that blood money up your greedy, dirty, stinking, lying asses! I couldn't believe what I was reading. And Vietnam vets later confirmed all this. A dear friend of mine recently related a story of a man he and his father knew during the Vietnam War, who took crates of plumbing and building supplies to the Saigon black market - and came home millionaires. My friend severed his friendship with this man.

But I was pissed. I learned not to read "Our Own Worst Enemy" at night. Because if I did, I didn't sleep - my mind and guts were churning so fast. South Vietnam was in no way committed to win this war. America was paying a ransom not only in dollars, but also in body counts. As an example, The U.S. Marines had a Combined Action Program with the South Vietnamese Popular Forces. It was a close relationship. Each man in the S.V.P.F. was allotted sixty pounds of food per month. But because the chain of responsibility broke down, the soldiers of the Popular Forces did not receive rations for six months. So one day, while out on patrol, the South Vietnamese deserted and went home. They were hungry and their families were starving. The Marines went out to relieve S.V.P.F., thinking they were out there, and were slaughtered by the Viet Cong. After an investigation, it was discovered that a U.S. Army major, responsible for food distribution, turned it over to a Vietnamese officer, who was charging money for the food instead of giving it to the Popular forces. When the Marines - before they were slaughtered - offered to deliver the food themselves, they were reprimanded and told that it was a lousy idea because it would show the South Vietnamese Army that they were mistrusted - bad public relations. So one guess what happened to almost 2,000 tons of food meant to go to the Popular Forces? The Vietnamese army, under the leadership of a General Lam, sold it all on the black market, including enough serum to inoculate 5,000 people.[26]

So while Mr. Lederer's book and all its revelations bothered me, it freed me from questioning my decision about not stepping forward. But it was an audition I had for a movie later that year in 1969, based on a book written by the film's director, that turned my thinking on its' heels. The man was Dalton Trumbo. His book... "Johnny Got His Gun."

Chapter Twenty-three

"If you agree to fight, you agree to die..."
- From Dalton Trumbo's *Johnny Got His Gun*

D alton Trumbo was a Hollywood screenwriter, part of the "Hollywood Ten" put on the honorary blacklist of Senator Joseph McCarthy. The Hollywood Ten were writers, producers and directors who were called up by the House Un-American Activities Committee for being members of the Communist Party. There were over 300 people on the list, but the Hollywood Ten refused to name names or admit to anything, standing on the Fifth Amendment. The HUAC denied that right, and these ten ended up going to prison, but not before they lost their jobs, their homes, and some, their families. Dalton went to prison for a year in 1950. When he got out, he moved to Mexico and wrote under pseudonyms in order to make a living. Ian McLellan Hunter (1915 - 1991), an English screenwriter, fronted for the blacklisted Dalton Trumbo as the credited writer of "Roman Holiday," for which Hunter won an Oscar in 1953. Hunter was himself later blacklisted. Trumbo won a second Oscar for "The Brave One" (1956), writing under the name of Robert Rich. Four years later, he finally wrote under his own name, thanks to the support of Kirk Douglas, who refused to play the lead role unless Dalton got screen credit. The movie? "Spartacus." [27]

That's where I first saw the name Dalton Trumbo. But I still didn't know who he was until I got a call from my agent to audition for a movie called "Johnny Got His Gun." It was based on the book published in 1939, written by Mr. Trumbo.

I had never heard of the book. But since my audition wasn't until the next day, I figured I'd better get a copy. I was reading for the part of someone named Joe Bonham. It wasn't an easy book to find - not even in San Francisco. I finally found it at a small bookstore in Mill Valley. By the time I got back to my apartment and sat down to read it, it was late afternoon. I figured I'd give it a quick skim to get an idea about this "Joe" character.

Five hours later, I was still sitting on my couch reading the book. I don't think I got up once. Simply put, it was the most astounding, terrifying, brilliant anti-war book ever written. In those five hours that I experienced "Johnny," I squirmed, I cried, I anguished. It was obvious why I'd never heard of this book prior to now. Definitely underground, it had to be kept off bookshelves during World War II and even the Korean War. But it came to light during the Vietnam War. And I found it. It changed my life forever.

Joe Bonham was a young man in 1918 living with his parents in Los Angeles. But when his country called him to fight in WWI, Joe got sucked into the whirlpool of patriotic hysteria. He said goodbye to his sweetheart and left for Europe. Then somewhere in a trench in France, a shell landed near Joe, and he exploded into red meat pulp. He was brought into a secluded, foreign hospital, where doctors proceeded to amputate both his arms and legs. Already missing his face, he couldn't see, hear, taste, talk, or smell. Thinking he was insane, the doctors kept him alive because he was such a medical phenomenon. A tube was put down his throat to keep him breathing; another tube in his stomach kept him nourished. But he had one thing the medical staff hadn't considered: A perfectly good brain. He could think. And with his mind, Joe takes us back to his past; and then his present, with all the horror of his situation. He establishes communication with doctors by tapping out Morse Code with what was left of his head. He wants to be sent out into the world so that people can see what war looks like. Of course the doctors refuse his request telling him that it's "against regulations."[28]But it was Chapter 10 - when he gives us his thoughts about war, "as a dead man," - that had the most powerful affect on me. I eventually memorized it word for word - the entire chapter. Never did I want to play a role more than I wanted the part of Joe Bonham.

The next day, late afternoon, I went to the Fairmont Hotel, where Dalton was holding screen tests. He was a man of about 65 years old; very gentle; very eloquent. He had a white mustache. I wanted to spend the day with him. I wanted to talk to him about his life, and tell him about mine - How I'd refused induction to the Vietnam War, and that his book was what I needed to stand my ground. But I was afraid if I told him, he wouldn't consider casting me fearing I'd be taken to prison during the middle of filming. So instead of saying, "Mr. Trumbo, anybody who wants this role, will have to fight me for it. No one can have this part but me," I did my screen test - even had a call back to do another one - and just hoped I would get it.

"Dear Bruce: Well, I tried, you tried, we all tried. And yet I've chosen another to play the role of Joe... Thank you for your talent, and great good luck. Sincerely, Dalton." Dalton Trumbo (personal letter, 1969)

That was the letter I received from him two weeks after my audition. Timothy Bottoms got the part. I was crushed. I've probably second guessed myself a thousand times about taking a plane to Los Angeles, planting myself at Mr. Trumbo's doorstep on St. Ives Drive, and insisting on the role. I don't have the letter anymore. I put it inside the soft-back copy of "Johnny..." that I had loaned to a friend to read. She never gave it back. We lost touch after I remembered she still had it. But to have met this wonderful man, who refused to crawl through the mud for the HUAC, and bring down people who had everything to lose, was such a privilege to me. His book became my bible, my inspiration, and my source of strength.

I've seen the movie *Spartacus* many times since 1969. There's a moment in the film when Caesar looks over the captured army of Spartacus, demanding to know "Who is Spartacus?" One by one, the men stand and proclaim, "I'm Spartacus." "I'm Spartacus." All were crucified. I always felt that was Dalton's statement to those Hollywood Ten who refused to betray their friends and co-workers. Joseph McCarthy and his band of Commie witch hunters destroyed more lives between 1947 and 1970, than did the Communist movement in the entire history of America.

1969 ended with anti-war demonstrations everywhere - the biggest one in Washington D.C. Ho Chi Minh died, though his death did not soften the conviction of North Vietnam to continue the fight, and perhaps the worst atrocity of the Vietnam War. It actually happened in March of 1968, but the story broke out in November of 1969 - the My

Lai massacre. Lieutenant William Calley and his "Butcher Brigade" entered a hamlet in the Quang Ngai province. Due to paranoia and sleep deprivation, they couldn't delineate who amongst 500 old men, women, and children were Viet Cong sympathizers. Better to be safe than sorry. They murdered all 500. It certainly produced an impressive body count for our military leaders, but witnesses recounted a horrible sight: A man thrown into a well, followed by a live grenade; women on their knees, praying, were shot in the backs of their heads; young boys and girls shot at point blank range. Calley himself grabbed a two year-old boy, running for his life, threw him in a ditch and shot him.

According to an article written in the Jurist, by Univ. Of Missouri Professor, Douglas Linder (March 2000), the cover-up began immediately after an Army official reported a great victory:128 enemy killed and only one American soldier wounded (the GI intentionally shooting himself in the foot). Twenty months later, thanks to helicopter pilot, Chief Warrant Officer Hugh Thompson's testimony, and another brave young man, 22 year-old ex-GI Ronald Ridenhour, who conducted his own investigation, writing letters to everyone in Washington until finally Morris Udall listened and called for an investigation - three mass graves were found containing the 500 dead bodies.

The final outcome was that 400 witnesses testified, 25 men were prosecuted, and only William Calley was found guilty. Even Calley's ranking officer, Ernest Medina, admitted he lied through his teeth about how many civilians were killed. It took thirteen days of deliberation for the longest court-martial in U.S. history to end. Calley became the Army's only scapegoat and was sentenced to life imprisonment. Within four years, he would be out on parole, married, and working in a jewelry shop.[29] God, ain't America grand?

I remember that while Calley was on trial, how he couldn't walk into a restaurant and pay for a thing. It angered me until I realized that the American people were finally waking up about this stinking war. The polls finally showed that this nation's people had had it. 80% were against it.

I read somewhere a long time ago that Calley's attorney called him "One of the nicest young boys I've ever known," Yeah... well so was I. Could I, too, have become a Calley had I gone to Vietnam? This would only help me when my day in court came. And it came - faster than I thought.

Dalton Trumbo, refusing to reveal names at the HUAC hearings

The bath tub – one of Dalton's favorite writing venues.

Lt. William Calley

Chapter Twenty-four
It's official! U.S. Declares War on Neckels

I can't even begin to describe what it's like to get that summons letter. And it was hand delivered. I had to sign for it. I was shaking when I opened and read it:

"The United States of America v. Bruce Howard Neckels." Jesus... The whole goddamn country was against me. I continued:

To Bruce Howard Neckels:

"You are hereby summoned to appear before the United States District Court for the Northern District of California at the U.S. Court House in the city of San Francisco on the 22 day of July, 1970, at 9:30 o'clock A.M. to answer to an Indictment charging you with Viol: T. 50.U.S.C. Sec. 462 - Refused to Submit to Induction." Dated: June 24, 1970 35 34. [30]

Reality had finally reared its' ugly head. I had one month to find an attorney to represent me. And I didn't have a lot of money.

I made an appointment to see an attorney who I'd read about in the paper - an anti-war advocate, Terrance Hallinan. But he wanted more money than I could afford at the time, and he guaranteed me nothing. I didn't get a good feeling from him, so I left. I think I called some anti-war hotline, told them what was happening. They informed me that if I didn't have an attorney or couldn't afford one, just show up in court, declare myself indigent and the court would appoint an attorney for me. So that was my plan of action. By this time, I was two weeks away.

July 22, 1970. Didn't sleep all night, wondering what kind of experience I'd have. By 8: 45 a.m. I took the 30 Stockton bus to the 47 Van Ness, which dropped me off across the street from the Federal Building. I was early. I was always early – no matter what. I'd rather be an hour early than a minute late. Guess that came from my Radio-TV training: When the second hand on that clock hits "12," it's action!

I was sent to the courtroom of Judge Sanford Levin. I walked through his door, and didn't notice a whole lot of activity going on. Judge Levin seemed like a very nice man. I sat quietly, nervously waiting for my name to be called. It was all so simple.

"Case number Cr. 70-489, the United States of America versus Bruce Howard Neckels."

I stood. "I'm here, Your Honor." I replied.

"Good morning, Mr. Neckels," said Judge Levin.

"Good Morning, sir." I replied.

"Mr. Neckels, you are here in violation T 50 U.S.C. Section 462 - refusal to submit to induction. Mr. Neckels, are you represented by an attorney?"

"No, I'm not, Your Honor. I can't afford one."

"Then if you have no objection, the court will appoint an attorney for you."

"Thank you. That will be fine."

The judge then looked at a man seated to my right in the front row. I don't remember the exact words, but he called him to step up. The attorney did so, introduced himself, and was given my case. Plea date was set for the following month and that was it. I walked out the door with my court-appointed attorney.

His name was Saul Holle. His home and office were in Oakland. I remember his curly hair, his sad-sack drooping eyelids. He always looked so tired. But I really liked him. He wasn't pushy. He was very soft spoken and very calm. He was the kind of man who would not be offensive to Judge Levin. I felt very positive. Even more-so two months later when we appeared back in court to enter my plea. To wit: Another CO was standing before Judge Levin when I entered and sat down. His attorney threw him on the mercy of the court stating he was going to the San Francisco Conservatory of Music, had two more years left, and was no threat to society. He was just simply against the Vietnam War. I couldn't believe it. Judge Levin gave him a two-year probation, made him promise to stay at the Conservatory and finish out his two years or he'd throw him into the military.

Once again, I was convinced there was a God. Levin was beautiful. I was sky-high encouraged and positive I wouldn't be doing any time.

I was guilty. I had no problem with that. I did indeed refuse induction into the military. Saul told Judge Levin that I was very willing to perform alternative service - that I didn't want to just walk away without serving in some capacity. Just non-combatant. The Judge would now await a pre-sentence report - psychological testing - all those trick questions which some FBI psychologist would interpret any way he wanted. So now another date was set for sentencing - for early December. I walked out the front door.

Two weeks later, I was back at the federal building, taking a 200-question psychological test for my pre-sentencing report. It was very confusing, cross-referencing, trick question kind of stuff: "I've never wanted to kill my father. " Yes or No. I answered no, because I really never wanted to kill my father. He was a gentle, kind man. However, the FBI psychologist saw it as a phony answer. He walked past me, talking to another officer as though I wasn't there.

"He says he never wanted to kill his father. Bullshit! I've never heard of a boy who didn't want to kill his ol' man at least once."

Well, had there been a question: "Did you ever feel like killing your stepmother?" My answer would have been "Yes" with my own written footnote:" Almost every day for nine years." I just didn't know how to answer the questions pertaining to violence. I hate hypothetical questions like that. How do you know what you'll do at a given time? I never thought I'd refuse to step forward - to be sent to a war to kill or be killed by someone I didn't know, and for no reason. But if I was walking down the street and someone attacked me, would I fight back to save my own life? If I answered, "Yes," would that eliminate me as non-violent person, against war? And if I answered the question, "What if we were attacked by alien beings from another planet and our world was at stake, would you fight?" - with a "Yes" answer, would that eliminate me as a CO?I mean, let's at least be realistic and stay within the realm of possibility. Besides, any enemy with the capability of traveling millions of miles to do battle with Planet Earth, I figure is going to win hands down, since our furthest venture putting a man on any terrestrial body, was the moon.

I walked out of that building still trying to answer those questions in my mind. I'd find out in December whether or not I passed.

Chapter Twenty-five
"Enjoy it while you can, Neckels."
FBI Agent Jones

By October of 1970, I'd received some residuals from a couple of TV commercials I'd done. My friend Frances had recently divorced, packed up her three children, and moved to New York. She invited me to come visit. I'd never seen the East Coast, so I hopped on the cheapest flight I could find and off I went.

My vacation lasted five weeks, only because I had a place to stay for free. And not knowing what my fate would be once I went to court for sentencing, I figured I'd better start piling up some good memories. The first two weeks in New York, I took in sights all over New York on my own: I saw several plays; went to museums, Central Park, the Statue of Liberty. Then one day Frances asked me to go with her to meet some lady who was helping her decide on a curtain pattern or carpet color. Frances was redecorating her apartment and apparently this lady, a recent graduate from a famous interior design college in New York, was already making a name for herself at the young age of 24. Her name was Colette. Born in France, moved to New York when she was 18, and within a matter of years, would become one of the top designers in America.

She was about 5'8" tall, soft blue eyes, long black hair, and very pretty – and with the most charming French Accent. Though we only exchanged hellos, within two years she would become one of the most thoughtful and loyal supporters in my life. But during this initial brief encounter, I merely stayed in the background while the two of them rifled through patterns and colors. All I wanted to do was get out of there. My best friend Terry, who drew military service in Arlington, West Virginia instead of Vietnam, was on his way to New York. Our plan was to take in a play that afternoon, then head for Boston the next day.

Our Boston trip lasted two days. Took the Freedom Trail, checked out Bunker Hill, and saw the Celtics play Atlanta. The day after I arrived back in New York, I drove to Arlington, W.V. and stayed with Terry and his wife Joanne, through Thanksgiving. I visited Washington D.C. daily, taking in all the museums. I went on a tour of the White House; watched a meeting in Congress; saw the original Constitution of the United States. I'll admit I had guilt feelings a couple of times about refusing to fight for my "country. "But I was able to snap out of it, knowing this current war was a big mistake. Terry and I spent a day in Williamsburg - the same day several limousines pulled up under heavy security. And who was our special guest? None other than Nguyen Van Thieu, current Head of State of South Vietnam. I'm sure we spent a few million for the privilege of entertaining him, while his generals and officials were continuing to bilk America out of billions of dollars.

I spent one more week in New York and arrived back in San Francisco the first week of December - time for sentencing. I contacted Saul to let him know I was home, and what time were we supposed to appear in court. But the sentencing date had been postponed. Hooray and Merry Christmas! The new date was set for March 26, 1971.I now had three months before sentencing.

But around February, I received a phone call - nothing that important to me at the time, but it came from someone who would help me keep my spirits alive months later. It was Colette, the French interior designer from New York. She was visiting San Francisco for a couple of days and staying at a boutique hotel up in Pacific Heights. Frances had given her my number.

"Bruce, hi, this is Colette. I met you in New York one day when Frances needed help picking out drape patterns."

She was alone and wanted to get together. All I could think was, "Oh, dear God. I can't have her in my life! Not now!" But I was being presumptuous. She wasn't there for romance. She was contemplating a move to San Francisco and was checking out locations to set up a studio. I happened to be driving around in a metallic blue 67 Mustang, which was handed over to me by my jazz piano playing friend, Jean Hoffman, as long as I'd make the monthly payments. So I figured why not, and picked her up. I don't really remember what we talked about, other than getting to know each other. The highlight of her visit was the two of us going out to dinner. We stopped at Colonel Sanders, picked up two boxes of chicken, two cokes and drove out to Marina Green. It was windy and cold that day, so we sat in the car, ate our dinner and looked out at Alcatraz and the Golden Gate Bridge. We discussed our aspirations—hers, interior design; mine, acting. I must have mentioned what I was going through regarding the Vietnam War, but that I hadn't been sentenced yet. I took her back to her hotel, said goodbye and please call me the next time you're in San Francisco, realizing of course, that there was a slim chance I wouldn't be around.

Okay, so times flies when you're having fun waiting for sentencing day to arrive. The real Christmas present would have been if Judge Levin HAD kept my appointment and sentenced me in December. I'm sure he would have given me probation and alternative service - maybe just probation. Because within days before the hearing – scheduled for March - my attorney called to inform me that we had been postponed once again until – June 11. Again, I was prematurely ecstatic because three months later, on June 5, Judge Sanford Levin died of a brain Tumor. Ohhhh shit! My mind immediately raced to a judge from Contra Costa County, recommended to President Richard Nixon by Governor Ronald Regan. His name was Samuel Conti. He was a tough Republican, ultra conservative who carried a gun underneath his robe. No dove, to be sure. He had been re-assigned to the Ninth District earlier in December and was told to crack down on draft dodgers and marijuana smokers. And the carrot being dangled in front of his nose was candidacy to the United States Supreme Court. Conti was not about to let Nixon down.

I had read about Conti in the San Francisco Chronicle. I remembered his picture - dark hair, that shit-eating grin, and the headline: "2-Year Terms For Four Draft Refusers." Even though my case was assigned to Judge Levin, I was in shock as I read the article, barely able to take in what I was reading. (You may recall this from earlier in my Prologue:)

"[xxxxxx], attorney for [xxxxx], termed draft refusal *"a crime of conscience, a crime with no person as a victim."* Judge Conti disagreed. *"He chose not to go, so someone else had to go and perhaps today, that person is maimed or dead."[31]*

What kind of logic was that? Does that mean I would've died or been maimed had I gone in my own place? How do you know the other guy died? Maybe he didn't even leave the states; maybe he spent time in another country besides Vietnam; maybe he went to Vietnam and never saw action or even fired his rifle; maybe he spent time in 'Nam drugged out on hashish or heroin every day; or helped run the corrupt black market; or how about he fathered ten Amer-Asians by several different Vietnamese women, causing those women and children to be scorned, beaten, kicked out of their homes. Maybe he fragged his First Lieutenant who was about to order him into a jungle fire-fight and certain death. He could have also been a "peace" soldier who fired his rifle way over the heads of the enemy so as not to hit anyone. Wouldn't that make him an even greater danger to his comrades who were fighting for their lives? Or maybe he turned into a killer and loved it, or became another William Calley did. Maybe he'll come home with PTSD. Now wouldn't that be something? He comes home with not enough debriefing - commits a felony, faces you, Conti, and you throw him in prison for ten years. Is that how you repay him for doing his duty?

Two days after Judge Levin's death, I went to the mailbox and opened a letter from my attorney. It was short and to the point:

"Dear Bruce, your sentencing date is set for Friday, June 11, 1971, at 10:00 a.m. The bad news is that we have drawn Conti's court."

I calmly put the letter down, picked up the telephone and began calling my friends. With no guarantee of bail or appeal, it was time to arrange for possible distribution of my belongings. I was definitely on my way to prison.

Chapter Twenty-six
"Maneater," by Hall & Oates, 1982

A stern warning to romantics like me, the song came years too late. But it was definitely written about... her.

Within days of the Conti article, I must have received a dozen phone calls from friends who also read it, and learned that I would be facing him.

"What are you going to do now, Bruce?"

"What's your plan of action, Bruce?"

"You going to Canada?"

I was going to face him. That's it. Ask for alternative service, and if he refused, which was 99%, I'd be depending on the strength of my solitude amongst madness from 2-5 years. Fortunately, I didn't have to sit around thinking about it. Walter Mirisch came to San Francisco to film a movie called, "The Organization." It starred Sydney Poitier and the late Raul Julia. I was Raul's stand in, as well as doing a few bit parts. On the production end, my job was to distribute time sheets/pay vouchers to the background atmosphere actors (extras). I also picked up the supporting actors from the hotel and drove them to the location.

It was the middle of May. We were doing an exterior night shoot on Broadway Street between Columbus and Washington - right in the heart of the strip joints - in front of the Condor Club. And there she was... Standing at the entrance of the Condor. Up to that time, the most beautiful looking lady I'd ever seen in my life. She had long, wavy, flowing blond hair; the most beautiful eyes and full lips. She was about 5'5."I fell instantly in love, but I didn't plan on doing anything about it. She was obviously employed at the Condor. And right now she was hosting at the door instead of stripping on stage. All I could think was, what a waste of a beautiful woman. I walked away without saying hello. I mean, why? I just figured I'd found someone to fantasize about while I was in prison. And as long as I didn't know her, I could create any kind of dream I wanted, until the fantasy wore off. But to be in love with someone who looked like her? To actually have known her? Made love to her? That would be torture, being confined, knowing she was out there. But that's what happened.

Two days later, we were on Market Street, shooting a chase scene that took us from Powell and Market, down into tunnels of the Bay Area Rapid Transit (BART), which was nowhere near completion at that time. There was a large casting call for background atmosphere. Having finished on the street, it was time to release the extras. I was calling out names, passing out vouchers. "Heather Canissi?"(fictitious name, for obvious reasons) Never heard of her. Must be someone new at the Brebner Agency.

"Here," came a soft reply.

I glanced up and there she was, sitting amongst a few other "extras." Wearing a light brown, soft leather, floppy hat, drawn slightly down over her eyes. And when she looked up at me, I may have smiled nicely, said hello, and handed her voucher, but my insides were churning, my heart was beating. I felt total exhilaration. She looked even more beautiful in the sunlight, and she wasn't a stripper after all! She was.... she was... an extra! Recently signed with the Brebner Agency.

As she was writing her telephone number on her pay voucher, I tried to maneuver around to see what it was. She looked up, smiled, and turned the voucher so I could see it. Holy shit! She just came onto me. I asked if it was okay if I called her. She said yes. And then I left. We went down into the tunnel to film and the minutes crawled like hours. But when the dinner break came, I found a pay phone on Market Street and called her. She was home. We talked for fifteen minutes, and in that time I got her to go to my apartment, get the spare key from my upstairs neighbor, and wait for me. We had to break at nine, and I'd be home before ten. She didn't hesitate. She wanted to do that.

Well, there was a slight bit of angst and confusion. I gave her the wrong apartment number. A four-fucking unit building; mine was number "1," and I tell her to go to number 2 instead of number 3. So no key; no one home in number 2, but there's Marcia up there in 3, waiting for Heather to ring the bell. Took two hours for them to connect, but they did, just before I got home. And when I knocked on my door, and Heather answered... we locked into each other like Rhett Butler and Scarlett O'Hara. And the rest of the night was pure magic. So was the next morning. And so was a weekend trip to Disneyland a few days later. But there was only one slight problem. She had brought a lot of scary baggage with her. Things about her past... and about her present.

She really had been working at the Condor Club. She swore she wasn't a stripper - it was a part-time job, being a hostess - and that she'd already quit. The 1st Assistant Director had seen her at the Condor the night before I did, and had already taken her to his place, screwed her once, then unloaded her. The reason she showed up on Market Street the next day was because he told the agency to keep her on payroll for a few days. Okay... we can work with that. If the A.D. finds out, I'll say Heather and I are in love and that's that. Fire me. I don't care. And he did find out but could have cared less. So that was easy.

But finding out that my little Sicilian had been married to a West Coast gangster, who was still angry at her—that could be a serious problem. And the fact she didn't come over one night, because someone had broken into her apartment and stolen a bag of "reds." I can't remember just what hallucinatory drug that was, but she obviously knew the perp 'cause she was trying to hunt him down. Instead of sensing the danger, I begged her to come live with me until I had to go to prison, which made her laugh. "Darling, you're too sweet a guy to go to prison." And she thought it was so "neat" that I did what I did - refusing induction. But do you think I noticed that she seemed to get a thrill out of hanging with guys on the wrong side of the law? No way. I was too much in love. I didn't even notice that the places she was always taking me to - a movie theater on Market Street, just next door to a bar where her ex used to hang out. To a restaurant in Sausalito - where her ex liked to dine. One Saturday afternoon, we double-dated with Heather's best friend, let's call her Reba - and her husband. We even saw his car parked in front of the restaurant.

"Heather, please," I heard Reba whisper. "Let's get the hell out of here."

"Relax. He's not going to do anything," said Heather.

We went inside the restaurant. He wasn't there. We had a very tense dinner. All four of us felt it. Heather pretended not to. I couldn't wait to get out of there. Fortunately for me, we did - and drove to her favorite nightclub in San Carlos... to hear her favorite local band. It was another place her ex liked to hang out. But he was in Sausalito... And Heather was sitting with me, but her eyes were on the door. Fortunately, he never walked in.

The next night, Heather couldn't be with me. So I was alone in my apartment when the phone rang. It was Reba. She got right to the point.

"Bruce, I have to talk to you, and please don't ever tell Heather I called. I love her very much. She's my best friend. But she's got a lot of problems.... Haven't you wondered why she keeps taking you to places where her ex goes? She wants to see what he does when he sees you. Do you know that right after they got married, they got in a big fight on the way to Vegas, he dragged her out of the car, tied her to a telephone pole and drove away? Bruce, he's a dangerous man. He could really hurt you.... You're the nicest guy Heather has ever had in her life, and I've known them all. But you're way too nice for her.... Please, if you're smart, you'll walk away."

Well... shit.... What do I do? It was Memorial Day weekend - still 11 days from my sentencing date. I was now praying to God that I'd live long enough to get to prison. June 11... That was also Heather's birthday.

Chapter Twenty-seven
God and Samuel Conti to the rescue....

Thursday night, June 10. I took Heather out to dinner for her birthday... A place in San Francisco where I liked to go. I was not in the best frame of mind, knowing that by this time tomorrow night, Vegas odds were that I'd be in a jail cell. But Heather kept laughing it off - She had the cutest, most mischievous laugh.

"Honey, I'm telling you, you're not going to jail. For what you did? Not wanting to kill anybody? We're going to celebrate my birthday in San Carlos at the club tomorrow night. I'm picking you up at six and we're going to have a great time."

Actually, once I was given my sentence, there was a 2 percent chance I could walk out of that courtroom after my attorney asked if I could remain free on my own recognizance pending appeal. For the rest of the night, Heather did her best to make me not think about the next day. But the next day came anyway. I was up by seven a.m., more nervous than I'd ever been in my life. After taking a shower, I had to really consider what to wear. A three-piece suit wasn't going to impress Conti. I didn't know what kind of jail uniform I'd be wearing, but I did know I'd wear the shoes I went in with, so whatever I wore, I'd have my Frye square-toed boots on. Something heavy, something solid. Two nights ago, while Heather was... somewhere... I watched a movie of the week on TV called "The Glass House," with Vic Morrow and Alan Alda. Scared the shit out of me. It was about a guy wrongly accused, thrown in prison, and having to face some real bad asses, led by Morrow. It was one of the most realistic movies I'd seen about prison. For the first time, I was really scared after seeing it, wondering if I would be challenged or put to any kind of "survival" test. And if Mr. C.O. here had to fight, I wanted to be wearing boots. So I dressed defensively.

I went to see my neighbors across the hall and upstairs, gave them keys with a list of instructions as to what to do about my apartment. I gave Marcia my check book with several signed checks in case I was gone for a while and she needed to pay bills and rent just to keep the place going until I got back. She was a dear friend and is still to this day - and I trusted her. But like Heather, she felt I'd be home by noon.

I don't remember where Heather and I went for breakfast - I think it was a pastry shop on Chestnut Street, just off Scott. And then she drove me to the Federal Building. I kissed her good-bye.

"I'll wait for you right here."

I told her to please go home and I'd call her as soon as I either got home or was allowed a phone call. She laughed.

"You're not going to ruin my birthday." I walked up the steps to the front entrance, then turned to see if she'd left. She was still in her car, staring at me. She blew me a kiss. "Go!" I mouthed, then went inside. The time had come.

Saul was sitting on a bench outside Conti's courtroom door, waiting for me. When I approached, he stood and we shook hands.

"It's not too late to be paroled into the military," he said. I shook my head.

"No." That's all I said.

Too much had happened in the last year. We invaded Cambodia, and now we had two corrupt governments to deal with. Universities all over America were demonstrating against this latest action. Richard Nixon's ratings were way down - a 70% disapproval; another 70% were against the war. America had finally awakened. And the biggest jolt they got was the demonstration at Kent State University on March 4, 1970, when Ohio National Guardsmen fired shots at rock-throwing anti-war demonstrators. Four students were killed and several more wounded. Kids in their late teens and early 20's, killed and wounded by other kids in their late teens and early 20's, who had joined the National Guard to avoid going to Vietnam[32]It was too insane. Even Judge Samuel Conti had to see that. But never underestimate the power of being considered for the United States Supreme Court.

As Saul and I walked into the courtroom, a hearing was in progress, involving another CO, Bill Gomez. He had already faced Conti once and was now on appeal. I remembered him from the article in the Chronicle months earlier. Bill was one of the first four CO's to face Conti, and now here he was again for his second dose of pain. His wife was seated on the right side of the courtroom in the front row. She was holding their baby, who was less than a year old. The attorney representing Bill was a total cripple, propped up by two crutches. His suit pants looked baggy on his fragile twig-like legs. But by no means did his physical challenge impair his eloquence as a legal representative. I listened and watched with admiration as he spoke, concluding with what I can only come close to remembering, but this was the gist of it:

"Your Honor," he said, "Mr. Gomez is a hard-working man with a wife and baby. If you sentence him to prison, then you also take away the income he provides for his family. She will have to go on welfare and be supported by the state. It will be an extreme hardship for them... I ask you to consider probation for Mr. Gomez." Conti looked coldly at Bill.

"Anything you want to say?" he asked.

"No, Your Honor," said Bill, softly.

"Then this court sentences you to two years in federal prison."

Well... Shit. I didn't even hear the rest of Conti's sentencing. I was stunned. A crippled lawyer; a wife sitting there sobbing, holding a baby?!Jesus, how much more did you need in sympathetic visuals? And Conti looked right through them as though they were glass. Bill was immediately approached by a courtroom marshal, who ordered him to hold out his hands. Bill was then handcuffed and led to a holding cell behind the courtroom.

Next case: The United States of America Versus Bruce Howard Neckels.

Why bother, I thought. Just put the cuffs on me now, because I'm going to jail.

San Francisco Chronicle
February 25, 1971 | San Francisco Cl

Joe Rosenthal / San Francisco Chronicle / Polaris

JUDGE SAMUEL CONTI
'A very serious crime'

2-Year Terms For 4 Draft Refusers

By William Cooney

Draft refusal is a "very, very serious crime," a new U.S. District Judge said here yesterday.

And then that judge, Samuel Conti, sentenced four draft refusers to prison for two years each, ordered them confined in jail immediately, denied them bail and said any appeal they made of their convictions "would be frivolous and only for the purpose of delay."

The attorneys said they would appeal immediately.

REFUSAL

~~————————~~, attorney for ~~————~~ termed draft refusal "a crime of conscience, a crime with no person as a victim."

Judge Conti disagreed. "He ~~————~~ chose not to go, so, someone else had to go and, perhaps, today that person is maimed or dead.

142

Chapter Twenty-eight
The speech I never gave.

Saul wasn't nearly as eloquent as Bill's attorney. But it didn't matter. He made a nice plea on my behalf, stating that I was willing to do alternative service. And as he spoke, a ray of hope suddenly appeared. I noticed that Conti was busily writing something. I couldn't tell what, but he was totally engrossed. Maybe he was authorizing probation and assigning me to a hospital. Perhaps I would be one of his exceptions. Saul finished. Conti kept writing. Didn't look up. And then he slightly lifted what he'd been writing on. It was a calendar... A fucking calendar! Conti had been lining up his lunch dates, dinner dates, tee-off time... target practice at some gun range with that 9mm he carried under his robe - fuck, I don't know. But it had nothing to do with me. And again, with that same, cold stare he gave Bill –

"Do you have anything to say?"

"Your Honor, I first read about you in the San Francisco Chronicle several months ago when you sentenced four CO's to prison - without bail. Sir, I've known for quite some time that I would be facing you with this knowledge. Yet here I am. I refused to run - knowing I could go to prison.

Your Honor, you made a comment that deeply bothers me, and I question your rationale. You were quoted as saying to CO Smith's attorney, 'Because your client refused induction into the service, someone else went in his place and died.' Well, sir, if you're so sure that other man died, then that means had I gone into the service, I would be dead. And the idea that I would have died because of that stinking Vietnam "police action," makes me glad I'm standing here.

Judge Conti, I've been studying about Vietnam. I've studied this war; spoken with Nam vets; read books. And I'm appalled at what I've learned. Sir, I will not support a country

*thousands of miles away whose crooked regimes are using us
to fill not only their pockets, but the coffers of the enemy. I will
not support American entrepreneurs pouring into Saigon with
fur coats, jewelry, blenders, liquor, cigarettes, plumbing parts,
merchandise irrelevant to winning a war - creating billions of
dollars' worth of black market products for South Vietnam,
which have been stolen or sold to North Vietnam, Laos,
Thailand, Cambodia - even Israel - then coming back to the
United States having made millions, while our young boys are
dying in the jungles, or coming home with arms and legs
missing. Coming home with their minds so torn, that they will
never be the same again. Am I afraid of dying or coming home
a cripple? Yes. Because I just don't know what I'm fighting for.
And when a president - not country - country is a place... a
word - orders me to join under the guise of patriotism, I have
to ask what that means. Does patriotism mean, "my country
right or wrong?" Well, according to today's polls, 80% of the
American people think this war is wrong. 80%! And the people
are the country. So does that mean most of the people are
unpatriotic? I don't think so. I'm not unpatriotic. I love this
country, and by refusing induction, I'm saying we're going
down the wrong path. But I am willing to stay here and
perform alternative service. Put me in a hospital or
convalescent home working for the aged, the lonely, or the ill.
I'll empty bedpans for five years, I don't care. But I will not
fight in an undeclared war. I will not fight for a president who,
in his 1968 campaign, lied about "having a secret plan to end
the war" just so he could get enough votes. He had nothing,
and 20,000 more of our men have died since that lie. He even
took the fight illegally into Cambodia. Your Honor, no
American president wants to lose the Vietnam War. But it's
time to cut our losses and come home."*

As we write in our soap opera scripts, "SMASH CUT BACK TO:
REALITY." Yeah.... Like hell I was going to say that – not to a judge
nicknamed "Maximum" Sam. I would've gotten five years from this

guy had I made that speech. So, I decided to cut my losses. The less offensive I was, I figured, the less of a sentence I would get. And so I cut to the chase:

"Your Honor, I am against this war, but I love my country. I'm willing to perform alternative service. Put me in a hospital. I'll empty bed pans for the old aged and invalid for five years if that be your decision. But I do want to serve in some way."

And Judge Conti wanted me to serve, too:
"This court sentences you to serve two years in federal prison."
Before he even finished the rest of his dialogue, I was descended upon by the Bailiff holding a pair of handcuffs. He asked me to extend my hands. I was handcuffed as Saul was asking that I be allowed to remain free on my own recognizance pending appeal.
"Denied." He said.
Saul then asked about posting bail.
"No bail," Conti blurted out. Jesus! No O.R.? No bail? I'm standing here because I didn't run, god-dammit! I'm not going anywhere! But that wasn't the issue. I had the audacity to challenge an order from the "United States of America" - that inanimate entity which speaks for everyone - more of a force than an ordinary man or government - and I was being treated like a mass murderer. I couldn't even get out on bail?!
Saul quickly told me he'd make an appeal to William O. Douglas, and see me that afternoon. I was then taken by one arm and led to the holding cell. The door to the courtroom closed behind me, and there was Bill, quietly seated on a bench in a small elevator-sized room. A cage, actually, with a cell door. In fact, it was an elevator, ready to take us down directly to a paddy wagon for transfer to the county jail. Bill and I exchanged looks as I entered. The bailiff opened the cell door; told me to have a seat next to Bill, then left.
Bill and I smiled meekly at each other.
"I'm Bruce Neckels. I'm a C.O., too."
"Bill Gomez."

"Yeah, I read about you a few months ago when Conti threw you in the first time. This was your appeal, huh?" Bill nodded.

"I'm sorry. Your lawyer made such a great speech. I was sure you'd get probation. Married, with a baby - I almost feel worse for you than I do myself."

Bill smiled. "Thanks," he said. "Your lawyer appealing now?"

"Yes."

"You'll be out by this afternoon," he said.

Bill seemed so sure about that, I felt tremendous relief.

We sat there talking for a while, then the bailiff entered, pushed the button to the elevator and sent us down to the main garage, where we were immediately put into a black and white paddy wagon, and on our way to the San Francisco County Jail. We had already missed lunch. Hopefully, I wouldn't be there for dinner.

Chapter Twenty-nine
But... as continued bad luck would have it...

When we reached the County Jail, we were taken to A-line, a row of holding cells in the quiet section of the jail. It's where new inmates stayed until they were either released on bail, own recognizance, or processed to the main line. This was as far as I wanted to go. Bill was stuck in one cell; I was put in with another inmate, in on a drug bust. A nice guy, Caucasian. He was making a deck of cards out of paper and a bar of soap, which was used to "wax" the cards, and make the paper more solid. This guy had done time before. We talked for a while; tested out his cards with a game of blackjack; then I tried to take a nap, hoping that I'd be awakened by a visit from Saul telling me I could go home.

Neither happened. Saul showed up around 4:00 with bad news. It was Friday and Justice William O. Douglas was no longer in his office. Not only was he gone for the weekend, he was starting a two-week vacation.

"He's in Washington State. I'll find out where and contact him. You could be in here for a few days. But then we have to get papers to him. He's got to sign them..."

My whole body caved in. A few days in this shit hole? Saul said he'd be in touch as soon as possible. I asked him if he'd speak to a guard about my one phone call I was allowed. He said he would and told me not to despair. I'd be out early next week. The problem was, now that I was there for at least the weekend, I would be processed and sent to the main line—C-line—where all the inmates were waiting to be transferred to state and federal prisons... Or just doing their six + month stints. That also meant I was about to find out for the first time in my life, what it would be like to be a minority.

Around 6:30 p.m. Friday evening, I was finally allowed my phone call. Of course, I called Heather.

"Where are you?" She asked in an upset tone of voice. "We're supposed to be in San Carlos by seven o'clock."

"Well, Heather, you're gonna have to go without me. I got thrown in with no bail. I'm here until my appeal papers can be signed. And that won't be until sometime during the next two weeks."

"Two weeks! Tonight's my birthday. Now it's ruined."

I tried to disregard her insensitivity. Lots of times we say stupid things in the midst of death, chaos, tragedy, or a shouting argument when we can no longer control our adrenaline flow.

"Sorry to ruin your birthday, sweetheart. But I still bet you're gonna have a better time tonight than I am. Now just listen... Because I won't be processed until tomorrow, I probably won't be allowed visitors until Wednesday, between one and three. I hope you'll come see me. I'll understand if you don't want to."

Heather saddened up on me. She felt horrible and promised to come visit me. I hung up feeling lonelier than ever. The idea that Heather was going to be without me tonight broke my heart. In an instant I understood why so many convicts doing long sentences - severed ties. It was just too painful, knowing you had someone on the outside, who would one day sever ties first. I felt lucky that I'd be with her again in just two weeks... Or less.

Dinner arrived: Hamburger patty, lettuce with oil, white bread, and yellow cake. Since they wouldn't be processing us onto the main line until Monday, I had tonight, Saturday, and Sunday, to eat in relative peace and quiet. Beginning Monday and for the rest of my stay at S.F. County, it would be noise and chaos.

Later that evening, just before "lights out," I got my first taste of jailhouse humor. Two African Americans were on either side of my cell. These guys obviously knew each other from the streets. Went something like this:

"Hey Aubrey!"

"Yeah?"

"You got any pictures of yo' girlfriend naked?"

Aubrey:(pissed off) "No, Man.... Shiiiit!"

There was a long pause then Jimmy says:

"Want one?"

Even my quiet, soft-spoken cellmate laughed his ass off with me on that one. I don't remember if I laughed again for the next two weeks.

Chapter Thirty
C-line, and Doo Wop City

T he bunk beds were made of metal, with thin mattresses and old, itchy army blankets. I didn't sleep all night. It was hard to just live in the moment. All I could do was wonder what each new step would bring for the day, tomorrow, next week, next month. I was already nervous about what to expect once I got to C-line. And it didn't happen until early Monday afternoon, after we were processed and ready to be moved.

Two guards arrived and escorted us into a check-in area next to the shower room, where we were told to strip down naked. Our clothes were turned over to a trustee behind a cage, except for our underwear and the shoes we were wearing, which were put over to one side.

"Line up in the shower area!" yelled one of the guards. There, four of us stripped naked, waiting to take our turn to be sprayed down and powdered with disinfectant. I remember one of the cops looking at me and shouting out, "This is Neckels. He's too big a chicken shit to fight for his country. He'd rather go to prison!" I took the high road and didn't say anything back to this moron. We dried off; got back into the jeans and shoes we came to jail in but were given blue denim shirts with "S.F. County Jail" stenciled on them. We were handed a blanket, toothbrush, toothpaste, then escorted to a big thick door. Up until then, it was rather quiet. But as soon as the door opened, the noise was deafening - inmates yelling back and forth from one cell to the other. Every other cell had at least one trio or quartet of guys singing doo-wop: The Pips, minus Gladys Knight; The Four Tops; The Jackson 5; The Temptations; Smokey Robinson and the Miracles... "Just My Imagination," "I'll Be There," "My Girl," "I Second That Emotion" - were all spilling into one discordant song, but no one seemed to even care.

I tried to look straight ahead, knowing that I was being watched and scrutinized by inmates checking out the new guy... And a white one at that. No question about it... For the first time in my life, I was a minority. Suddenly, I heard someone yell out:

"Hey! Mod Squad! Mod Squad!"

I turned to see that an inmate in a cell slightly ahead of me was yelling at me.

"You that guy on Mod Squad?"

And then I realized: I was wearing a blue denim shirt; my hair was long and slightly curled; and I was wearing round, rose-colored glasses. He thought I was Michael Cole, who played Pete Cochran on the ABC hit series, *The Mod Squad*. Well, what the hell! Might as well play along with it. If word got out I was a celebrity, maybe I'd get some respect around this place. So I gave him a quick smile which he translated as an affirmative, and moved on down the line, hearing this guy in the background, yelling:

"Hey, man, we got Mod Squad in here with us!"

We finally reached my assigned cell. The guard opened the cell door. I stepped inside and he closed it behind me. I just stood there checking it all out. Two long, narrow rooms - about 10 x 20 feet, each. The one I was standing in was where everyone slept. At the far end on the right were two sets of metal bunk beds, one in front of the other; in the middle, far end against the wall was a toilet; about five feet away from the bottom bunk. And on the far left against the wall, was a sink. And in front of the sink, working our way back toward me, were two more sets of bunk beds along the left wall. It was an eight-man cell. Now, in the other cell, separated by bars, was a long metal table and benches, bolted into the floor, running right down the middle of the cell. At the far-left end, was a shower. To the right of the shower was another toilet. Normally, this room was for eating meals and showering. But because of a run on crime, due I'm sure to the terrible heat wave we were experiencing in San Francisco - it was now June, 14 - and that cell was filled with inmates sleeping on the floor on mattresses.

So, there I was with fifteen other inmates. Twelve were black; a couple Hispanics; and I was one of two white boys.

After standing there a few seconds, a black inmate approached me. He was about three inches shorter than me. I probably outweighed him by 30 pounds, even though I'm sure he could've torn me a new asshole if I'd pissed him off. He came up to me, and in a soft voice, said:

"What it is, Peckerwood?"

What it is? Never heard that before. What-it-is? I loved that. Still use it today. But "Peckerwood"... I guess at one time, the definition of peckerwood was a low class, rural, white Southerner. But now, during the 60's and early 70's, and the evolution of civil rights movement and the Black Panther Party, it was analogous to a white man calling a black "nigger." Okay, not nearly as bad. But 'what it is?' I needed an equally cool answer. I looked down at him, smiled, and said...

"It ain't what I want it to be." Seriously, how cool was that?

"I can dig it," he said. "What are you in here for?"

"I'm a conscientious objector to the Vietnam War. I chose prison instead."

He smiled up at me then turned around to all the other inmates, and yelled out:

"Hey man, this dude's okay. He's a political prisoner, just like us!"

As I stood there wondering just where in the hell I was going to sleep, I suddenly locked on to an open bunk! I couldn't believe it. Guys sleeping everywhere, but there was an open lower bunk, with a thin mattress rolled up." Is that bunk being used?" I asked the inmate who had greeted me.

"No, it's yours if you want it." He replied. I noticed a couple of the other inmates grinning.

"Nobody wants to sleep across from the toilet, huh?"

"That toilet ain't the problem," another inmate chimed in.

"It's the toilet on top of that bunk that's the problem."

A few inmates started laughing. I looked at the top bunk and saw a man sound asleep. He was black and looked to be very tall.

"Who is he? What's the problem?"

"His name's Jerry Samone. He sleeps all day, and farts... Right through his mattress to whoever's sleeping underneath. Then he stays awake all night and talks. Fucker's crazy and nobody wants to mess with him."

"Well... There's no place else to sleep," I said. "I don't have much of a choice."

I walked over to the bunk, and stared at this Jerry, who had his back to me, sleeping on his side, snoring. I put my towel, toothpaste and toothbrush, in a small cubby-hole on the frame of my bunk, rolled out the mattress, put my blanket on it, and laid down... and waited for that first fart to arrive.

Chapter Thirty-one
Jerry... my guardian angel

S ure enough, Jerry slept the entire afternoon... What farting he did, I could handle. Finally, trustees arrived with their dinner carts: Lettuce with oil and vinegar dressing - always served with dinner. Not sure what the main course was, but with white bread, and yellow cake for desert.

Jerry got up, didn't even notice me, and went to the front of the cell and waited for the food to be handed though the door slot. He quickly ate without speaking to anyone, then sat on the toilet, took a crap, and went to bed. I was seated in the other cell room where the dining tables were, so I didn't have to witness that. But what was starting to bother me was in only a matter of time, I'd need to go, and how weird was that going to be with all those guys hanging around within a few feet of me. It wasn't like going to Giants game and using the urinal at Candlestick Park! And man, did I have to go! I hadn't been to the bathroom, other than to piss, in three days. Nerves and no appetite, I guess. But I held it until around ten o'clock that night, when everyone was lying down. And then I went. I thought no one even noticed, but then I suddenly heard someone yell at me from one of the bunks:

"Hey man... Down one, drown one!"

I immediately knew what that meant because it made sense. Before that turd even hits the water, be flushing it down to avoid as much smell as possible. Now that was 40 years ago, and to this day, whenever I'm in a public restroom, (and most of the time at home), I make damn sure I've got one hand on the flush handle.

And so I laid down in my bunk... Underneath Jerry Samone, sound asleep in the top bunk. The lights in all the cells went out, leaving only the corridor lights on. A guard made one final pass, then disappeared, the heavy steel door, slamming shut in the distance with an eerie reverberation. I was physically exhausted, but my mind was wide-awake, and my stomach was churning. Not that I was worried about getting stabbed in my sleep, but this place was a dump, a fucking, filthy dump! There was no place to go, no privacy, and of course the unknowns. And Jesus, you can't imagine the thoughts that creep into your head. First, the basic practical thoughts, like, how long will I be in here? Will my attorney be in tomorrow to tell me I've been released on my own recognizance by Justice William O. Douglas, and now I can go home? Has William O. Douglas even been contacted yet, and if so, how long will it take before the papers are signed? If I'm still here Wednesday, will Heather come visit me? Or any of my friends who know I'm here? From there, the thoughts became paranoid: Will the guards purposely make it tough on me because I'm a "chicken shit who refused to fight for his country?" Have the guards told one of the inmates to pick a fight with me to see if I'm really a pacifist?

My thoughts were interrupted when Jerry Samone sat up, and suddenly these two huge feet were dangling off the side of the bunk, right in front of my face. He sat motionless and quiet for about a minute, and then he began to sing:

"She stood there...." Then he paused...

Whoa, do I sense an icebreaker here? I knew the song! Rock n' roll oldies music was my passion. I won radio contests when I was sixteen, just hearing a fraction of a second of three songs meshed together! Three phone calls to KYOS in Merced, guessing three sets of three meshed songs, and I won three used cars from Moombeam's Used Car Lot! In 1967, I won $960.00 On KFRC, hearing one second of the Zombies singing "She's Not There." I mean, I knew this shit! Those were the opening lyrics to a Doc Levine's song "Our Last Goodbye," backed by Tab Rauls, an unknown at the time of that recording. So I blurted out, in tune, on the same note:

"at my door..."

There were a couple seconds of silence, then I swear to God, simultaneously Jerry and I sang:

"Lookin' prettier'n I'd ever - seen her before." Then:

Jerry:" But I could tell…!"

Me: "by the look in her eye…"

Jerry/me: "She was only here to share our - last goodbye"

Jerry started laughing, then put his huge hand, palm up, down to me for a five and yelled out:

"Mother-fucker! I finally got me a good one!"

I slapped his hand, and as Jerry jumped down from the bunk, I heard one pissed-off inmate toward the front of the cage loudly lament:

"Ahhh. Goddammit! Now there's two of 'em!"

"Who I got down here with me?"

Jerry squatted down, looked at me, and said,

"No shit! A white boy! What's your name, man?"

"Bruce Neckels. And you're Jerry."

We shook hands. He couldn't believe someone who looked like me, was in jail, and assumed I'd been busted on a marijuana charge. When I told him was opposed to the Vietnam War, and refused induction, he shook my hand again and said,

"That's bullshit. So, you're a federal prisoner. Means they'll send you to minimum security... Maybe Lompoc down south, or Safford, in Arizona."

So until four o'clock in the morning we talked about rock and roll music, movies, Vietnam, his life as a criminal... I don't even remember what else. But it was great. It was genuinely great. Jerry put my mind at ease. And when he finally crawled back up to his bunk, I felt relaxed and safe enough to say:

"Jerry, do me a favor."

"Yeah, what it is?" (Yup, there is was again - "What it is")

"When you fart, you think you might point your ass up to the ceiling?"

Jerry laughed.

"If I'm awake, I'll do that."

With that, he went right to sleep. I'd made my first friend at San Francisco County Jail, and I couldn't have had a better one. I didn't care how much he farted. The place was a shithole anyway. Three hours later, the lights went on; the main cell door clanged open, and a guard yelled, "Breakfast!"

Oatmeal and black coffee... The perfect laxative. I remained in the adjacent cell with bolted-in tables while it seemed every inmate took a nice shit five feet away from my bed. Didn't bother Jerry, though. He was sound asleep. An hour or so later, a trustee came by with a commissary cart. Inmates who had filled out an order slip the night before, were able to purchase candy bars, pastry, orange juice, a newspaper. I'd missed out on it. So while most inmates were eating something palatable, I was about to face a full day in Cell 14, hoping to God I'd get a visit from my lawyer with good news.

And at noon, I did get a visit from my lawyer. Only it wasn't good news. Justice Douglas was still somewhere in the forests of Washington State, hunting Bambi's father. My appeal was sent to his office, but it could be a week before he even saw it. Talk about a low point lower than the one I was already in. But tomorrow was Wednesday, and Saul did let my friends and Heather know it was visiting day, as well as Sunday. I asked Saul to put twenty bucks into my commissary fund, then went back to my cell, having missed lunch, and with the apprehension that my friends and Heather might not show up, or that the visiting line would be so long that they'd never get in.

I was already so nervous about the next day. And paranoid. I didn't even want to have another inmate think I was looking at him wrong or give anyone reason to want to pick a fight with me. So I lay down in my bunk and just kept quiet, not caring that Jerry was farting his brains out just above me.

There was a lot of activity that afternoon. Several inmates had been transferred out, either being released, on their way to state prison, or just to another cell. But I remember the one kid who came in. He was Hispanic, let's call him Jesse, and he was scared on his ass. The thing is, he was about 6' 1" tall and looked to be in pretty good shape. He was about 22 years old. Once he found a place to lay his mattress, all he did was pace... And smoke. There were no anti-smoking laws back then, especially in jail. The place reeked with cigarette smoke. Everyone smoked. I was the only one who didn't. But with second-hand smoke, I probably inhaled a pack a day.

It wasn't until that night after a great meal of hamburger patty, string beans and white bread that Jesse finally began to open up. He was anguishing, speaking to no one in particular. However, Jerry was now awake and prowling about. And he was listening to Jesse's diatribe, stemmed around "The Glass House," a riveting prison drama which had shown on television several nights before I spent my first day in jail. Apparently poor Jesse saw it, too.

To refresh your memory, in "The Glass House," Alan Alda plays some poor schmuk who gets sent to a violent state prison for a crime he didn't commit. The king rat, or bully of the prison is an inmate played by Vic Morrow, a good actor and a nice guy who I had the privilege to work with several years later in the movie "Dirty Mary, Crazy Larry." Long story short, Alda gets on Morrow's bad side, and it ends up being in a fight to the death, with a black inmate teaching Alda how to kill. The movie was a terrifying account of prison survival, and was very realistic. It sure scared the hell out of me. But not like it scared Jesse.

"Shit, man, I saw this movie, "The Glass House," about this dude in prison. He was innocent, and trying to survive. Fuck man, why didn't I take karate? All my friends wanted me to take karate with 'em about a year ago, and I didn't wanta do it. Now I wish I'd done it, man 'cause I'd be able to protect myself."

Well, you knew who'd already done time in state penitentiaries just by the guys who were laughing at poor, terrified Jesse. And here comes Jerry's line.

"You dumb motherfucker! Karate? What the fuck you gonna do with karate when six 250-pound niggah weightlifters decide they wanta fuck you in the ass!? You ain't gonna do shit with your karate!" End of conversation. After I finished stifling my laughter, I realized that wasn't funny. Please God... don't let me encounter that!

I didn't sleep much that night, thinking about Heather and my friends, and wondering who'd visit me tomorrow. As soon as the lights came on in the morning, I went to take a shower... There was a small shower in the adjoining cell. More on that later, but when I saw what the inside of it looked like, I couldn't finish showering fast enough. And now that I had money in my commissary, I was able to supplement my breakfast of corn flakes and white bread, with orange juice, and a packaged pastry. And even though we were several hours from visiting time, I was already a nervous wreck.

Finally, the visitors were lined up outside, and it was time. It was agonizing as guards came down the main line, yelling out names: "Rodney Jones!" "Benny Lopez!" "Daniel Lee!" - the names came pouring in, and every time the guard came toward our cell, my heart raced. Fifteen minutes went by, and nothing. Finally... "Neckels! You have a visit!" My adrenaline was flowing like a tidal wave. Who was waiting for me out there? As I walked down the aisle, I could hear that one inmate yelling at me:

"Hey! Mod Squad you still here, man! How come you ain't out yet? You're famous!"

I walked into a huge room separated by a wall of windows, narrow counters with phones and chairs. The officer pointed to my seat and told me to sit down. And there she was. Heather... And God, was she beautiful... Wearing of all things, a khaki green jacket, with her blond hair draped over her shoulders. I picked up the phone, and she immediately started fighting back tears. But through the admitted heartache and loneliness, she did say something rather alarming:

"As soon as you get out..."

With one of her hands, she made a motion of an airplane taking off, and made a "whooshing" sound. I got the message.

"No, Heather... We're not running away or leaving the country. I won't put myself in a position where I can't come back. We just have to hope I win my appeal."

I let her know my attorney was working on getting me out on my own recognizance, and I should be out by the weekend. And then she hit me with another one:

"There's a guard here named Larry. I used to go out with him. I just talked to him and told him about you. I asked him to keep an eye on you and make sure you were safe."

She dated a guard at S.F. County jail???Why? How did that initial meeting occur? And who broke up with whom? Because if she cut out on Lt. Larry, then I wasn't feeling all that comfortable. And I had no doubt that's what happened. Somewhere in the past, she had come in to visit someone else, maybe her husband; maybe she'd been busted on drugs - who knows - but somehow they met, and he fell head over heels in love with her, not knowing what he was getting into. And sure enough, she fucked him over, and his badge, his gun, his phallic symbol of a baton, couldn't do a thing about it.

I had a nice day of visits that Wednesday afternoon. And as I went back to my cell to the cries of "Hey Mod Squad? How come you ain't outta here yet, man? You a TV star," all I could think about was, when am I gonna meet Lt. Larry?"

It didn't take long. About a half hour after visits were over, two guards walked by. They looked inside, one whispered to the other, and I was marked. That's really all there was to it for the day. No, I was never taken to a private cell and beaten.... nothing that dramatic or brutal. The only confrontation I had with Larry was the next day. I was sitting at the table playing solitaire and whistling. Keep in mind that in other cells, there was yelling back and forth, and doo wop singing everywhere. Lt. Larry walked by, heard me whistling, and yelled, "Hey Neckels! Shut the fuck up!"

"Yes, Sir. Sorry." I replied. I was right... Lt. Larry was still in pain from Heather dumping on him once upon a time in the past. The last thing he was going to do was a favor for her, by keeping an eye on me. And believe me, I understood. And it wouldn't long before I'd be feeling his pain. But in the meantime, I experienced other jailhouse ironies aside from the Larry-Heather connection. One of those occurred a few nights after I first got there...about 1:00 a.m. in the morning. I couldn't sleep, but I lay in my bunk. Jerry was in the bunk above, sound asleep, which was totally not him. But there was one inmate who was pacing up and down the cell, stopping on occasion to try and peek down the C-Line walkway, as though he was expecting someone. I kept peeking from under my blanket, and it wasn't long before I hear footsteps coming down the line. My cellmate quickly moved up, and within seconds a guard appeared, carrying a rolled up white towel. He handed it between the bars to the inmate without saying a word, and walked away. The inmate walked toward the end of the cell, right across from me, and crouched down between the last bunk and the sink. He reached over and grabbed a roll of toilet paper and began wrapping the roll sheets tightly around his hand. When he removed the toilet paper, he had created a tightly wound "donut." He set the donut in a small dinner tray he'd confiscated earlier that evening then unwrapped the towel. Inside the towel was a package of heroin, a syringe, and a rubber hose. The inmate took a book of matches out of his shirt pocket and lit the toilet paper "donut." It made a perfect little burner. It was about this time I decided what the hell? I've got to really watch this. So I raised my head from out of the covers and looked right at him. He glanced up at me and gave no reaction that I was even watching. So, I thought what the hell again.

"Mind if I watch?"

He didn't care. So, I sat on the floor, a few feet away from him and watched him as he tied the rubber hose tightly around his arm, creating a nice full blue vein. Then he put heroin on the spoon, balanced it on his burner, then readied his syringe. When the heroin turned to liquid, he sucked it up with his syringe, then shot it into his vein.

"How the hell did you get this in here?" I asked him.

"I got girls working the streets for me. They get the heroin, give it to a cop, along with a couple hundred dollars cash, and he brings it in to me."

I must mention that the inmate was black; the cop was white. Talk about your double oppression! Not only is the cop guarding the inmate; he keeps him fucked up and addicted on heroin and makes a ton of money from the prostitutes the inmate still has working for him! And my ass is in jail because I'm a moral conscientious objector, against killing or harming another human being. And this cop, whose duty it was to protect and serve, found a way to serve himself up a nice wad of cash from a black drug addict who was probably busted for that very thing. I don't deserve this! Yeah, like deserve's got anything to do with it.

Chapter Thirty-two
Elevated status..... Cum clean

By the end of my second week, I was a veteran. Through the process of seniority, i.e. inmates being hauled off to state prison, or out on bail, we all advanced one bunk, each time, one bunk forward. I had a top bunk. I also had my commissary food; my morning San Francisco Chronicle; used the toilet without intimidation; and got my ass kicked no matter who I played in chess. Yes, chess. Those blacks could play prison chess! They even taught me how to play "Tonk," a popular "black" card game. Never won a game. I also witnessed two fights, one in the cell across from me at 3:00 a.m. in the morning, which just sounded brutal with fist hitting flesh; and the second one between Edson, an Asian and Jerome, a black. Their field of battle was on the table, damn near stepping on my plate and smashing my hot dog! Which is why these two dip shits were fighting in the first place. Earlier in the day they were playing a game of dominos. They had a small bet: the winner got the loser's hot dog at dinner.

Well, Edson won, but Jerome was starving by dinner time, and refused to give up that hot dog. Edson asked for the dog a couple of times, but was refused. Each time Jerome tried to put the hot dog up to his mouth, Edson tried to slap it out. And a fight ensued. Edson lost, in spite of the fact that he knew karate—a wake-up call for Jesse. I know that, because I used to watch Edson go through his exercises. But something happens to a street fighter who knows karate without all the mental discipline... He forgets about the karate, reverts more to street fighting, making it a level playing field. Jerome kicked his ass. It was a bad deal all around: the hot dogs ended up on the floor; neither pugilist got a thing to eat; Edson flattened out a spoon and for hours, scraped it across the concrete floor, trying to make a shank out of it. Jerome stayed awake all night, thinking he was going to be stabbed to death; meanwhile, Edson was sound asleep, having long given up trying to make a knife out of a spoon.

And me... I was such a wreck out of it all, I didn't sleep either. I just laid there, thinking... much like every night I was in that jail. And of course, the predominant theme of thought was, "how long before I set my foot on free ground again? Two years... 24 months... 730 days... 17,520 hours. And the endless possibilities of things that could happen to me that I'd have to deal with. And for what? An undeclared, corrupt war, started by one of the most beloved presidents in our history, and promulgated years later by lies from one of the most corrupt... a candidate with polls so dead-even, that he lied about having a plan to end the war in order to get a winning edge. But what was the use rehashing that. It was my choice when it all came down it. My biggest problem was constantly trying to block out the claustrophobia I was starting to feel. Something I hadn't considered when I chose prison as opposed to killing some Asian who only wanted to live on his land in peace. The best way I found to block it out was to make my space smaller. That was my bunk. Stay there until I absolutely had to move, then get up. Little did I know I was preparing myself for an even smaller space which I would occupy sixteen months from now.

There was an area for privacy in our cell: The shower. It was a cubicle, 4 feet wide on all sides. The shower door is a plastic mattress cover from a single size mattress used on the jail bunks. It's not see-through, so inmates did have privacy while taking a shower. And this one was filthy; thick with old soap and grime... just like the walls.

I went up to the cell door and waited for a trustee to come by. I asked if I could get a bucket with a scrub brush and soap. About ten minutes later, he arrived with an officer who opened the cell and handed me what I'd asked for. It took me over an hour to clean that stall, and I seemed to be getting through it all right until one inmate yelled out, "Hey, man, be sure an' get all the cum stains off dem walls! I know I got about a quart in there." Yes, I'm sure 5,000 inmates had masturbated in that shower since it was last cleaned.

And that was the last favor I did for the S.F. County Jail.

Chapter Thirty-three
Same ol' same ol'....

I couldn't fucking believe it! It was Friday. I'd been in this shithole for two weeks. Seemed like a month. Another weekend was upon us and still no word from William O. Douglas, and when Friday afternoon came and Saul, my attorney, paid me a visit, the news was bad. Douglas was still on vacation but would be back next week. But when next week; he didn't know. I was looking at the weekend and at least three more days after that until all the papers were looked at, signed, sent, and whatever else kind of bureaucratic bullshit had to take place. I didn't know what real depression was until that moment. Christ, that meant tomorrow morning, if we cleaned our cell like good little criminals, they'd roll the TV up to our cell and let us vote on what to watch. Gee, what would win? A pro baseball game... Or "Soul Train?" I mean, for the first time, I wanted to cry. But that's one vulnerability you never want to expose in jail.

However, on the upside, it meant I'd be having more visitors. Heather showed up again, asked if Lt. Larry was looking out for me. I just told her I hadn't had any trouble with anyone. I don't know what we talked about, but I let her know I'd probably be out next week. I had two or three more visits from friends, who tried to pump me up. They were always in touch with Saul and he pretty much filled them in on what was happening. All we could do was keep good thoughts that the next time I saw them, would be back at my apartment.

And so, for the next several days, it was more of the same: inhaling a pack a day of everyone else's cigarette smoke; the noise, noise, noise; somebody wanting to kill someone else who took two pieces of yellow cake instead of one; the C-line doo-wop groups—and "niggah" this, and "niggah" that. And to this day, even though the word "nigger" is used all the time on television, movies, stand-up comedy, and rap music - I still heard it more in my two weeks in jail, than I've heard it spoken in the last 47 years. I didn't bother asking any "black" inmate why they used the word themselves so freely when it was such a taboo-ugly word throughout American history. Though the slaves did use it all the time referring to themselves, so as to "show" their masters and bosses that they accepted their roles servants and slaves, and posed no threat. Perhaps black inmates used it because they wanted to take control of it and make it theirs. And it seemed to be a term of endearment. The perception of the word had been regarded by many white people of their times throughout the last 100 years as derogatory –a "nigger" was inferior, stupid, lazy—and were the major criminals of our society.

I'm sure the word originally held no negative connotation during the settling of America. It's from the Spanish word *Negro* which came from the Latin word *niger*. Now imagine that as the Negro was being shipped over to the colonies from Africa to work the plantations, they were greeted by the Dutch, Germans, French, Scottish, Irish, English - and look at all the different dialects pronouncing the word Negro:"Nigra (long i)" "Nagra (long a)," "Negra (long e)," Add the "r" to it and now it's "niger," "nager," "neg'gar" "nee'ger," and as we got into the Southern dialects, "nigger" finally became the lazy-mouthed way to say "Negro." [33]

By the 1800's, the word took on its present pejorative meaning - all the way up to my present moment at S.F. County in 1971. When I heard the word nigger, it was still synonymous with hangings, tar and feathering, whipping, beating, shooting, "back of the bus," separate water fountains. Not "colored," nor "black," nor "African American" will ever render that word archaic. It's part of their history. Comedian Dick Gregory wrote a book in the 60's called "Nigger." One of my heroes during that time, Muhammed Ali, refused induction to fight in Vietnam, saying, "No Vietnamese ever called me "nigger." I learned later that he was fed that line by his mentor, Abdul Rahaman, from the Nation of Islam, which was somewhat disappointing to me. But when he said it, the whole world was watching. Comedian Lenny Bruce used it in his comedy routines back in the 60's. He felt the more it was used and heard, the less powerful it would be. George Carlin said it was only a word and that the context in which it was used was offensive.

Well, here it is, the 21st Century, and even though the word "nigger" is used in rap songs, movies, and stand-up comedy – and mainly by black singers, actors and comedians – it's still very taboo. For fear of vilification, it's been reduced to "The N word." A few years ago, Actor Damon Wayans of the Wayans Brothers, tried to get a trademark on "Nigga" for products he planned to market. The U.S. Patent and Trademark Office rejected his application, saying that the law prohibited trademarks that are immoral and scandalous. A politician in Texas went on television to say that anyone caught using that word should be fined.[34](He didn't say whether that included African Americans using "niggah" with each other.)

But, back to 1971. I was not about to use that word with my cellmate soul brothers, no matter how much they regarded me as a "political prisoner, just like them." All I wanted to do was get through what would hopefully be my last few days. And I lived them one minute at a time. And then the moment came...

Saturday morning, 6:00 a.m., June 26. I was awakened by the sound of the steel door of my cell, sliding open and coming to a loud slam. Then I heard:

"Neckels! Roll up!!"

My heart was pounding. I'd heard those words "roll up" several times during my stay. It meant, get your belongings together because you're leaving! At fucking last, William O Douglas had signed the papers to let me out on my own recognizance—O.R. they called it. I couldn't wait to get back to my beautiful little apartment in the Marina. I figured Saul would probably drive me home. I couldn't wait to get my own clothes back on, get home, then head on over to Doidges on Chestnut Street for a pastry and cup of French Roast coffee..

Jerry Samone came up to me and I gave him a hug, thanked him helping me through this ordeal. The guard once again yelled out:

"Come on, Neckels!!FBI's waiting for you!"

My entire body wanted to cave in. My mind became so twisted up and frazzled and shocked, I couldn't even think! I don't know how I looked at Jerry, but he could see my devastation.

"You gonna be all right, man." He said very calmly.

I nodded and walked out into the corridor. How did it come to this? It couldn't be more than a couple of fucking days before Justice

Douglas would get the papers in for my release. Can't they just leave me here?

We went down the main line and out to the admitting/release area. And there they were—Two FBI Agents—One in his 40's, flat-top haircut, looked ex-military – I'm guessing the Korean War. His counterpart was in his late 20's. Standing next to them were Bill Gomez and Pete Sanders. Both were handcuffed and leg-ironed, and they were waiting for me.

"Here you go, Neckels." One of the guards said, handing me my jeans and shirt. I got dressed. They told me to stand next to the other two prisoners, then proceeded to handcuff, leg-iron, then chain all three of us together. We exchanged meek hellos, then were led into the parking structure and put into the back seat of a late model Ford LTD. It was crowded to say the least. It was a few minutes before the officers got in the car, so I asked Bill and Pete where we were going. Both felt we'd be going to Safford Federal Prison in Arizona. Lompoc in Southern California was Federal, too, but for younger inmates. At this point, I didn't much give a shit. I'd just as soon stay in California. Safford was one thousand miles away—far enough without being handcuffed and leg-ironed.

The agents got into the car. Charlie, the older of the two, was the driver, and John rode passenger. The only instruction they gave us was to keep quiet unless we were spoken to or needed to go to the bathroom. It would be an hour down the road before they let us know we'd be going to Safford, Arizona.

Chapter Thirty-four
Travels with Charlie

R emember the first Charlie who said I raised too much corn and
not enough hell? Well now I was with the third Charlie in my
life, taking me to prison for raising too <u>much</u> hell! We drove down
Highway 99, heading toward Los Angeles. We'd gone over a hundred
miles and were about 30 miles from Merced, my hometown. I was
praying to God that our FBI escorts weren't going to decide to make
that a bathroom stop. Because they wouldn't have let us go, one at a
time. We'd have all gotten out of the car together, handcuffed and leg-
ironed, and marched into a gas station bathroom, and taken turns. The
idea that someone I knew would spot me, then call my dad, had my
stomach in knots.

"Hey Howard, I think I just saw your son chained together with
two prisoners, taking a piss at the Richfield station."

Fortunately, we passed through Merced and didn't go through the
embarrassment until we got to Fresno. And it was weird and people in
the nearby area did stop whatever they were doing to google at us. I
didn't care. At least it wasn't Merced.

Three hours later we arrived through earthquake-torn Los Angeles.
I remember getting through the grapevine into the San Fernando
Valley and seeing the bridge and freeway devastation. Once again we
endured the indignity of being led out of the car and marched to the
men's room at some Union 76 station. Of course, being L.A., these
lookie-loos were taking pictures. I wonder if, 47 years later, sitting in a
drawer somewhere, or tucked away in a box up in an attic, long
forgotten, is a picture of me, Pete and Bill, chained together, heading
for the bathroom.

By now, we were all pretty hungry, but none of us wanted to walk
into a restaurant, not that it would've happened. Charlie pulled into an
A&W Drive-In, where we could order from the car. I'll never forget
that young, un-intimidated free spirit of a waitress who took our
orders. She had to have been a model-actress, and this was her side

job. When she looked in the back seat and saw us handcuffed and leg-ironed, her take was hilarious!

"Hi, what can I get you gentle- whoaa!" And she didn't back off. "Prisoners, huh?" I waited for Charlie or John to say. "Miss, please don't talk them. Just take their orders." But I guess they just wanted to watch us squirm.

"So what are you guys in for? What'd you do?" I wasn't going to say anything, but Pete blurted out, "Bank robbery."

Then Bill chimed in with, "Narcotics."

What the hell, it was my turn, so I said:

"I killed a waitress who brought me the wrong order."

I could see Charlie and John, and they didn't crack a smile. Of course, the waitress knew I was kidding, and went along with it.

"Well, I'll be sure and get your order right!"

After the difficult ordeal of balancing burgers, fries and drinks—don't forget we were handcuffed—we finally continued our journey. It was now the hottest part of the day, and heading southeast toward Blythe, California and beyond, it was only going to get hotter. It had to be at least 110 degrees outside. That's when Charlie and John decided to fuck with our heads. Instead of rolling up the windows and turning on the air conditioner, they rolled the windows down and Charlie put the pedal to the metal, going anywhere from 80 to 110 miles per hour. Within minutes we were sweating our asses off. It was like being trapped in a wind tunnel, with temperatures exceeding 150 degrees. It was suffocating. One of the guys asked Charlie if he could roll up the windows and hit the A.C., but Charlie pontificated how much gas an air conditioner uses up. I see... But going 110 mph didn't!?And I believe it was somewhere between Blythe, California, and the Arizona border when I experienced a transcendental state of mind. Our FBI escorts were kind enough to keep the radio on, and that's when I heard, "the song" I mentioned earlier—that beautiful acoustic guitar and the mellow, soothing voice of James Taylor singing, "You've Got a Friend."

The lyrics to that song came right out of that radio and into my heart. Because right about that time, I knew my closest friends were at the San Francisco County jail, standing in a long line waiting to see me. And by now they'd learned that I was gone, and no one would give them information. I knew they were worried about me – that I was being thought of...

Even now, whenever I hear "You've Got A Friend," I think of that day and I don't know if there could have been a better place to hear that song for the first time, and have it carry the meaning that it does to this very day.

It was getting to be late in the afternoon when our escorts decided they'd done enough driving for the afternoon. We'd reached Arizona and would finish the drive to Safford Federal Prison in the morning. While Charlie and John would be kicking it in a motel, we stayed at a county jail in some dink-ass town. The front office was modern, but once we went back into the cell area, we entered the late 1800's—bars built into the rocks. It reeked of musk and mildew. I'm sure that place entertained many a bank robber, gunfighter, drunk and disorderly cowboy, and even a few Indians, in its' time. It was obviously not the main line, just a few holding cells. And today, us peaceniks were the only criminals there, and we each got our own cell. That is, until about one hour later. While we were eating the dinner they fed us, they brought in another prisoner—a kid in his late teens-early 20's... and all hell broke loose.

We never found out why the kid was arrested, but he had apparently swallowed some peyote buttons, mescaline, or acid—because a few minutes after they stuck him in with Bill, the drug kicked in and he started hallucinating. He was seeing strange patterns and designs on the walls, which in his mind, began to start closing in on him. Before we knew it, he was running from side to side, trying to hold the walls back. But that wasn't working, so he began slamming his body against the walls, trying to stop them from crushing him. A couple of times, his momentum caused his head to hit the walls, and his face was bleeding. We tried to get him calmed down, but he wouldn't listen, so we started screaming and whistling for the guards. But they didn't hear us.... And then he went into an epileptic seizure. He fell to the floor and began shaking violently. We told Bill to try and stick a spoon in his mouth so he wouldn't swallow his tongue. Bill was making a valiant effort at it, then finally our yelling brought three officers in. They quickly opened the cell and removed the badly self-destructed inmate, bringing an end to a very long day.

Charlie and John must have picked us up around 9:00 a.m. the next morning, because this town to Safford was around 356 miles, and I remember getting to the prison at 3:00 p.m. that afternoon. But let's not get ahead of ourselves. Still one more minor incident:

The drive to Safford from this dink-ass town took us through a lonely stretch of road. I'm sure it looks better today. But Charlie couldn't hold it any longer. He started asking us why we thought we were too good to do our duty to our country. We tried to explain that it wasn't our country we were being asked to serve, but leaders who were waging an illegal, undeclared war. I honestly can't remember how long we stayed on the subject, or what was further discussed. But I do remember one of my fellow prisoners having to urinate badly, and we were miles from a gas station. So Charlie pulled off to the side of the road and ordered us all out, saying we should all try to go at the same time so he wouldn't have to make separate stops. We got out of the car, and they led us to these bushes. They waited as we went behind them. Well, we were pissing away for a few seconds, then suddenly Charlie says, "I sure wish you guys would try to make a run for it." I don't remember what our expressions were when we looked at each other, but we all had the same thought: How easy it would be on this stretch of road for those guys to just shoot us and say we were trying to escape. And they could make it look believable, too. But we knew they wouldn't. Both were upstanding guys. Still, it was disconcerting to think that Charlie might be having a Korean War flashback about holding one of his bleeding comrades, who died in his arms. And now here he was, hauling CO's to prison. It had to grate on him that Pete worked for the government when he refused induction and had a higher G-rating than Charlie did. But nonetheless, I said:

"Sir, the reason we're here with you today, is because we didn't run."

We got back in the car and drove away. I couldn't wait to get to prison.

Chapter Thirty-five
Well.... Maybe I could.

We finally pulled into the town of Safford without further incident. Safford Federal Prison Camp—now called the Federal Correctional Institution—was seven miles south of town. I was now getting anxious. What would this prison experience be like? What kind of inmates would be waiting and barking out catcalls as we walked down the line? I remember Jerry Samone saying it'd be minimum security. What exactly did that mean?

But as we got within a quarter mile of the prison, I could see it was indeed minimum security. There were no gun towers, which immediately set my mind at ease. There weren't even any high walls for that matter. It was a simple administration building, one story high. There was a small lawn in front of it, as well as a stretch of green grass in front of the parking lot filled with cars.

The three of us were led into the main building, still handcuffed and leg-ironed. I remember passing by a large glass display case, where inmates presented their handmade crafts for sale: Purses, wallets, and belts. We clanked our way up to the admittance window. We could hear music coming from outside a door on the left which I later learned was the visiting area. I got a peek out the glass door leading to the compound: dormitory buildings on either side of a cemented area that had bolted-in benches and tables. This area was covered by an arbor, to offer protection from the sun. There were two televisions mounted on high beams, with a few inmates watching whatever was on. I was immediately relieved to see that there was no "gauntlet" of inmates lined up for us to pass between. It was very quiet. Thank God.

After our shackles were taken off, the sergeant at the desk began with the processing. Charlie and John said their curt good-byes and insincere good lucks and left. That was our final touch with the outside world, such as they were. We were now official residents of Safford Federal Prison Camp, former home of David Harris, political activist and husband to folksinger Joan Baez... And future home of one of Richard Nixon's cohorts in the famous Watergate cover-up scandal.

Next up... A meeting with one Mr. William Cunningham, the prison's Senior Case Worker. He would talk to each of us individually. While we waited, an inmate walked out of the visiting area. The first thing we noticed is that he was wearing an army uniform—not combat fatigues, but light brown pants and a short-sleeved matching shirt— nevertheless, ironic. He came up to us, asked if we were draft resistors. We replied affirmative. He replied that he was too, and as though acting the spokesman for all CO's at the prison, let us know that our job was not yet finished.

"We still need to raise hell in here, and give the guards a hard time," he said.

Why would we want to do that? It's going to be tough enough in here, I thought. Would giving them a hard time do anything to get our guys back home from Vietnam any faster... Or get me out of here sooner? Were the guards going to throw up their arms and say, "Oh, those darn CO's! They're so rowdy. We quit! We can't take it anymore – we're out of here!" No, when I was found guilty and hauled to prison, my protest against the war was declared and official. It was now time to figure out how the hell I was going to get through this experience with as little physical and emotional damage as possible.

The inmate then went on to let us know the man we were about to meet was a first-class ass-hole—that he had nothing but contempt for draft dodgers.

"He'll berate you, insult you, but tell him he'll still be here long after you're gone."

At that moment, Cunningham came out of his office, looked at the inmate and told him to get the away from the new prisoners. The inmate just turned and walked away. Cunningham stared up at us. He was a stocky man about 5'9", white flattop haircut. His cheeks were plump and red, like he was about to explode. He didn't seem at all like a very pleasant man. Pete was the first one in. Five minutes later he was out. Cunningham couldn't see that Pete just looked at us and rolled his eyes and sat down. Cunningham called for Bill next. After a few minutes, Bill came out showing no emotion one way or the other. But at least I never heard any yelling while either of them were in there.

"Bruce Neckels?!" Cunningham barked.

It's amazing what a handshake and a smile will do in even the direst situations. Cunningham stood by the door as I passed by him and entered his office. When he closed the door and turned, I was standing there with my hand extended and a soft smile on my face.

"How do you do, Mr. Cunningham. I'm Bruce Neckels. I can't say it's a pleasure to meet you."

I really didn't expect the guy to shake my hand, but surprise, surprise, he let my comment sink in, gave me a very thin smile, then shook my hand.

"Have a seat, Neckels." For what it was worth, I had broken the ice.

He looked at my file, realized I was awaiting appeal. I mentioned that when they woke me up at the San Francisco County jail yesterday morning, I thought my attorney had heard from William O. Douglas and that I was going home. But instead... here I am, and I expect to probably hear something this week. Cunningham said that I needed to be processed and assigned a dorm, but that he'd wait this next week before assigning me a job. He then asked why I refused induction. I told him I'd studied the history of Vietnam; that I felt it was an illegal, undeclared war. I mentioned my arm, and how the pre-induction physical ignored my injury. He offered no smiles or words of understanding. But then he asked:

"Why didn't you offer to do alternative service?" Great question!

I responded that I offered to serve in a hospital for five years, emptying bedpans for the sick and elderly, but was refused. Cunningham made a notation and that was pretty much it. I was assigned a dorm, then, Bill, Pete and I were escorted out into the compound by a guard. Most of the inmates watching TV outdoors were Mexican. There were a few Caucasian inmates straggling about—including the guy who we'd met in the main office—but none of them felt threatening at all.

We were taken to a dorm where they had several beds reserved for new inmates—until they were given work assignments. Then they'd be transferred to a permanent dorm. I wouldn't be going anywhere for a week. Pete and Bill would be employed the next day. Immediately inside the entrance of the dorm were two rooms with no doors. One had several showers. The other had a half dozen or so toilets lined next to each other, offering no privacy. The main room housing prisoners was long and divided down the middle by a partition maybe four feet high. Each side had two rows of beds and lockers, making four rows—I'd guess about 20 beds and lockers to a row.

We were shown our beds, then taken to the barbershop, where I was able to convince an inmate barber to not cut my hair real short since I was on appeal. Surprisingly, and with no objection from the guard, I was granted that request, though he still cut it a little too short. Next, we had our pictures taken and prison numbers issued, then led to the laundry room, where we took off and turned in our street clothes, then dressed up in prison army uniforms. We were given our sheets, pillows, and blankets, and sent back to our dorm to make our beds and settle in. After the journey we'd been on for the last two days, we were totally exhausted. But no sooner were we settled than other CO's, coming in from the visiting area, came into the dorm to meet us and see who we were. Suddenly the place seemed like a fraternity club, as all the CO's were educated, intelligent—most of them had graduated from college. They were from all over—Iowa, Utah, California, and Arizona. I finally felt relaxed after two weeks of hell at San Francisco County and a 1,000-mile journey. But all I wanted now was to take that 1,000-mile trip back to San Francisco.

And four days later, it happened. But those were four of the longest, most frustrating, angst-filled days. Not that I ever felt in any danger. It was waiting for that goddamn phone call informing me that I would be released OR (own recognizance) pending an appeal. But to pass the time, I learned what I could about Safford Federal Prison Camp.

And that started Monday morning, my first full day there. The prison whistle sounded at 6:00 a.m. Everyone had a half-hour for breakfast, then most of the inmates got on trucks and were herded out to work detail. Inmates remaining at the camp either worked camp maintenance, kitchen duty, the glove factory, or were powerhouse employees - more on that later.

The kitchen-duty inmates also broke up into three shifts. According to a much older inmate who had spent about thirty years in Leavenworth and was now being weaned for freedom by coming to this minimum-security camp, Safford Federal Prison food was the worst in the entire federal prison system. I didn't find the food that bad—other than lots of starch and carbs. But it made sense that the maximum-security federal prisons would have good food. When you're spending time behind bars, living in small cells for years, the least you can do to keep inmates from rioting is serve good food. But in all fairness to the kitchen staff at Safford, most of the cooks were Mexicans who were only doing six-month stints for trying to illegally cross the border, so they really didn't really have time to hone in on their gourmet cooking skills.

The glove factory was the best paying job and why many Mexicans tried to get caught coming across the border. They made $26.00 a month, which they sent back to their families in Mexico. They had three square meals a day, clean uniforms and underwear every day, clean beds to sleep in, and showers every day. This was a better life than most of them had on the outside, sans freedom. But the work detail outside the camp—hard work to be sure—was rather amusing. From what I'd learned, the prison camp was originally built so that cheap labor could build a road from Safford to a mountain resort area, which included a lake. However, with the equipment at hand to build this road, we calculated that it would take 126 years to complete the job.

My attorney did call late Monday morning, telling me he was aware of where I'd been taken, but still no word from Douglas. And that's when I really got nervous. All along it seemed imminent that I would be released. But what if it didn't happen? What if Conti was somehow able to deny my release? After all, he did throw me in without bail. Could he somehow override Douglas? Did Douglas already have his quota of OR's filled? What the hell did I know about the law?!Jesus, this could be it. I could be here for two years. Tuesday was worse. I didn't get a phone call at all, one way or the other. Nor did one come on Wednesday. It was June 30th. The Fourth of July would fall on a Sunday, and I wanted to be home. But it didn't look good. If I didn't hear from my attorney by Friday, I'd be here another weekend. And then it came. Thursday afternoon, the Sergeant's voice over the camp loudspeaker:

"Neckels, report to control! Neckels, to control!"

My heart was ready to jump out of my skin. I quickly walked up to the control room, and Mr. Cunningham was standing there, with a thin smile on his face.

"In my office... You have a phone call." He said. We went into his office, where he handed me the phone.

"Hello?" It was my lawyer.

"You ready to come home?"

I wanted to start crying, I was so happy. But I kept my cool and very flippantly said, "Sure."

Saul then told me that William O. Douglas had granted my appeal. Saul had also spoken with Mr. Cunningham regarding arrangements for my release. I would leave on a bus from Safford to Phoenix, then catch a plane to San Francisco.... Tomorrow morning. I asked Saul to notify my friends who had kept in touch with him. But he had already done so. I thanked him and hung up. Free at last, free at last. Cunningham congratulated me and told me he'd have his office set up my travel plans for tomorrow, then call me back with the information. I thanked him, but thinking I'd be up in front of Judge Conti again, told him I'd more than likely be coming back.

"Well then, we'll make the best of it," Cunningham replied.

I walked out of the control room, trying to remain calm. Paranoia was already setting in. I didn't want to appear too happy in case some angry inmate looking at five years was watching and wanted to stab me in my sleep to keep me from being free. I went to my dorm and just sat quietly on my bed. Within the hour I was called back to the control office and given my travel plans. I'd be catching a bus from Safford to Phoenix early in the morning, then fly to San Francisco. I'd be home by 3:00 p.m. Friday afternoon. I was already making plans in my mind. I'd call Heather as soon as I got to Safford, have her pick me up at the airport, and then spend 4th of July weekend with her. We'd open up a bottle of BV Georges De Latour Private Reserve Cabernet Sauvignon, smoke a couple of joints; then Marcia, Susan, Barbara,

Brad, Heather, and I would head to Gatsby's Friday night in Sausalito, and listen to the Jean Hoffman Trio. Known as the "Miss Oscar Peterson of Jazz," Jean was one of the most shit-kicking extemporaneous piano players I've ever heard. My buddy Al, Marcia's boyfriend, was the drummer, and Nat Johnson played standing bass and had a voice like Nat King Cole.

The road crew hadn't returned to the camp yet. Pete and Bill were on that detail, and I couldn't tell them until dinner. It was kind of sad for me because I'd met two guys who helped me get through a most incredible journey. A journey they would take for the last time until their release, but one that I could, God forbid, be destined to repeat.

After dinner, I walked with Pete to his dorm. We'd been talking about San Francisco during the last few days, and it just so happened that his girlfriend lived in the Cow Hollow district, just above the Marina where I lived. He gave me her address and phone number and asked me to call her and even go pay her a visit. Pete was such a mellow, confident, upstanding guy, and I appreciated his trust in me, and moreover, his trust in her. I told him I would. The saving grace about this prison camp was that we didn't have to stay in our dorms after the 9:00 o'clock count. After the inmates were accounted for, we could come back outside. I talked with some of the CO's until around midnight, then went to my dorm. I was so excited about going home, I couldn't sleep. Besides, I was afraid of being stabbed in my sleep, remember?

Friday morning, and I was up with the six o'clock whistle. I had breakfast with Pete and Bill, then said goodbye to them. I'd be in San Francisco by the time they got back from road detail.

"Neckels, report to the laundry room. Neckels to the laundry room." Music to my ears. I turned in my bedding, the uniform I was wearing, and got into my own clothes. I then went to the control room, where I was handed my wallet, which still contained the cash I'd brought with me when I first entered SF County Jail. I was told to have a seat and a guard would be up in a few minutes to take me to the Safford bus depot. My bus departure was 10 a.m., and now I was paranoid that they'd purposely make me late so I'd have to wait hours for the next bus and then miss my flight.

But that didn't happen. A guard moved in and said, "Let's go." How great it was to get into a car without being handcuffed and leg-ironed. Within minutes we arrived at the Safford Bus Depot. My ticket was already paid for and waiting. I thanked the guard. He wished me luck and drove off. I was standing there alone in a small-town bus depot, never happier in my life. I went inside the bus station and picked up my ticket. Talk about government waste! If they'd just let me stay at S. F. County for one more week, they wouldn't have had to have paid two FBI officers time, food, and gas mileage, plus a bus ticket, plus airfare. But what the hell, it was what it was. Within a half hour I was on a greyhound headed for Phoenix - a three-hour trip through some pretty desolate country—rough, dry terrain and saguaro cactus.

It was July 2nd, 1971.Even though we were still two years away from bringing the boys home, we had lost 55,000 of our own men, and probably four million North and South Vietnamese combined army and civilians. 1971 would be the last year that our country would lose over a thousand men per year. We suffered 2,350 casualties that year—as opposed to 16,600 in 1968. California led the way in number of soldiers to die in Vietnam, with over 5,000; American soldiers 19 - 21 years old sustained the most casualties with over 33,000. There was a huge cry about the number of African Americans sent to die in the jungles of Vietnam—over 7,000 – but the ratio was fair. Caucasian deaths were over 30,000. American casualties in '72 dropped to 640; then to 168 in 1973. And even though the troops finally came home in 1973, with the war ending officially in April of 1975, we lost another 1,300 men. In the post-war years of 76 and 77, we lost 173.[35] Can you imagine your child, husband, brother, friend, being the last soldier to die in a stinking, worthless, illegal war after it was over?

But sitting on that bus, heading for the airport, then home, my life was still up in the air. Nothing had been settled. I would now have to go through the appeal process, whenever that would be—in one month or one year—and if I lost, it meant that I was going to have to go through this shit one more time. Hopefully, I wouldn't. The mood in this country by 1971 had changed even more dramatically. In April of that year, the Vietnam Veterans against the War helped lead a half million demonstrators in Washington DC. They had appealed to Congress to urge Nixon the put a halt to this military madness.

And what had I done to help bring an end to the war? Up to then, nothing as a single individual. But as part of a collective consciousness—i. e., the Students for a Democratic Society (SDS); those who fled to Canada, faked injuries; faked being drug addicts and homosexuals; mothers of sons killed in Vietnam, and now the Vietnam Veterans Against the War—the guys who really put their lives on the line, many of whom had to demonstrate in wheelchairs—and yes, guys like me, and other CO's who were willing to choose prison—the message was loud and clear.

Entrance to Safford Federal Prison

Chapter Thirty-six
Goodbye Stormy Heather...

N ow, if I was writing a movie script here, and wanted to give you a happy ending, you'd see me in a SERIES OF DISSOLVES and CUT-TO'S:DISSOLVE TO: The bus arriving in Phoenix. CUT TO: me getting in a cab; CUT TO: me getting out of the cab at the Phoenix Airport; CUT TO: me on the plane heading for San Francisco. My eyes are closed and I'm smiling. DISSOLVE TO: me, moving briskly down the aisle to the terminal; suddenly I stop, looking straight ahead. POV: There's Heather, standing there waiting for me, tears in her eyes. We run into each other's arms and melt into a passionate kiss. She pulls back and says, "Welcome home, darling. I'm never letting you out of my sight again." And as we walk away from camera, these words appear on screen:

"Bruce and Heather were married one month later. Bruce's appeal hearing came in December, but by then the war was over, thanks to efforts of so many who opposed it. The three appellate judges saw no reason to send Bruce back to prison."

But this ain't the movies, folks. I got off the plane full of expectations, but Heather wasn't waiting. Since I didn't have any luggage, I went straight out to the "Arrivals." The place was a logjam, what with holiday weekend upon us. I looked around but didn't see Heather and her yellow Pontiac convertible anywhere. But I didn't have to wait long. There she was, coming around the curve. I waved, she saw me and pulled up. I got into the car. I looked at her face... And she was pissed.

"Your plane was late. I had to drive around three times."

"Oh, I'm sorry... So, hello."

We gave each other a kiss, then headed for my apartment. Again, my expectations were soaring, but I could see she was very irritated. I asked her why and she said it was because she was right in the middle of helping her best friend move into a new apartment in Pacifica—and then they were going to spend the 4th of July weekend somewhere in Marin County.

"They?" Not "we?"

"You can come if you want to. I just thought you'd want to be with your friends."

Which was sort of what I had in mind. Only I wanted Heather to be with me. We arrived at my apartment on Scott Street. God, it was fabulous! To smell the salt air; hear the foghorns on the bay. She came inside with me, and I immediately saw that someone had gotten the place really cleaned up, with fresh flowers on the top of my stereo console—along with a new album, left as a gift, Graham Nash's "Simple Man," which included the song, "Military Madness."

Heather couldn't stay—had to get back to Pacifica. She invited me again, but I really wanted to see my friends. I wanted to sleep in my own apartment tonight. I asked her to please come back when she finished helping her friend move. She said she'd call me and we'd work it out. Then she left. This just wasn't right—not how I'd planned it all. It was almost as though she couldn't wait to get away. She was a very mysterious girl, and who knows what could've happened in her life in the three weeks I was in jail.

She didn't call that night. She didn't call Saturday, July 3. And what made that weekend even more painful was the news that Jim Morrison, lead singer of the Doors, had been found dead of an apparent heart attack in Paris, France – lying naked in a bathtub. Another rock icon, gone. Jimi Hendrix had died on September, 1970; Janis Joplin followed less than three weeks later in October. The three of them in less than a year. The hippie/acid rock/anti-war counter culture had taken quite a hit. The lingering 60's, to me, had officially signed off.

However, on Monday, I contacted Pete's girlfriend. I told her who I was; the trip Pete and I made together to Safford, and how I promised him I'd give her a call and maybe get together. She invited me over that afternoon. We sat around and talked, smoked some weed, drank wine. She was a very pretty, confident, practical, soft-spoken lady—and a most interesting match for Pete. She was on the hippie side; he, a CO who had worked for the government. She promised to stay in touch with me and let me know when she heard from Pete. I left, wishing Heather could have been as together.

The following week Heather surfaced again, but there was nothing romantic. I remember it was cold that day, and she didn't have a jacket, so I gave her my junior college letter jacket with leather sleeves. After she left, I tried calling her for days and she never returned my calls. Then one day, she picked up the phone assuming it was another guy and said his name. "No, Heather, it's Bruce." She hung up. This was one troubled lady, and drugs had a lot to do with it. It was time for me to go. I borrowed a car, then drove to her house—and waited—for at least two hours. Finally, she pulled up, and when she got out of the car, I moved up and asked just why the hell she was treating me like this. She replied that she was scared that I would have to face prison again and just didn't want to go through it all over. I believed her on that one. After all she did have a new boyfriend, and I made her admit it. She cried and apologized. And I said good-bye. Strangely, she was wearing my letter jacket and wanted to give it back. But like a dumb shithead, I told her to keep it, thinking it would always remind her of me, and that maybe one day she'd come back.

But God was still looking out for me. Had Heather come back to me, I'd have never left San Francisco. Because what happened between the time I walked away from her and my appeal five months later was the most amazing acting experience I would ever have. And if I had any misgivings about choosing prison over going to Vietnam, they would be put to rest by students, teachers, parents, and even a few Vietnam Vets all across this nation and Canada. And all it cost me were a few weeks of emotional turmoil getting over her, and of course... my letter jacket.

Chapter Thirty-seven
Hello college coeds...

For the next month, all I did was hang out with friends and rehash the "experience." My attorney even came over one night and joined several of us for dinner. He assured me that my appeal date wouldn't come for a few months, which made me happy. I didn't want to spend Christmas in prison, should I lose. I wanted to get back on the audition trail and hopefully pick up a national commercial or two, and whatever else came along in the way of TV or movies. It was the third week of August. I'd celebrated my birthday the week before, and what I really needed to do was get back to the fitness club and start working out again. But I just couldn't seem to get off my ass and get over there. Well, timing is everything.

It was Friday, August 27. Normally, I worked out in the morning... But I didn't get there until about three o'clock in the afternoon. There weren't a lot of people in the club. I was well into my workout, when one of the trainers walked in and saw me. He moved up, said hello and wanted to know where the hell I'd been for the last two months. I told him all about it– from courtroom to County jail, the trip handcuffed and leg-ironed to Safford Prison. The trainer kept asking me questions. He was fascinated. And unbeknownst to me, so was another guy who happened to be there working out. I didn't notice him, but he was eavesdropping in on every word. By the time I walked out of the gym and headed for home, that normal routine I was hoping to get back to was not going to happen. And as crazy as it sounds, going to jail was a pre-requisite to the whirlwind journey I was about to embark upon.

I wasn't back at my apartment for five minutes when the phone rang. It was the trainer from the fitness club. Apparently after I left, a man came up to him, inquiring about me.

"He'd like to know if you could meet him at the Chestnut Street Bar and Grill. He wants to talk to you about maybe going out on some kind of tour. His name's Jack. He'll be at the bar having a beer."

Well, how enticing was that? I was out the door just out of curiosity. He could've been Jack the fucking ripper as far as I knew.

I walked in the bar. It was practically empty, and there he was, this mousy-looking, chunky character, about 5'8", at the counter with a mug of beer. As soon as he saw me, he smiled. I went over to him and we made our introductions. His name was Jack Clemons. He was tour manager for a theatre group of ex-convicts called the Barbwire Theatre. He had overheard my conversation about going to prison and wanted to know if I'd ever done any acting. When I told him I was a professional actor who'd' done theater, movies, and commercials, his eyes lit up. He then asked me if I'd be interested in auditioning for a chance to go out on a nation-wide tour of colleges with a 90-minute one-act prison drama called *The Cage*. I hadn't heard of the play, so Jack gave me a brief history about it. The tour itself was three-part package: The actors performed mainly at colleges, starting off with classroom visitations during the day—classes like sociology, psychology, law, drama—where they talked about the prison system in its current state of insanity, and their personal experiences in prison. Part two was the performance of the play that evening. Part three of the program was the actors coming back out on stage for a Q and A with the audience about the play, and more prison talk.

I told Jack it sounded fascinating, but that I'd be a risk, because my appeal could come up within the next few months and I'd have to leave. He didn't care about that. He told me that one of the actors, also the producer of the show, was tired of touring and wanted to stay home in San Francisco, write plays, and be with his wife.

Jack had a copy of the play in his car. He went and got it; told me to look it over. The college fall semester was just around the corner and they had gotten a last minute request to do the play at a college in Monterey County early next week, due to the Aug. 21 murder of George Jackson in San Quentin Prison. Jackson was a former member of the Soledad Brothers, a trio of inmates who murdered a guard in Soledad Prison in 1970. A black militant member of the Black Panther Party, he was gunned down during an alleged escape attempt. According to prison officials, Jackson's activist attorney smuggled a pistol to Jackson hidden in a tape recorder which Jackson then hid underneath his Afro hair wig. There were several controversial stories surrounding this report. Many felt it was impossible to hide an Astra 9-mm semi-automatic in a tape recorder or the wig; and that Jackson was set up to be murdered because his two books, "Blood In My Eye," and "Soledad Brother: The Prison Letters of George Jackson," were making him too famous, and the FBI and Quentin officials wanted to destroy the Panthers and the civil rights movement.[36] Others claimed that his major rival, Huey Newton, had him eliminated to gain control over the Black Panthers, and all that royalty money from his books, would support the Panthers.[37] At any rate, it was a national topic, ripe for the Barbwire Theatre and their prison package.

"I'll call you Wednesday. That should give you plenty of time. If you're interested, we'll set up an audition."

I asked him if there was any particular role I should be focusing on and he said, "Yeah... Hatchet." I figured why the hell not. Even though I'd only been in jail for a month, the fact that I'd be able to face all those college students, and tell them that I'd more than likely be going back to prison, could have some sympathetic value. Besides, the 60's were over. All the "peace and groovy love" was starting to trail off. The summer of 71 had been tumultuous to say the least. America's attitude toward the Vietnam War had swung left because of student protests; the Supreme Court ordered busing of students to racially integrate schools; and with all that social pressure, culminating with George Jackson's murder, even prison inmates were now getting into the act and wanted their rights recognized. This could be an interesting time. In addition, I'd made my personal statement, and to be honest, I wanted to see how the youth of America felt about what I'd done. But first things first. I had to get the part. So I read the play, and what a mind blower. I mean, this fucking thing was sick!

The Cage is a gritty prison drama about three inmates doing life in an isolated prison cell. It was a six-character play, with two sadistic guards and four inmates: Hatchet, totally insane, schizophrenic, mass murderer, who thinks he's Jesus Christ, a Civil War general, and a Supreme Court judge; Al, a crippled homosexual, afraid to death of Hatchet, and gives himself over for sexual favors to Doc for protection; Doc, who is more humored by Hatchet than anything and

187

actually enjoys playing Hatchet's games. Into their mix comes a new young inmate, Jive, who may or may not have killed his girlfriend. The play is about Jive trying to survive in this dungeon of insanity and madness. The centerpiece of the play is a toilet bowl, which is used first as a baptismal bowl, where Hatchet, as the Christ figure, gets Jive to confess his guilt, then baptizes him in toilet water. Later, it becomes the Supreme Court bench on which Hatchet stands for Jive's trial. Doc, who wants this "fresh meat" spared for future sexual gratification, serves as Jive's lawyer. Al, jealous of Doc's feelings for this new inmate, becomes the prosecutor, and wants Jive found guilty, knowing the severity of his punishment, should Hatchet find him guilty. In the end, Jive is found guilty, and though he begs for Hatchet to help him, Hatchet mercifully strangles Jive to death, then proclaims to the audience, *"I have done your will. Your will!"*[38] Inferring that as a society, we build these iron jungles without any idea of what we're creating inside. Therefore, through our indifference and neglect, whatever happens, we're all to blame. The role of Hatchet had more levels than I wanted to count. It scared the shit out of me because I didn't know if I could pull it off. Jack called me the following Wednesday morning, the night after the play. Apparently, the theatre was filled to capacity with students anxious to talk about Jackson's murder at San Quentin. Jack asked if I'd had a chance to read the play.

"About five times," I replied. "I wanta do it."

Jack said he'd set up an appointment for the next day, to meet Ben Niems and Ken Whelan, *The Cage* producers. In fact, Ken was the one currently playing the role of Hatchet.

Thursday afternoon, I arrived at the Barbwire Theater office on Geary Street. There was no one else there to audition. I got the feeling I was it. Ben and Ken were there waiting for me. Ken was this big, burly Orson Wells type, and I just couldn't imagine taking over his role. We were so different physically, vocally, and even in age. Already I was apprehensive. But we talked for a while—about my acting career, mainly my theatre experience, and my prison experience—then Ken asked me to open up the script and read a long monologue—one where Hatchet confronts his audience. Though terrifying and mad, it was a beautiful monologue. I read well enough for them to want me to meet the author, Rick Cluchey, who had also played the role of Hatchet. I don't know if I was really that good, or if Ken saw enough to indicate that I could be directed, so he could get off the tour. I would meet Rick the next day, Friday September 3. He was on his way in from Modesto, Calif., where he was currently raising Doberman Pinchers.

The next day, I was back in the office. I read for Rick, and the part was mine. He had no problem with the fact that I'd only been in jail for less than a month. I was really more of a ringer than anything else, and with that in mind, Rick felt my crime was too soft and suggested that maybe I could change it to a drug bust. I absolutely refused, saying that because the Vietnam War was the most major topic of protest in America, that college students would want to hear from someone who'd experienced what I was going through. It made perfectly good sense to Rick and that was the end of that. Though he couldn't be there, Rick wanted me to come to a brush-up rehearsal of the play, where I would meet the cast with whom I'd be touring. They would be leaving for the Midwest next week to start the fall tour. I panicked. There's no way I could be ready, plus I had to make arrangements for someone to watch my apartment, make bank deposits from checks I'd be sending them, and pay bills. Ken set my mind at ease. The plan was to start rehearsing with Ben on Monday, September 6, until I was fairly comfortable with the role, then Rick would come back the second week and really add on the layers to my character.

"They'll work with you for two weeks before you join the tour. You'll have a chance to see several performances and rehearse with us for two weeks. It'll be a month before you even go on. "I felt better. One month was plenty of time for me. Little did I realize it was all bullshit.

I went home that Friday afternoon and started learning my lines. I was a quick study back then and by Monday's rehearsal I had the play practically memorized. I hated to rehearse with a script in my hand, especially a play as physical as *The Cage*. I always tried to get off book as quickly as possible so I could have more freedom. We rehearsed in Ben's office, which was very small so movement was very limited and awkward. Ben was quite impressed that I already had

189

my lines. Tuesday's rehearsal was better and that night I showed up at the Barbwire Theatre rehearsal hall with Jack. It was an upstairs, one-room space in the Tenderloin District of San Francisco, one of the worst areas in town. Fortunately, it was still light outside. I don't think I would've shown up had it been night. Well, it was a complete waste of time. Rehearsal had been cancelled, only Ken forget to tell Jack and two other cast members- Terry, who played one of the guards, and Gary, who played Jive. Ken decided he'd rather spend his last night with his wife before hitting the road the next day. I was wondering just what the hell I was getting involved in. I was really frustrated because I wanted to see this play on its legs. So on Wednesday, *The Cage* cast set out in two station wagons to begin the tour. I rehearsed with Ben for a couple of hours, then went home.

The next day, all hell broke loose at a maximum-security prison 30 miles south of Buffalo, New York: The Attica Prison Riot. Apparently, tensions had been running high for quite some time due to the horrid living conditions. Things like inmates being allowed only one shower per week; one roll of toilet paper per month, and with overcrowding exceeding the capacity limit by 40%, the inmate population consisting mainly of Puerto Ricans and African Americans had finally reached boiling point. The riot lasted for five days. One thousand inmates took control of the prison and held 40 hostages. Guards were beaten with pipes, chains, and bats. One guard died. The inmates demanded to see Governor Nelson Rockefeller to discuss better conditions, brutality by the administrative staff, and the expulsion of the current prison superintendent. But Rockefeller refused, fearing some kind of domino effect. So instead, he ordered State Troopers to retake the prison on Sept. 13. The result? Ten hostages and twenty-nine inmates lay dead. It was revealed that all the hostages died by gunshots from the troopers and guards.[39] At any rate, the Attica Riot took the Vietnam War off the front pages of every paper in the country. And the topic couldn't have been more perfect for The Cage tour that was just under way. Extra bookings poured in to the Barbwire Theatre Office between September 9 - 13. And on Friday morning, September 10, Ben called from his office.

"You're leaving for the tour next Wednesday."

I went into panic mode. I told Ben I wasn't ready yet.

"You're ready. You'll fly to Milwaukee and meet up with the cast there. You'll rehearse for two weeks before you do your first show."

Did I say earlier it was all bullshit?

That night Rick wanted me to have dinner with him at his apartment in Pacifica. He wanted to get to know me better, talk to me about the play, my character, etc. It was important for me, too, because even though Ben said I was ready and obviously told Rick, I felt so unprepared. During rehearsals with Ben, I'd gotten away with technical and intuitive skills, but I couldn't find the core of this character.

After spending four hours with Rick that night, I could've patterned the character of Hatchet just by observing Rick as himself— the way he listened to me; eyed me with his piercing blue eyes; those deadly pauses before answering questions I asked him; his facial reactions—absolutely unnerving! And I wanted Jive, the new inmate in The Cage, to feel the same way about Hatchet. Yes, it was still technical, but I sensed the painful past that Rick had experienced, as well as a man who was redefining himself as a free spirit; a creative artist who had found theatre as a way to change a hideous prison system that in his own words, *"chewed people up and spit them out"* - and what was needed went way beyond punishment, and he had written a vehicle to drive the point home. But I had no doubt this man had heard it and seen it all and could spot bullshit a mile away.

In 1954, Rick Cluchey was 21 years old when he was given a life sentence in San Quentin without the possibility of parole. His crime was armed robbery, aggravated assault, and kidnapping. From what I heard the gun he was carrying accidentally discharged, hitting his captive in the foot. Three years later, in 1957, the San Francisco Drama Workshop came in with a production of Samuel Beckett's *Waiting for Godot,* and what better play for a prison audience than one which depicts the hopelessness of man's future. But it rejuvenated Rick's life. He had found the theatre. He formed the San Quentin Drama Workshop and began producing, directing, and performing in plays by Beckett. Then in 1965, he wrote "The Cage" and handed it over to the San Francisco Drama Workshop, who staged the original production. Sitting in the audience was a drama critic from the San Jose Mercury. She was so blown away by the play; she had to meet the "lifer" who wrote it. She paid a visit to Rick at San Quentin and thus began a one-woman campaign to commute his sentence. It didn't take long. In 1966 Governor Pat Brown made Rick eligible for parole. And in one more year, Rick was released from prison and formed the Barbwire Theatre in San Francisco. With a grant from the United States Government, he mounted a production of *The Cage* with a cast of ex-convicts and began performing his play at college campuses throughout the country. An amazing story... And I was about to become a part of it. That night, I called Pete's girlfriend and let her know what had transpired, and that I'd be out on a tour for a while. I told her I'd call her as soon as I got back.

The following Wednesday morning, me, my one big piece of luggage, a brief case which included a copy of Ramsey Clark's "Crime In America," and 500 copies of the play sealed up in two boxes, to be sold after each performance—were on our way to what would be one of the single most memorable experiences of my life.

Chapter Thirty-eight
The setup…

I arrived in Milwaukee, Wisconsin, around 6:00 p.m., two hours before Showtime. Gary and Terry showed up in one of the cars to pick me up. We drove directly to the college where I was escorted to the dorm room where I'd be staying for the night, then went to meet the other members of the cast, who were having dinner in the cafeteria. I said hello to Ken and Jack who introduced me to the other cast members I hadn't yet met: Don, who was playing the role of "Doc;" and Henry, who played one of the sadistic guards. Now with the exception of Jack, who would be taking over as tour manager, and Ken, who happily would be going home soon, none of the other actors seemed that happy to see me. Ken had been a real father figure to these guys for a long time, not to mention his wit and brilliant mind. As I was to learn later, he was very well educated and could converse on any subject, especially theology, psychology, and of course, our failing prison system. I couldn't imagine why he ended up in San Quentin. But apparently one night he walked into a super market and robbed it, threading the fine line of genius and insanity. And while the terrified cashiers were filling his bag with money, Ken was singing opera, which gave him the nomenclature of "The Singing Bandit." His criminal career didn't last long, however, until he found himself in San Quentin with Rick. They worked together in prison mounting productions for the San Quentin Drama Workshop. Rick was released first, then Ken joined him later at the Barbwire Theatre, where they continued mounting touring productions of *The Cage.*

I accompanied the cast to the theatre, where hundreds of students had already lined up to see the play. We were still an hour away from curtain, so while the guys went off to get into costume, I took a seat a few rows from the front with my note pad and pencil. I planned on taking blocking notes and scribbling down ideas for my character. I sat there alone for a good half hour, staring at an eerie stage, with one,

193

lone toilet bowl as the only prop, with a dim, blue light glowing from inside the bowl.

But once the audience filed in and the play started, all note taking went out the window. It was mesmerizing to watch. And to see Ken up there playing the role that I would be taking over, quite frankly scared the hell out of me. He didn't even have to open his mouth. His presence was so intimidating. There was no way I could pull off Hatchet the way he did.

The play ended to a standing ovation, and now I was really scared. The actors quickly went backstage, wiped the sweat off, and came back out for the second part of the show, which was the audience Q&A. Ken came out first and talked about the origin of the play, then introduced each cast member who took their seats on stage, and the questions and answers began. All the guys had their own wrap down, whether they discussed Attica, George Jackson; the prison system, or their own experiences. The students were so interested and attentive, they could have asked questions for three hours, but the cast cut it off after an hour. And while they were selling copies of "The Cage," I hauled ass to my dorm room, opened up the script and started making notes, figuring out what the hell to do.

A half hour later, there came a knock on my door. It was Ken, wearing a huge grin on his face.

"Well, Johnny, what'd you think?" he quipped. He loved to call me "Johnny."

"I think I want to go home," I replied. He started laughing.

"Ken, I could never play that role the way you do. I didn't learn a damn thing tonight.

"Yes, you did," he replied. "You learned you can't play Hatchet like me. Play it like Rick does. Think jungle cat waiting to pounce; Charles Manson. Don't worry about it. The audiences who see you won't be comparing it to me. You'll make it your own."

Make it my own? Well, shit.... I know that! I'm an actor! I've studied drama. It's just that right now, I don't remember a goddamn line in the play! But fortunately, I have a month to calm down.

Then it came... The "set-up."

"So listen, Johnny," Ken Continued. "Tomorrow I have to go to Whitewater. I'm sitting on a panel for a Crime Commission seminar. I'll be gone all day, so I want you to go with the cast to St. Norbert College at De Pere (we're still in Wisconsin here). You can help Baghdad (that's Henry's middle name) unload and setup the stage while the other guys are doing classroom visits. I think the last class is at 3:00. I'll tell them to meet you at the theatre, and you can get on your feet and do a rehearsal with them. Play doesn't start until 8:00 p.m. I'll be back in plenty of time."

And it really wasn't a bad idea. I kind of wanted to see what it'd be like with these guys on stage. Besides, I was at least two weeks away from doing a performance. Ken left and I immediately started going over my lines and making blocking notes. But about ten minutes after Ken left, I got one those paranoid feelings.

The following morning we all met for breakfast at a local I-Hop or whatever the hell chain restaurant they had back there in the Midwest. Ken instructed the other cast members to do a run-through with me when we got to St. Norbert College. Told us he'd be back by 6:00 p.m. to do the play. I felt a little less paranoid.

De Pere, Wisconsin, training camp for the Green Bay Packers, was a very beautiful, quaint little town, population of around 12,000 people. It was nestled alongside the Fox River, but we were a few months too early for ice fishing. It was overcast, with the wind blowing and the leaves turning colors—a beautiful autumn day. St. Norbert College was a Catholic Liberal Arts and Sciences school—I believe that today it's ranked as one of the top Liberal Arts Colleges in the nation.

We checked in at a local motel then went to the school. Gary, Terry, Jack, and Don, went and did their classroom visits while Bags and I set the stage and ran light cues. Later, the guys showed up and we got into our prison uniforms and ran the show once with me playing Hatchet. We had to stop a few times to clean up physical moves and blocking, but it went surprisingly well. It even prompted Don, who seemed the most distant with me, to say, "It was different, but I think we've got a good show here." It was exhausting, but I felt with a few more rehearsals, I could possibly be ready to go in another week.

I didn't get that luxury. 6:00 p.m. rolled around and no Ken in sight. The other guys had gone to dinner, but I was too nervous. I had a feeling that I might have to go on. I stayed in the theatre and just went over the lines. Jack returned to the theatre by himself. I was already in the dressing room, putting on my prison coveralls, which were still wet from the sweat of our earlier rehearsal. I was so nervous, I'd already sat on the real toilet with diarrhea.

"Have you heard from Ken?" I asked.

"No.... He'll be here. We still have an hour. But you should get ready in case."

I tried to act cool and cavalier about it, but I had a butterfly in my stomach with a twelve-foot wingspan. Hundreds of students were already lined up outside the theatre to see the play. So I opened my makeup kit, grayed my hair; I put a pancake base on my face and hands that had a yellow tone to it. Hatchet hadn't seen the light of day in years and I wanted him to look sickly and pale. I darkened the creases in my face to look older, then another trip to the bathroom.

The other cast members arrived and still no Ken. They didn't seem fazed by it because they all thought the rehearsal was good and if I had to go on, we'd get through it. By now, the students had filed into the theatre and every seat was filled. It was noisy with general hubbub. I didn't want to run lines because my voice was tired from the rehearsal and I wanted to save it. I sat by myself and quietly meditated. Then, at 7:45 p.m., Ken walked in. He looked at me and started laughing.

"Well, Johnny? Ready to go on?" All I could do was look at him and give him a sick smile.

"You fucker," I said. "You've been here all along, haven't you? I'll bet you didn't even leave town!"

Again he laughed, but said that he really had gone to Whitewater. I tried to get him to admit he'd been back for hours, but he wouldn't cop to it. He then said he'd go on if I wanted him to.

"No, hell no!" I said. "I'm all psyched up to go on. If I don't then I'm gonna feel a real let down." He knew damn well what my answer would be.

So I went on that night, and I think I only made one mistake, but it wasn't noticeable. It was a damn good performance given the situation, — seven on a scale of ten. The audience gave us a sustained standing ovation. What the hell. But like Ken said, I was the only actor they'd ever seen in the role.

But what happened next was something no one expected. Don went out on stage and gave an introduction and history of the "The Cage" and the Barbwire Theater. He then brought out the other actors to begin the question/answer segment of the evening. Baghdad and I weren't introduced because we were loading up the van. But when we finished, we waited in the wings of the stage, and when Don saw us, he brought us out. He first introduced Baghdad. I was actually just as nervous about going out there as I was doing the play.

"This next guy just flew in from San Francisco last night," Don said. "We only had one rehearsal with him this afternoon and tonight was his first performance." Okay, a few "oohs" and "ahhs" and a nice round of applause; then Don leaned over to Jack and I heard him sotto voce. "What's that guy's name?"

Jack told him and Don introduced me as "Bruce Nichols." Close enough. I came on stage and took the last chair. And then someone in the audience raised their hand and asked:

"How long were you guys in prison and what were your crimes?"

The answers started at the other end: Check forgery, drug dealing, armed robbery, pimping and pandering, bank robbery.... and everyone in the audience remained silent as they listened to the answers. Then came me.

"Well, I was only in for a month. I'm out on appeal and will probably be back in prison by the end of the year. I'm a conscientious objector to the Vietnam War."

The place erupted! The audience stood and cheered and applauded. None of us on stage expected that. I had the chills. I didn't know what to do or how to react. But when the applause stopped and the audience sat down, the questions were now coming at me, and suddenly I had my own story to tell, my own answers to give: "How were you treated in prison?" "What was it like when you didn't step forward at the induction center?" "If you know you're going back to jail, why don't you go underground?" These students wanted to know, because as long as the war was still going on, this was something they would have to face if they chose not to go.

The confrontation ended, and we started selling copies of "The Cage." I must've signed a hundred autographs. It was exhilarating and the other actors felt it, too. I thought back to that day three weeks ago when I walked into the production office—when Ken and Rick asked me to come up with a more dangerous crime, and I refused. I was right….I had the perfect crime for the time.

The next morning, Ken came to my dorm room.

"I'm going back to San Francisco after breakfast. You did a good job last night considering the pressure you were under. It'll only get easier. Don't be afraid to try something new every night and keep throwing surprises at those guys."

And so Ken flew home to San Francisco, while the rest of the cast and I drove to Oshkosh, Wisconsin to perform at Wisconsin St. University. One week later came what turned out to be the highlight of my short tour: Two Friday performances at the University of Wisconsin in Madison – one of the main antiwar-political hotbed colleges in the country. Once again, the response I received when I announced "my crime" was well received. In fact, the next morning one of the actors put a copy of the Wisconsin State Journal at my hotel room door, and there I was – a huge picture of me on the front page.

For the next month, we played many colleges all over the Midwest. Without fail, when it was my turn during the after-show Q&A to state my crime, I got standing ovations and long sustained cheering. I was never booed or made to feel ashamed. And these students were from all over the United States.

In early October, we went into Canada, and performed at the University of Edmonton, Brandon University, and then spent three days at the University of Winnipeg, where we gave five performances. But before returning to the United States, we gave an afternoon performance at a boys reform school, which I believe scared the hell out of those kids—our version of "Scared Straight." And that evening, we performed at Headingly Correctional Center. We got a standing ovation from our inmate audience, thank God. From what the other guys in the cast and one of the Headingly guards told me - if a prison audience doesn't like a show, you know about it!

After the performance, I met two guys - both draft resistors from the United States. One of them was fortunate to get a job working as a recreational director at the prison; but the other wasn't as fortunate. He had committed a crime while in Canada and was an inmate at Headingly. He'd served a couple of years and in just one week, was going to be deported back to the U.S., where he would serve another sentence for draft evasion. I felt so sorry for him. Five other inmates had recently jumped him while he was sleeping. They beat the hell out of him and shaved his head. He didn't look so good. His hair was growing back, but he still had a couple of bumps on his face and five stitches under his eye. I know that if I'd been with him privately, he'd have broken down and cried, but he managed to hold back.

My personal experiences at the colleges in Canada where we performed were no less than positive. Not only did I receive sustained applause or standing ovations, I was offered sanctuary. Quite a few college coeds and a few male students invited me to come live with them. Local merchants offered me jobs. But I refused them all, explaining that I didn't want to put myself in a position where I couldn't come home to my family and friends, nor did I want to jeopardize the Barbwire Theatre and their program operating under a government grant. But I also loved my country and even though I knew I'd be going back to prison, I still had to show my patriotism by opposing an unjust war. I didn't run from my first court appearance, and wouldn't do it for my appeal.

By October 9 (1971), we were back in the USA—in Bemidji, Minnesota. I know my attorney was so grateful to know I was back... Because he let me know that my appeals hearing would take place on November 11. You gotta be shittin' me! Veteran's Day? As if the odds aren't already stacked against me, I'm to face three judges to appeal my prison sentence for being a draft resistor—on Veteran's Day. Give me a fucking break!

I called San Francisco and notified Ken, Rick, and Ben about my appeal hearing date. Ken said he'd contact one of their former actors and have him join us as soon as possible and asked me to continue the tour. And so I did. We performed throughout Minnesota, Illinois, Iowa—and on October 22, 1971, on a rainy day in Washington DC, we did a command performance in the Great Hall of Justice, for a few senators, congressman, and law makers. There were only about 40 or 50 in the audience because of the lousy weather, but I remember how weird it was performing on a very small space, I think the floor was marble, but here was our toilet in the middle with two huge statues— one of them Blind Lady Justice, holding her balanced scales, looking down upon us. I found the irony so amusing, that it was supposed to represent equality in justice, but to me, it meant just the opposite.

That night we went to Dulles Airport and performed a "dinner theatre" of sorts for the FBI National Crime Convention. More irony, getting drunk with FBI agents and other lawmakers after the play, them knowing I was a CO, me knowing I was probably going back to prison—and yet treating me very politely, wishing me luck—and basically not making a very big deal out of it. And for some reason, I didn't ask if there was a possibility they could write letters for me to the Ninth District Court of Appeals, or to my attorney to pass on to the three judges who'd be deciding my fate for the second time. I can't explain it, really. I just didn't feel good about asking anyone to "bail" me out. I felt I had to be responsible for my choice.

The next day, Saturday, October 23, we flew back to Minnesota to pick up our cars, then head for a performance in St. Cloud. A black actor named Bobby Drake joined up with us there the next day. He's the one who's going to take my place. He'd played the role of Hatchet a couple of years ago. This guy was cool! He was going to travel with us for a week, rehearse a couple of times, then I would head for home the following weekend. But first, I had a performance at the University of Nebraska in Lincoln, then three in Omaha.

As soon as we arrived in Lincoln and settled in, I called Marcia in San Francisco, to let her know I'd be home this weekend. She'd been watching my apartment for me. Well, she had a surprise for me. Apparently, a girl from Texas who had gotten a job at Marcia's firm, had just broken off with some guy and needed a place to stay. So Marcia let her stay at my apartment until she could find her own place. I had no problem with that. In fact, my mind was racing! If I lost my appeal and went back to prison, she could just rent my place out and keep it for me for when I got back. This could be perfect. My only question was, how long will we be roommates before I leave—if I leave—and what if I couldn't stand this girl? Marcia replied in a very "suggestive" tone:

"Oh, don't worry... You won't mind having her around at all." Now I couldn't wait to get home!

The afternoon performance in Lincoln was the best one yet. On October 27, we did another afternoon performance in Omaha, which was filmed by CBS Evening News with Roger Mudd. I remember seeing it on CBS a couple of hours before our 8:00 p.m. performance and I looked like one, crazy, insane, son of a bitch! When I arrived at the theatre at 7:00 p.m., it was cold and raining so they had already let the audience in, and it was filled to capacity. The next night, we performed in front of 2,000 people. The Attica Prison riot was still the hot topic of the month, and our play was riding that wave. It was incredible. But the next morning was not. Bobby suddenly decided he didn't want to do the play. He realized in just a few days he didn't want the rigors of travel. He had a wife and a good job as a boys' counselor. He was ready to go home. Well, so was I. I called Ken and gave him the news. I don't know why he didn't try and persuade Bobby to do the show for a few days, but by Oct. 30, Bobby was gone. Ken asked me to do the play until he could get there on - November 3. What else could I do? I called Marcia and let her know I'd be a few days late.

I gave my final three performances at the University of Illinois, in Chicago; drove 300 miles to Andrewsville and the University of Southern Illinois; then drove another 293 miles to Dubuque, Iowa, where I gave my last performance on November 3. Ken was there, ready to take over. We had a farewell party at the hotel lounge and the next day I took a cab to the local municipal airport and hopped on an Ozark twin-prop airplane to Omaha. From there I flew United back to San Francisco. My friend, Joanne, was there to pick me up and take me to my apartment in the Marina. It was early afternoon, and Marcia had left my key under the doormat. I was so glad to be home. Whoever my temporary roommate was, sure had the place looking nice. My stash of wine was still in the closet, so I cracked open a BV Burgundy and poured myself a glass. Then I got on the phone and called my attorney to let him know I was home.

He gave me some good news. The court realized they'd made a scheduling error for November 11. It was a holiday. They pushed it back to December 2. I asked if I'd be in prison before Christmas, should they deny my appeal. He said more than likely, no—but that he'd make a request that, should I lose, my incarceration not happen until January. I had almost a month before my court date. The only question now was, who's the girl I'd be living with during that time?

PRISON DRAMA — San Franciscan Bruce Neckels, an ex-inmate of California's San Quentin Prison, plays a crazed killer-rapist in the drama "The Cage" presented Friday before University of Wisconsin audiences. The production, designed to provide a glimpse into the conditions that spark prison revolts, was part of a two-day symposium on prison reform sponsored by the Wisconsin Student Assn. and the Student Bar Assn.

—State Journal Photo by Steven L. Raymer

Front page picture of my performance at the University of Wisconsin. Mistakenly written as "ex-inmate of California's San Quentin Prison."

Chapter Thirty-nine
Well, howdy... simply howdy!

P icture a blond with a Texas drawl, who looked like a 22 year-old Faye Dunaway. Well, that's who walked through my door around 6:00 p.m.. Marcia was with her and introduced me. Her name was Amy, and after two minutes, there was just no doubt we were going to hit it off. And we did. Suffice to say, she certainly took the edge and worry off my upcoming appeal hearing... for two whole months.

But around two days after I adjusted to my return home, I called Pete's girlfriend, to let her know I was home, and got the nicest surprise.

"Peter's back in San Francisco. He volunteered for a NASA project and was accepted. He's at the U.S. Public Health Hospital doing this bed rest study. You should go see him." I immediately headed for the hospital.

It was located on 15th Avenue and Lake St., just below the Presidio. I found Peter and two other CO's from Safford flat on their backs in hospital beds. It was great to see Peter again, but I was anxious to know just what the hell this volunteer program was all about and how he became a part of a program that would keep him in bed for five months. I will save this explanation for a more appropriate time. But Peter felt it was well worth it. One, it got him home and away from prison; and two, he was getting paid $100.00 a week. Pete and I talked for quite a while. I told him about my adventures touring with The Cage, and my upcoming appeal in December. He told me that if I lost my appeal, he'd be happy to recommend me to the doctors in charge of the program, for their next study. I jumped on the idea. I didn't relish the thought of being confined to a bed for 150 days, but if it could bring me back to San Francisco, then I'd go for it. But maybe I wouldn't be going back to prison. I just wasn't sure anymore which way the pendulum would swing. It was the end of 1971. The presidential election was coming up in '72; Nixon was weak; more people than ever hated the war. Who were the three judges I would face? All right -wing republicans? Did they consider Daniel Ellsberg's leaking of the "Pentagon Papers," detailing secrets of the Vietnam War, a breach of national security? Did this make Ellsberg and all us other left-wing, anti-war supporters, traitors? Or was there even a point to sending me back to jail?

#

Daniel Ellsberg was a Harvard graduate who actually favored the Vietnam War when America first got involved. He worked at the Defense Department for Secretary of Defense, Robert McNamara. In fact, it was McNamara who wanted these rotten little secrets put into written form. How could he predict that Danny's loyalty would shift to the anti-war movement? But it did, and Daniel had the final draft in his hot little hands right about the time Robert Kennedy had announced his candidacy for president. Ellsberg began campaigning for Kennedy and was going to turn these documents over to him, but Kennedy was assassinated. Two years later Ellsberg decided the people had a right to know and turned the papers over to the New York Times. This fueled the flames for Attorney General, John Mitchell, who picked up McCarthy's fallen flag. Once again there was a communist conspiracy in America, only this time the antiwar movement was behind it. That's all Nixon and his cabinet needed to hear because it justified breaking the law for the sake of national security. They began making a list of "enemies of the state"— public figures consisting of actors, politicians, authors, and whoever else they could nail.[40] Nixon was now reaching paranoia levels of Shakespearean characters - Othello, Macbeth and Hamlet, all rolled into one.

A couple of days before my hearing, I went to Saul's office for a last-minute consultation and surprise, surprise. He introduced me to his new associate, Pat, who had just passed the bar and would be joining the firm. Also, Pat was going get his feet wet by handling my appeal... if that was okay with me. I didn't know what the hell to say. The court was paying them, I wasn't. Saul hadn't been successful the first time out with Conti. Maybe the judges would reward the new kid with a "welcome to the bar" victory. He was a nice guy, good energy. I decided to let him handle it. What the fuck—it was only my life at stake. So I spent some time with Pat, told him about my tour with The Cage; how the job was still waiting for me if I won my appeal; how it was good alternative service because it contributed to national awareness of our prison system. I wanted to give him enough material to build a case, whether he used it or not. Then came the inevitable day. I'm not sure where it was I went for my appeal, but it wasn't a courtroom. It was more like an office, and I'm not sure if it was the Federal District Court Building, or an Appellate Court Building, if there is such a place. Pat and Saul were waiting for me when I arrived. Pat was nervous. When I shook his hand, it was moist from sweat. We were summoned into the room. There I stood - an actor, an antiwar activist, about to face three judges, one of them from Georgia. Hell, why didn't we just leave the Nov. 11 date alone? I was dead in the water anyway.

Chapter Forty
A lawyer's debut...

S ometimes being an actor can have its drawbacks. What I mean is, I'll often catch myself listening to the way someone delivers a line or speech, and less attention to what they're saying. And so it was that day when Pat delivered his speech on my behalf to the three judges. He was very articulate; I believe he mentioned the fact that I'd been on tour on behalf of prison reform, and how I should be able to continue that endeavor because I was educating the youth of America, some shit like that. He even did what every Public Speaking 101 student learns to do: Recite a quotation from someone great, relevant to your speech. "In conclusion, Your Honors, if I may quote the great Mohandas K. Gandhi, etc. etc..."The problem is, he spoke so goddamn fast that I couldn't keep up with what he was saying, and I doubt the judges could either. He was like a kid in his first elementary school play in front of a live audience, whose main objective was not to color or give meaning to his dialogue, but rather to get the words out as fast as he could, so as not to forget his lines.

Well, it didn't take long for the Court of Appeals to make their decision. And it was based on my previous elbow injury, rather than my opposition to the war. They only had one of the two doctors letters I'd submitted, and it wasn't the one that favored me. I had been declared fit for duty by army medical doctors and that took precedence. One week later, the wheels of justice had continued turning. I lost by a vote of 2-1. It was time to put me and my heinous crime back where I belonged... Prison. I was going to have to go through this shit all over again, starting with the San Francisco County Jail. I'd have to endure that madness once more until the FBI came to transfer me to Safford. Only now I was going for the duration. Two years. However, the judges did allow me to spend Christmas at home. I was to report to the Federal Building on Monday, January 3, at 10:00 a.m. With time off for good behavior, I wouldn't be seeing the streets again until middle of 1973. On Friday, December 31, 1971, my friends threw a New Year's Eve "Oldies but Goodies" party for me. They rented an old Wurlitzer Bubbler loaded with 45 rpm records from the 50's and we tried to enjoy ourselves as best we could. But the fact was, I'd be gone in two days, and none of us really had that great a time. On Monday morning, a very tearful Amy and I said good-bye. She was going stay in my apartment and pay the rent. We had become very close. She promised she'd visit me at the jail, and even travel to Safford Federal Prison to see me. And so I hopped on the 30 Stockton bus, transferred to the 47 Van Ness, which took me right to the Federal Building.

I walked up to the FBI floor, and hit the door buzzer that would allow me entrance into the main room. One of the officers glanced up at me from his desk, said something to one of his cohorts, who also looked up. I couldn't hear what they were saying, but it appeared as though no one was expecting me. Finally, they hit the buzzer and let me in. I walked to the far end of the room and up to the desk. One of the officers was waiting for me.

"Can I help you?"

"Yeah, I'm Bruce Neckels. I'm supposed to turn myself in." He gave me a puzzled look.

"For what?" he asked.

"Refusing induction into the military. I lost my appeal in December and was told to turn myself in today at 10:00 a.m."

The officer looked at his watch.

"It's 9:50. You're early." He turned to his cohorts.

"Bruce Neckels is here to turn himself in today. Draft evasion."

A couple of them shrugged while another officer picked up some kind of manifest chart and scanned.

"Yeah, here it is. Bruce Neckels. But we've got him scheduled to come in next Monday... The 10th."

The officer at the desk turned to me.

"Wow... You're REALLY early. We appreciate you making it so easy for us, but the10th is the day we were given. Looks like you got yourself another week of freedom?"

I couldn't fucking believe this!

"You mean I can just turn around and go home?"

"That's right."

"But... I'm here! Can't we just start my sentence a week early? Just take me to County jail right now."

The agent, Phil was his name, laughed.

"No, I'm afraid we can't do that. And they wouldn't have you on their processing list either."

"Well, I don't wanta spend a day in that shithole anyway? What if I just hopped on a plane, flew to Phoenix, then took a bus to Safford and turned myself in there?"

By now, every officer in there was paying attention and laughing their asses off.

"Neckels, I'm afraid you can't do that either, but we really do appreciate your enthusiasm. Just go on home and we'll see you one week from today."

"Well... Okay... See you guys later."

I left, not quite knowing how to feel. Yes, I had one more week of freedom, but that meant I'd have to suffer the anxiety of going back to jail for one more week. But Amy and my other friends were ecstatic with joy. And we made the best of it. We got stoned a lot; drank nice wines; ate at our favorite restaurants, saw a couple of movies. The week went by very fast. And the following Monday, January 10th, acting like a veteran of the prison system, I put enough money in my wallet to use for the jail commissary, kissed Amy goodbye, and off I went. Only this time I wasn't coming back. The FBI guys welcomed me back, thanked me for showing up on time, stuck me in a holding cell....

Chapter Forty-one
... and it's Déjà Vu all over again

I really don't know if I have the stomach to go through what it was like at the San Francisco County Jail for a second time. There was no Jerry Samone-like ally in there, but I knew how to handle myself, which was basically this: keep your mouth shut; don't argue with anybody; if some greedy asshole wanted to take two pieces of yellow cake off the dessert tray, instead of his allotted one, then rather than watch two guys beat the shit over each other for it, just take mine. However, it was still twice as bad this time because I wasn't in there for two weeks. I was there for a whole month before the FBI came to get me on Saturday, February 12. By the second week, with inmates being transferred to maximum security prisons, I worked my way up the chain to a bunk more toward the front, away from the toilet, and a top bunk at that; I had visitors every Wednesday and Saturday, and once again that dose of "Soul Train" on Saturdays. Now that Amy was living in my apartment, she brought me any personal mail, which the guards handed me later. My favorite letter came from my dad and step-mom—my dad had remarried in 1967, and he really picked a gem. Her name was LaVon, and if she'd have been my stepmother when I was younger, I have no doubt that I would've had the happiest childhood imaginable. But anyway, they had no idea that I was in jail. In fact, I don't know if they were even aware I was in jail the first time. But LaVon wrote the letter from Reno, Nevada. To wit:

"Hi, honey. Your father and I took a little vacation to Reno. Having a good time but haven't had very good luck at the tables... Lost about two hundred dollars. Give us a call. Let us know how you are. Love, Mother and Dad."

So I bought one of those pre-posted lick'em shut letters from the commissary and wrote back:

"Dear Mom and Dad: Got your letter from Reno. Sorry you didn't win at the tables but let me tell you—I kinda crapped out myself. Fill you in once I've reached my final destination. Don't worry. I'm fine. Love, Bruce."

I put down my home address and sent it off.

It's strange, but I never really kept my parents in the loop about what was happening with me during this whole experience. I felt that the less they knew, the less they'd worry. I didn't realize that the FBI had visited my mother, Janet, who was living in Elk Grove, California at the time, a year earlier. It wasn't until after I finally got out of prison, that mom told me how terrified she was the day they knocked on her door and asked all kinds of questions about me. Knowing my mom, I'm sure she almost had a nervous breakdown over it. My dad was much cooler. When the FBI visited him, he told them that I was never a troublemaker; that I loved my country but felt the war was wrong, and that he respected my decision. I have a 26-year-old daughter as of this writing. I worry when she drives one mile to work by herself. Yet for two years, from 1971 to 1972, I didn't give it a moment's thought that every day my parents were worried sick about what I was going through.

But there I was, sitting in that stinking shithole of a jail, counting the days when I would hear what this time around, would be the magic words... "Neckels, roll up!"

Finally, on Saturday morning, February 12, 1972, those words echoed up and down B-line. I said a quick good-bye to anyone who was awake, and was escorted to the main desk, where I would get into my street clothes, and then into my shackles. Two FBI officers were waiting for me. The younger officer's name was John, nice guy, soft spoken. But who do you think the lead officer was? Phil - the guy who I met up in the Federal building when I showed up a week early. He gave me a thin smile.

"Hello, Bruce," he said.

"Hi, Phil. Sure wish YOU would've shown up a week early."

I swear, he wanted to laugh, but had to hold his ground.

"Well, get dressed and let's get going."

And so once again, there I was in the back seat of a four-door sedan, heading for Safford Prison, hand-cuffed and leg-ironed to two other prisoners: Jim was a CO and on his way to Safford with me; the other was a prisoner they were taking to a maximum security prison in Long Beach, Terminal Island - T.I. as it's called. And that's where we went first - and where we spent the night. Now that was scary—rows and tiers of cells and bars. We were put up in holding cells away from the main line, so thank God, none of the lifers and hard-core inmates even knew we were there. The next morning, Sunday, February 13, we had breakfast and Jim and I were picked up around 8:00 a.m. It was a lot more comfortable with only two of us shackled together in the back seat. Safford Prison was a 550-mile trip. Going the speed limit, it'd take us about nine hours to get there. The way these guys drove though, maybe seven. But there was only one problem. We weren't going to Safford. The officers aren't allowed to give us their traveling itinerary, at least not until we're in the car and well on our way. And that's when Phil told us we were on our way to Las Vegas, to pick up another prisoner and take him to Florence Prison in Arizona. I couldn't believe it! Vegas was 287 miles away; and from there to Safford, another 460 miles. 750 miles in one day! Four hours to Vegas; another eight to Safford—That's twelve hours, going the speed limit. And unless our two escorts planned on averaging 100 miles per hour and get to Safford in eight hours, there's no way they were going to do all that driving. Which meant we'd be spending the night in another goddamn jail somewhere. And that was guaranteed when we pulled in to Las Vegas SIX hours later. It was Valentine's Day weekend and traffic to Vegas was bumper to bumper. Thousands pouring in to gamble, see shows, get married, or get divorced. We pulled in around 2:00 p.m., stopped at a drive-in for lunch, then went to the Las Vegas jail to pick up our prisoner. By the time he was processed out, then shackled to Jim and me, it was almost 3:00 p.m. Sure enough, Phil drove for another hour and a half to Kingman, Arizona, and that was it for the day. Welcome to Kingman, Arizona, home of Andy Devine and, according to original road positions, the "Heart of Historical Route 66." We were put behind bars at the Kingman County Jail until tomorrow morning. Next stop, Safford Federal Prison.

Chapter Forty-two
Home sweet home.... I don't think so.

H appy Valentine's Day! We pulled into Safford Federal Prison sometime in mid-afternoon. Bob, the same guard who was there last year, was at the glass-enclosed station. However, this time there was a different inmate, Tom, standing there to greet us. And thank god, he didn't expound about how our job as CO's wasn't finished. We exchanged hellos, then he was told to back off while they disconnected Jim and I from the other prisoner, who still had a drive ahead of him. Phil shook my hand and quietly wished me good luck. I told him I'd drop by and see him when I got back to San Francisco - maybe we'd go have a beef dip sandwich at Tommy's Joynt. He nodded politely. We both knew that was never gonna happen. I know it sounds strange, given the situation, but I never considered him "the enemy." He and John were both quite respectable and civil throughout the entire trip. They turned and left, leaving me to complete the final chapter of my almost four-year ordeal.

We were told to be seated. The Senior Case Manager would be with us in a few minutes. That would be Mr. Cunningham. Once again I was going to see him. He was very cordial the last time I saw him, but I wondered how he'd treat me now that I was officially "guilty" and serving out my time in his prison. I remember how inmates thought he was the biggest asshole at the prison. But then, I figured it was a given that they all were, until proven otherwise. After all, this wasn't summer camp, and there was definitely a separation of power. Horror stories existed even in minimum security prisons. It remained to be seen if there would be any here. I remembered reading in "Life" or "Time" magazine, an interview with singer Joan Baez, who was married to draft resistor David Harris, who had been an inmate here at Safford. Was what he wrote to her in a prison letter, true? That late at night you could hear prisoners being rubber hosed by the guards? If so, what would I be facing with these guards? I'm sure they were all rednecks; some of them probably fought in Vietnam. Would they try to provoke me into a fight? I didn't get a sense of that the first time I was here, but now I belonged to them, and power on any level, comes with arrogance. And intelligence, or lack thereof, combined with power, doesn't guarantee freedom from cruelty. A Stanford University Prison Experiment proved that in the summer of 1971. And the only reason I knew about this was because of touring with *The Cage*. It was something that our actor/ex-cons discussed with audiences everywhere we performed. Here's how it went:

#

In the summer of 1971, a newspaper ad was issued in Palo Alto, Ca., asking for volunteers for a two-week experiment, on the study of the psychological effects of prison life. Pay was involved. Those who showed up went through a battery of personality tests, so that they could weed out candidates who had criminal records, medical or mental problems, or were fucked up on drugs. The research team finally came up with two dozen people who seemed very normal. Their contact information was gathered and then they were dismissed. All were adult males.

The consultants, who were used to assist in helping the psychologists assimilate prison life, were former correctional officers, and actual inmates who'd done a lot of time. The "prison" was constructed in a basement corridor at Stanford's Psychology Department. The rooms were converted into prison cells. The actual doors were removed and replaced by doors with steel bars. Unbeknownst to the prisoners, the "cells" were bugged so that the research team could listen in on their conversations. They also secretly video-taped what was going on. The corridor was the only place else "prisoners" could go to exercise or walk around. If they had to go to the bathroom, they were blindfolded and led to the bathrooms. They even took a dinky closet and called it "the hole" which they used for solitary confinement for unruly inmates.

Now as I remember, by way of a coin toss, it was decided who would be guards and who would be inmates. About one week after the interviews, early one Sunday morning, The Palo Alto Police, who agreed to assist in the study, showed up at the homes of the chosen "criminals," sirens blasting. They dragged the volunteers out onto the street, handcuffed them, and threw them into the back of police cars and drove off. It was very humiliating for these poor people who weren't quite sure this was what they'd signed up for. They were then read their rights, booked, fingerprinted, then taken to "holding" cells and blindfolded. They remained in these holding cells while the research team added the final touches to Stanford County Jail. Then the prisoners were brought to "jail" one by one, where they met the "warden," who reprimanded them for their crimes. They were then taken away to be stripped naked, searched, then sprayed with germ and lice disinfectant. They were issued smocks with ID numbers; no underwear; chains on one ankle—I can't remember what other shit was laid on them, but it was all done to humiliate them. They were called by their ID numbers and never their names. I don't believe their heads were shaved; but they were forced to wear caps made out of women's nylons—totally emasculating. Now here comes the fun part: The Guards—and remember, normal, intelligent human beings—were allowed to make up their own rules to maintain order in the prison, within reason. And of course, the "inmate" volunteers figured there'd be some minimal punishments handed out to make it as real as possible. Wrong. The guards became sadistic after two days. They played inmates against each other; made them defecate and urinate in buckets in their cells, then refused to allow inmates to empty them into the toilet. Prisoners staged a rebellion which took extra "guards" to quell. Guards who had worked the night shift had to work overtime just to help out. And when they caught the ringleader who came up with the rebellion idea, they made it hell for him. Even parents and friends who were allowed visits, were put through hell until they threatened to get lawyers; one inmate had a nervous breakdown after two days and was released. They had parole hearings for inmates by a mock parole board. Inmates offered to give the money back they'd be earning in exchange for an early release. One inmate who was denied "parole," went into hysterics.

Before one week was up, things unraveled so badly, the experiment had to be stopped. Volunteers had lost their identities and were taking on the personae of real inmates and guards.[41, 42] They were dehumanized in less than one week! Is it understandable why our prison system has failed so miserably?

#

After a few minutes, Cunningham came out of his office. This time, I was the first one in. He closed the door behind me, and to my surprise, gave me a faint smile.

"So, you're back."

"Yes, Sir," I replied. "Lost by a vote of two to one."

"Well, let's make the best of it then." He had said that the first time I was there.

I sat down and once again, Cunningham was very civil, as we got down to business, starting with the basic rules. I believe the first was... any attempt to escape would result in another five years tacked onto my sentence.

"Hardly seems worth the risk," I said. I assured him he wouldn't have a problem, then told him about how I showed up a week early to turn myself in. He actually laughed. We then discussed what kind of job I would have while I was here. There were several: you remember the road crew? Where inmates were building a road to a lake resort, which by our calculations, given the equipment provided, would take 126 years to build? Kitchen duty; laundry; the glove factory, which was filled up; prison ground maintenance. And then there was the power house. There were three shifts: 6:00 a.m. - 2:00 p.m.; 2:00 p.m. - 10:00 p.m.; and the graveyard shift - 10:00 p.m. - 6:00 a.m. I told Cunningham that I still experienced occasional bursitis in my elbow from years ago when I slammed it against a basketball pole. So maybe the road crew wouldn't work. I told him that I'd be glad to work graveyard shift at the power house. I had learned during my short stay in July of 1971, that a powerhouse job working night or graveyard shifts would put me in a room with two other inmates - instead of having to sleep in a 80-man dorm. But there was only a day shift opening. Cunningham gave me that assignment and said he'd move me to the graveyard shift as soon as there was a spot available.

After all the rules and regulations were explained, Cunningham then told me that the six weeks I'd already spent in prison would be deducted from my two-year sentence. So with 22 1/2 months left to serve with time off for good behavior, I'd be out June 2, 1973. Jesus, I was already counting the days, and I had 474 to go, provided I behaved myself. That's the carrot the prison system dangles over your head. I was then escorted to Dorm 5 and my bunk. Since Valentine's Day was considered a holiday, there were visitors out in the enclosed patio, but many more in the main compound. I was eyeballed all the way to my dorm. Unfortunately, it wasn't a dorm that housed most of the CO's. Just about every one of my roommates were Mexican, who spoke little or no English. I was now the minority, listening to everyone talk about me and not knowing what they're saying. But within seconds after the guard left, inmate Tom came in, and I'd made my first friend, other than Jim, my traveling companion. By 4:00 p.m. that afternoon, after visiting hours were over, I would meet at least twenty more CO's. Some I remembered from my first visit to Safford. But all of them, within a week became a core of friends...Our own band of brothers, not to mention, a very interesting cast of characters. There was Mike, from Tempe, Arizona. He had a great smile, his blond hair brushed off to one side; a good guitar player who loved Crosby, Stills, Nash, and Young - and who predicted in 1972 that Bruce Springsteen would one day be bigger than Bob Dylan. Mike was politically outspoken, with a biting sense of humor. Tom, who greeted me at the control center, was from Iowa. Very soft-spoken, but inside of him was an anti-government protestor screaming to be let out. In a few months, Tom and I would share an interesting experience together. There was Sean, the prison poet, who wrote the "campus" newspaper. Craig, from San Diego, whose mind was all over the place. You never knew what was going to come out of his mouth. He once spent three years in a seminary, as he put it, "dipped in a great vat of papal blubber, coated with a thin, holy shell... All bullshit." However, in just a few months after his release, he would be working his way back to spiritual fulfillment; another Tom, I think from LA, who would keep us all horny as hell by reading letters his girlfriend would send him - describing how she would ravish his body. There was redheaded Dave, with a red moustache, who was into cross-country running. He had a connection to some sporting outlet and would have running shoes sent into the prison. John - this guy looked like a fucking movie star. I swear he drove into Safford Prison on a motorcycle, and when he was released, he left on it. Pat was Korean? Asian? Hawaiian - can't remember, but a real nice guy. Steve - "moustache" we called him for obvious reasons. Somehow, he was the only CO in prison who was able to keep that "hippie" look. Must have been the red bandana he wore around his head. Steve was the total opposite from one of my favorite characters, Spencer—the "King Rat" of Safford. Spence was always dressed and groomed immaculately. He paid someone who worked in the laundry room (with cigarettes or commissary supplies) to starch his shirts and pants, shine his shoes, and make sure that his Khaki clothes were the newest. I think he also gave a pack of cigarettes to the prison barber, for trimming his hair once a week. All totaled, there were about forty inmates at Safford who were CO's, including Pete, Steve, and Richard, who would be finishing up their NASA stint at the U.S. Public Health Service Hospital, by the end of March. And every one of these guys were strong, intelligent, and well read. Most were college graduates. Imprisonment consisted of a two-part plan: punishment and "rehabilitation." Rehabilitate means "restore to good repute"-to re-qualify oneself. So to a bunch of well-educated COs, that meant absolutely nothing. It's a worthless word. When I get out of prison, does that mean I've learned my lesson and will fight in the next unjust, immoral war? No, we were there because nobody likes a smart-ass! And we all stuck together. There was always someone there to lend moral support to the other. And it wasn't all serious, guarded conversation, looking over our shoulders. Many of these guys, including myself, had a great sense of humor, and we needed that to get through all the bullshit. I know many of our friends and family would go home after a visit and tell their friends, "Oh, it's like a country club." Trust me, it was no resort. The discipline was very strict; so were the rules. There was plenty of tension, and there was tragedy. It was lonely and a long way from home – and a fucking waste of time. And it sure didn't help when I picked up the Arizona Republic newspaper a couple of days later to read the following:

"Tucson - A 41 year-old Tucson man was placed on five years' probation yesterday on a guilty plea to the charge of manslaughter in the stabbing death of his wife. ..... pleaded guilty of the charge before Pine County Superior Court Judge..."[43] Unfucking real! The police find her body lying in a pool of blood. He admits killing her; gets probation and we're sitting in prison because we didn't want to kill anybody! But one must accept injustice and move on. Perhaps I should have told the court that my refusing induction was a crime of passion.

That night, I was called to the control office. They were allowing me to receive a phone call, normally against regulations because I hadn't even been there a week. It was from Marcia and Amy. They were calling to make sure I was okay, to hear my voice, and for Amy to tell me she was going to try and visit me this weekend. Mr. Cunningham and Warden Tom Lanier, had already given her permission. Visiting days were Saturday and Sunday. I thought an inmate had to be there at least a month before visits were allowed. But because I was under two years, visits started immediately. However, Saturday came and went, and no Amy. Well, she said she'd "try." I was pretty depressed. But the next day, I got that call from the control office. "Neckels, report to control. You have a visit." I hauled ass to the control reception area and there she was, looking drop dead gorgeous with the biggest smile on her face. And... she had brought my Martin guitar. We were allowed a quick hug and a kiss, and after they checked my guitar case for contraband, then put it in a holding area, we went into the courtyard.

She explained that she couldn't get off work until Saturday afternoon, then caught a plane to Phoenix; a bus to Safford, then got a room at the Desert Inn of Safford. What a trooper! It took quite an effort on her part to get here. I figured the lady must love me. Then she looked around and said in her Texas drawl:

"This ain't s'bad, baby... It's like a country club." Ohhhhh-kayyy...

Chapter Forty-three
Love Letters in the Sand

R omantic song, but not when the sand surrounds a prison, with me in it. And here's where I start dragging out the letters I've been saving for the last forty-seven years... about 300 of them. My parents sent a few; my San Francisco friends sent many; quite a few from inmates who got out before I did but stayed in touch. I received several from girls I'd met while touring with *The Cage*. Most of the letters – 96 to be exact – came from...Colette. But for now, let's get Amy out of the way, because that's kind of what happened and so I pass on this tip to all you future CO's, should that day ever come: Don't be in love before you go to prison. And as I will relate a tragic story later on, it might be a good idea that you're not even married.

This was by no means Amy's first letter to me during my incarceration, but she wrote from the Desert Inn of Safford, dated February 20, 1972.

> *"Dear Bruce- in only 5 hrs I'm gonna give you the biggest, tightest hug & sexiest kiss you've ever had! ... I can hardly wait to see your beautiful, brown eyes & your sexy body! Ummmm - I can't stand it! ... Bruce you've been gone a month now (actually, it was six weeks). It hasn't been lots of fun but it hasn't been so bad that I couldn't handle it - know what I mean? Anyway, I think my feelings for you have doubled in size a million times* [doubled in size a million times???]*What I'm trying to say is it just won't be that hard to wait for you. Why should I want anyone else when I have the best? Plus my mama always said "Now Amy Honey, if it's worth having, it's worth waiting for."' And I just happen to think you're worth it! I love you, cutie pie. Tomorrow – oops, I mean today - is going to be heaven! All my love, Amy."*[44]

Now, this one came three days after our visit, when she got home to San Francisco, dated Feb. 23:

"... Bruce, this weekend just really blew my mind. I've never in my life felt so close to a guy. It was like a reservoir of emotions, ideas & love finally letting loose ... What can I say - except I'm in love with you. My confidence in our relationship can't be shook - I know it will work - if you love me only half as much as I love you. ... It won't be long again, before we're together. I promise. All my love and kisses, Amy. "[45]

Well, for the next two months it was nothing but love letters. But that came to a screeching halt, in a letter dated April 19th. She'd been applying for jobs as a flight attendant. Got turned down by Delta; United said she needed to drop some weight to meet their height and weight requirements; and two other interviews with World Charter Airways and American in May. Her life, as she put it, just wasn't complete and flying, she thought, was the answer.

"Dear Bruce - I've needed to write a real 'heart to heart' letter for quite some time, so here goes. Presently, I'm very dissatisfied with my life - I'm happy yet not completely together ... Naturally, with all of my personal indecision our relationship is up in the air. I have to date and need someone in my present and daily life. I'll be the first to admit I need a man. I'm not looking for a husband presently, so that won't harm us.)I want to see you & give things a chance after everything is complete. Yet in the meantime I can't promise to be true-blue ... Please understand that I'm not saying, "it was fun but now it's over" because I'm not. I'm only saying I don't know about anything, only time will tell. Unfortunately, there are no absolutes or concrete situations in my life. I'd be lying to say I'll wait. I can only honestly say that I want to give it a try when we can. Hope I've made some sense in my confused honesty. ... I love you and care about you, but I've got a lot of my life to work out. Much love, Amy. "[46]

That was enough for me. I wrote her back and was rather mean. I told her if she wanted a job as a stewardess, but needed to lose weight, perhaps she should stop fucking long enough to concentrate on dropping a few pounds. Her final response to me was much more mature.

> *"Dear Bruce - Ouch! I guess truth hurts, huh? ... Thank you for your honest feelings. On many points you were exactly right. Bruce, I don't know what I want or where I'm going. Guess I'm a little directionless. I'm only sorry that in my searching I unintentionally (please believe that) have hurt someone besides myself. ... Apparently I'm incapable of love or responsibility - I don't know if I'll ever achieve either ... I don't ask your forgiveness because it isn't deserved ... Wish I could undo everything and every way I touched your life. But I do thank you for the many beautiful memories and for some realizations ... You're such a strong, beautiful being that you will survive whatever comes. Please don't let this episode embitter you..."*

Her three pages of clichéd mea culpas—which I do believe were sincere—ended with *"... I did love you with all my heart and at the time meant everything. Please be happy and believe I'm sorry. Amy."*[47]

And that was the end of that. Nothing left for me to do now but "be happy." She left my apartment and Marcia thankfully found someone who needed a place to stay and rented it out. Someone I didn't even know, who was using my furniture, was occupying my apartment and my belongings were stuffed in boxes and stuck out in a back shed. For the first time, I finally felt disconnected from my home.

But it's not like I hadn't been fully involved and acclimated to prison life. Going back to February, two days after my arrival, one of the members of the prison basketball team came back from a game with a broken wrist. They needed another player for a game two nights later. Normally, an inmate had to have been there for at least a month before being allowed to participate in activities held away from the prison. But because I had played college basketball, I was given the green light by the Correctional Supervisor, Tom Lanier. Again, like Cunningham, here was a guy all the inmates hated. And indeed, he was humorless, unbending, and quite caustic. But yet, after consulting with Cunningham, both felt I was absolutely not a flight risk. So for the last month of the season I played on the Safford Prison basketball team. The division of teams came from Safford, from a junior college, and another prison. Our first game that I played was against the first place team who had beaten us once already. But with my defensive ability, hitting some key shots, plus two clutch free throws toward the end of the game, we beat them. I was heralded as the missing link that would win us the division, but sadly my game went to hell. I'd had my glasses knocked off during the second game I played, and since they were my only pair, I played without them. Fucked up my shooting - the basket was slightly blurry from beyond ten feet, and I just couldn't find the range with my outside jump shot. We still came in second, thanks in large part to a CO named Gary, who averaged about 30 points a game. He was so good that our guard/coach, Officer Kenske, contacted colleges in Arizona to come see him play. He was released a week after the final game. I don't think he went to college, though. He went home.

By the middle of March, I knew who all the prison guards were, and their attitudes. I guess I could thank my love for theatre, but I decided to conduct my own "Stanford Experiment." After all, weren't they playing roles? I wanted every guard in that prison to respect me. I absolutely would not be intimidated by any of them. Whenever they approached me, I would greet them as though they were equals. If I was denied something, it didn't matter. Whenever I felt something was done as a form of intimidation, I would understand that this was the role they had to play and diffuse any attempt. This was my way of softening the feeling of institutionalization. Spence's way was keeping well-groomed and going with the flow. Old Mr. Simmons had Chess Club on Tuesdays, and Bridge Club on Thursdays. Some of us even spent two hours with a local visiting guru from Tempe every Wednesday afternoon. He always brought a healthy rice dish with him. I lasted two weeks with this guy and that was it. On his second visit, he wanted us to close our eyes, concentrate and see the "blue circle of light." When I confessed that I couldn't see it, he took his thumb and middle finger and placed them on the outside edges of each eye and squeezed them toward the bridge of my nose. I saw the circle all right, but it was white! I thought my eyeballs were going to pop out, or that I'd at least go blind. It was my last session with that 20th Century skyhook to God.

Given the fact that Cunningham and Lanier, the two top dogs, had already proven to be quite civil to me, I didn't really need to do much except just be me. Kenske was the oldest guard and very laid back, so he was easy. Yes, I was once accused of "raising too much corn, and not enough hell," but I'd made my statement in court. Now it was time to just grow some corn. At least I was aware of what I was doing. And I experienced some rather touching moments.

This would never have worked in a hardcore maximum security prison, where a few men have to control many. There was really no need for "divide and conquer" games here - playing one inmate against the other. There were no Mexican gangs; no neo Nazi gangs; no Black Panther Party gangs, and no CO gangs. Mexicans made up 70% of the prisoners. They didn't care for us gringos, but they kept to themselves, with a few exceptions. And most of the CO's were pretty laid-back guys.

By the end of March, I was working a graveyard shift at the powerhouse - 10:00 p.m. to 6:00 a.m. Hallelujah! One of the inmates was released and I got his job. I might add, it was a rather prestigious job and I followed on the heels of good company. I sat in the same chair as the aforementioned anti-war protestor David Harris. David wasn't getting enough publicity at Safford, and really wanted out of there. Legend has it he did it in a very unique way, not by screaming and yelling in protest about Vietnam, but rather his gardening skills. He got permission one day to go out and trim the hedges in front of the compound. With pruning shears, he shaped one of the hedges into a penis with balls. He was transferred to a medium security Federal Correctional Institution in Latuna, Texas, for destruction of property

The powerhouse held the boiler tanks that ran water into the dorms, laundry room, kitchen, and administration building. Water came to these boilers via a water tower. It was a 24-hour a day operation, which required workers for three eight hour shifts - two workers per shift. They had to keep water in the tower, so that it could provide the smaller boiler tanks with water. There was a powerhouse supervisor—a government civilian, Mr. Danner—whose team of inmate employees had to supply chemicals to the water –then run tests to make sure water was hot, cold, softened, and drinkable. They also had to keep the pumps running in the cesspool. Samples had to be taken from the cesspool, then tested and chemically treated. It was a very important job. So important that we were paid five dollars a month. But I didn't care. To me, this job may have well been my salvation. My sanity would be somewhat preserved by the fact that four powerhouse guys, and two early morning kitchen chefs shared two rooms. I'd be sharing one of them with two other inmates instead of being in a dorm with eighty. However, I was warned by my roommates that I should be prepared to be busted in on at any given time by a guard named Ron, who took sadistic pleasure out of emptying drawers, turning mattresses upside down, rifling through books, magazines, drawers, looking for contraband, and leaving the room in a mess when he left. I was actually looking forward to dealing with him.

Anyway, back to the graveyard shift. Other than the guards, I'd be the only one awake, and when my shift was over, I'd be one of the only inmates around the prison yard while everyone else was at work building that lake resort highway or working in the glove factory. I was the guy who blew the prison whistle at 6:00 a.m., waking not only the prison inmates, but the town of Safford itself, seven miles away. As soon as the day shift inmate arrived, I'd go join my CO buddies for breakfast. And when everyone left for work detail at 7:00 a.m., the prison was pretty much empty and I'd go to bed. But when I wasn't sleeping, I'd go to the library; shoot hoops at the outdoor court; work out with weights, or lie out in the sun with my jar of iced Tang, and get a tan. And of all things, it was the tanning that got me in deep water.

About the third week there, I walked over to the powerhouse and found a nice little patch of land behind the building. I laid down on my towel and fell asleep - right through the whistle that blew at noon for count time. That meant everyone had to get back to their dorms, while a guard came by to take role. Well, I wasn't there, and they called for me over the loudspeaker. When I didn't show up, I was put on "escape

228

alert." A couple of the guards got in a jeep and started driving around the camp. When they came around to the powerhouse, I was just getting up. One of the guards, Bob, from the front desk, stood up in the moving jeep and yelled. "Neckels, what the hell are you doing?"

"Just getting a tan," I yelled back.

"Well, you're on escape alert! You missed count. Now get your ass to the control office!"

I must admit I was scared. But once I arrived and they all realized what had happened, they were very relieved. They gave me a harsh reprimand and told me never to do that again. I didn't have to be told twice. And it certainly didn't put me in bad standing, because a week after that, they called me in again. Checking my files and seeing I was an actor and had been in movies and television, they put me and another inmate, Gary, in charge of ordering the next three months' worth of prison movies, which were shown every Saturday and Sunday night in the auditorium. Lanier handed us a four-page list of movies, current and classic, gave us a small budget, and sent us on our way. It wasn't much to work with, and we tried to gear it toward a majority prison population of Mexicans whenever we could. But we also had to consider that there were a lot of pretty savvy CO's in there, too. What we also took into consideration was the length of each movie. The longer the film, the more time the inmates had to be out of their dorms. So we were looking for movies that were at least two hours long. We picked *"Treasure of the Sierra Madre,"* which the Mexicans loved, and *"Casablanca,"* which was slightly under two hours, but that one was a no-brainer. However, the one that brought me the highest acclaim as a film booker amongst my CO buddies, but booed by the Mexican population, was an anti-war movie of sorts, which told of the lunacy of battle, Paddy Chayefsky's *"The Americanization of Emily."* But my personal best pick, which started off the Safford Federal Prison Film Festival, was *"Once Upon A Time In the West,"* starring Charles Bronson, Henry Fonda, Jason Robards, and Claudia Cardinale. Based on the book, "Man with the Harmonica," it was about a stranger seeking revenge. Fonda was brilliant as the bad guy. Even though it came out in 1968, I'd never seen it. And sitting in the front row of the prison auditorium, watching it for the first time, I felt as though I was in that screen, riding my horse alongside those guys. But that could be because four hours prior to the movie, I had taken a tab of mescaline.

Love letters, suddenly washed away

Chapter Forty-four
The Visit, bad poetry, and
Once Upon A Time in the Psychedelic West.

It was Saturday and I had a visit from my dear friends, Susan and Mark, who didn't realize that it was okay to bring food. So Susan asked one of the guards if it was okay if she went into Safford and got a pizza. He gave her the okay and she left. Now mind you, Safford was only about seven minutes away from the prison camp. Susan was gone for two hours. Why? Well, as she related the story to me years later—before she got to Safford Prison, she decided to pull over to the side of the road and hide a couple of tabs of mescaline under a rock. I guess she suddenly got paranoid that she'd be searched, body and purse. But now that she'd been through the first time, she felt safe enough to go get it and bring it in. Now I don't know if it was on her way to get the pizza or on her way back, but when she stopped to get the mescaline, she looked out there and couldn't remember exactly under which rock she'd hidden it. That stretch of road between Safford Prison and the town was pretty desolate landscape with sand, cactus and rocks, and it all looked pretty much the same—kind of like that scene in "Fargo," where the guy is hiding a briefcase full of money, and as he's digging a hole in the snow, he looks in both directions and sees nothing but snow and fence posts, and it all looks the same. So he leaves a marker. Susan didn't do that. Dressed in a pink mini-skirt and thin blouse, she crawled around the desert turning over rock after rock looking for that fucking mescaline. How she avoided being stung by a scorpion or bitten by a rattlesnake, I'll never know. But she finally found the mescaline, swallowed one of the tabs, then stuck the other one in the middle of a Milky Way candy bar. Miraculously unbitten or unstung by a desert predator, she arrived with pizza and candy bar in hand. The guard looked her, flirtatiously - because she did look very sexy, and asked if he could have a bite of that candy bar. Susan said she started to panic. If he'd taken a bite, he'd have had that capsule right in his mouth.

But Susan giggled, said something silly, and he let her by. I didn't know any of that at the time, but then she set the pizza down, and said, "Brusso, I think you could use this." She then took a nice bite of the Milky Way, then pulled my face right up to her lips and gave me a kiss, sliding that candy right into my mouth. When she pulled her tongue out, I knew I had more than a bite of candy. I swallowed it and just decided to let it happen. I'd never taken hallucinogenic drugs before. I'd heard all about acid trips from my hippie actor friends in San Francisco, and about 45 minutes later, I was about to go on an amazing journey unlike anything I'd ever experienced, and I didn't have to leave prison to do it.

In that time, the mind allowed all five senses of sight, hearing, taste, touch and smell, to enhance a hundred-fold. Different emotions came at different times, starting with laughter with my visiting friends, that was so filled with joy, to the point of tears. My head became light and free. Things became brighter; sounds more clear. When I looked across the patio at other inmates forty feet away, I swear I could hear their conversations, even though they were speaking very quietly. Every inanimate object I looked at appeared to be alive. Peeling a fucking orange was the most amazing thing I'd ever experienced—watching the skin separate from the pulp in slow motion, revealing the orange fruit. And when I cradled the orange in both hands and put my two thumbs in the button of the orange and gently broke it open, it was like a miniature, slow motion explosion of the sun. And when that happened I could feel that sensation in my stomach—you know the feeling you get when you're so happy your insides tickle - I believe it's known as a "peak experience"—a joy that took me away from captivity. And for the next 18 hours, I would have a "peek" into the "eternal realm of Being."[which was a hell of a lot more than I got from that Guru who damn near popped my eyeballs out of their sockets].But first, I had to test my ability to appear normal, by getting past the guards when visiting hours were over. My two friends were nervous for me, and told me they'd drive just a ways down the road then wait for me to appear in the compound. There was a place where they'd be visible to me and I could wave to them that I was okay. The guests all left first, then the inmates were searched head to toe by the guards. Had they only known about the psychedelic contraband in my brain! I got through with no problem and entered the compound. Most of the inmates were out at the recreation areas, playing softball, soccer, basketball, lifting weights, so it was unusually quiet. I walked past the first dorm on my left then turned and headed for the boundary wall. I looked across the desert a quarter mile away toward the road leading away from prison. And there they were, standing outside of their car, looking for a sign of me. I waved at them, and they waved back.

After minute or so, they got into their car and drove away. I watched until the car was out of sight, and then.... I just started bawling. I was into phase two of my mescaline trip - the release of all that pent-up emotion that I hadn't expressed in four years - through the whole induction-refusal process; the court sentencing; then having to maintain a tough skin during my two stints at the county jail; my preoccupation with the "Cage" tour - I finally released all the pain, the hurt, and the loneliness that I'd been afraid to show. And I just let it flow, constantly looking around to make sure I wasn't being watched. I thought about my mom and dad, who I had been putting through hell, but never stopped to consider what they might be feeling. My dad was a bartender. Everyone in town knew him, and I wondered how many behind-the-back comments had been made about his son, who was in prison because he wouldn't fight in Vietnam. I'm sure my mother, who was married to a highway construction redneck, was taking a lot of shit from him. I felt sorry for myself because I was out of the anti-war fight, no longer part of the protest masses. And except for my friends, who really knew I was in prison or even gave a damn? My career as an actor had been gaining momentum, and now was put on hold. Prison was absolutely no place for CO's. This was purgatory... A total waste of human life.

So after I got through the "poor, poor, pitiful me" stage - I found a patch of grass, laid down, and looked up at the sky. It was the most beautiful blue, with puffs of clouds that were the purest white I'd ever seen. And that's when Mescaline Phase III kicked in. I started watching two clouds that seemed to be working their way toward each other. My eyes were so sharp that I could see every strand of mist that made up each cloud. Now that, coupled with the emotional flood of tears I had just experienced, took me to Mescaline Phase IV—the poet in me just screaming to be let out.

I walked to my dorm room. My roommates weren't there. I had the place to myself. I took out a piece of paper and pen—and proceeded to write just about the shittiest, most maudlin piece of poetry in the history of mankind. Etheridge Knight and his book of prison poems written in 1968 did not have to worry about me. Nor did George F. Root, who wrote *Tramp! Tramp! Tramp!* still considered the greatest prison poem-to-song, ever written.

And I'll be damned if I still don't have that poem. I found it nestled between the letters I'd saved. And when I read it again, my brain began puking. But against my better judgment, I'll share it with you, simply because I take no responsibility for writing it. It was the mescaline working, and the inspiration came when I was lying on the ground earlier looking up at those clouds. It's a simile - and had I left out the word "like" - a metaphor, about love. And here it is:

Love is like the joining of
two clouds who meet after
a long and sensuous dance
starting from a distance
until finally, the initial touch -
soft, delicate - and ever so slowly
prolonging the brief moment
of their existence
blending, sharing, and being inside
each other until the beauty of
what they have given to the world
evaporates, yet leaves a space for some
new love to follow.

I am as embarrassed at this moment writing it again, as I was when I read it the next day after I came down off my mescaline trip 45 years ago. I wrote a couple of other poems that day but had the sense enough to throw them away.

The Camp horn sounded, signifying count time, then dinner. After roll was taken I went into the cafeteria, and just spaced out at the weird things my food was doing. It was like faux art, only moving. It didn't gross me out. I was fascinated by it—the yellow, melted butter, blending in with the mashed potatoes—farrrrrr out, in hippie vernacular.

But dinner was over and now came the moment we were all waiting for: It was Saturday night. Opening night of the Safford Federal Prison Film Festival. My first entry as movie manager was Sergio Leone's *Once Upon A Time In the West*, to this day, the greatest western I've ever seen in my life. I've probably seen it a hundred times. I've put it above *High Noon, Shane, Magnificent Seven, The Man Who Shot Liberty Valence, The Good, the Bad, and the Ugly, The Unforgiven.* Seeing it on mescaline first probably had something to do with it, but it's endured throughout time—unlike the poem I wrote.

Me and some of my buddies got to the auditorium early so we could grab front row seats, and for the next two hours, I experienced Mescaline Phase V. My entire being was inside that movie screen. There was nothing going on in the planet except that film. And the music! The soundtrack was written by Ennio Morricone. The four main characters had their own theme song, and the main theme was simply the most beautiful music in the history of westerns, including the song, which led up to the greatest western gun duel ever staged. I often wonder if I'd seen it straight, if it would have had the staying power with me that it still has.

The movie lasted three hours, but my mescaline trip was on its seventh hour and not even half over. I was now into the darkness of the desert, with the moon and stars carrying me right into the universe. Fortunately, I had the capacity to find my way to the power house. My shift was about to begin. How in the hell was I going to get through it? Fortunately, there were two of us on duty and between my partner and I, the chemicals we put in the water were perfect; the samples from the cesspool were correctly filed in tubes. We never let the water tower overflow; didn't miss two count times; and I saw the most beautiful Arizona sunrise you could imagine. I was also into Mescaline Phase

VI - wired for sound, wide-awake, but starting to crash. My journey outside the prison without even leaving lasted about 18 hours. It was Sunday and that meant another day of visitors. My two friends would be coming back for another visit, so I went back to my room, hid the horrible poetry I had written the night before, and went to sleep for a few hours.

My next visit with them went "normally." They both had trouble sleeping last night, worried that the mescaline may have had a negative reaction. They were extremely relieved that I had gotten through it and enjoyed my retelling of the experience. Later that afternoon, after they left, I felt completely normal. In fact, once again they parked by the roadside a quarter of a mile away and waited to wave goodbye to me from a distance. I saw them, waved back without shedding a single tear. I couldn't wait to see *Once Upon A Time In the West* again. I wanted to make sure it was as great seeing it straight. It was.

And that was the last time I ever tried mescaline. However, I did have one more experience during my prison stay. Several of the inmates came up with very creative ways to smuggle marijuana and several types of psychedelics in. My favorite was blotter acid. One of the inmates had a friend who would write a letter with a mixture of LSD and blue food coloring. They'd leave a cryptic message as to how many lines would do the trick. Simply tear off x-amount of letter, wad it up and chew on it for a while, then swallow the juice created from the saliva. I actually tried it. Don't remember much about the trip, other than playing a game of basketball and hitting about eighteen shots in a row. Me, the ball, and the hoop were all connected into one cosmic entity. I couldn't miss. What was great about this trip, though, was that several of us were on it at the same time, and it just happened to be rock and roll night in the patio. That meant, the rednecks weren't there because they were only into Country Western—Merle Haggard/Johnny Cash music, and had their two nights a week to enjoy it; the Mexicans were only into Mexican music. They had three nights in the courtyard because there were more of them. So us CO's and drug dealers, who had the other two nights of the week, sat there with our snacks and jars of Tang, and tripped out on CSN&Y, Springsteen, Led Zeppelin, Santana, Grateful Dead, The Band, Dylan, Steve Miller,

Jefferson Airplane, Janis, Hendrix, Chapin, Joni Mitchell. And I didn't have to work the powerhouse that night. By this time, my roommate and I wised up. Two guys weren't needed to work the graveyard shift. So we did one week on, one week off. It was great. Every other week, I didn't have to do shit, and this was my week off.

Crazy.....When I was on the outside, I never had a desire to do psychedelic drugs. I had to go to prison to experience them for the first time.

Chapter Forty-five
Hope is a good thing.

A nd so came the merry month of May, which brought an abrupt end to my "tripping out" phase—for three very important reasons, other than that I was stupid to even risk it in the first place.

Cunningham called me into his office to let me know that the U.S. Parole Board would be arriving on June 8 to consider inmates for early parole, and that I would be interviewing. According to a Sentence Data Summary I was given when I arrived, I could be eligible as early as August 26. I was stunned. It was as though I'd been handed a gift but wasn't allowed to open it just yet. As it stood with Expected Good Time, I would be out by June 2, 1973. Hell, now I could be out in less than four months! Cunningham told me not to get my hopes up for Aug. 26. Doing eight months on a two-year sentence was thus far unheard of.

Second reason, and I must say it put me in a quandary. Though it wasn't official, the last NASA study at the U.S. Public Health Hospital in San Francisco was about to end and doctors would be arriving at Safford on June 15, to get three more volunteers. Pete had really put in a good word for me to be selected for the next five-month program, starting July 1 and ending in December.

But what if I got paroled during that time? I couldn't just walk away from the study; I'd have to commit to it. I'd actually counted on making the July study, but there was no way I'd be notified as to whether I made parole or not. Nevertheless, I still planned on putting my name in so I could at least meet the doctors. I explained my dilemma to Mr. Cunningham, and he also agreed that I should pass up the next study. I knew I'd be pissed if I went to my parole hearing, got turned down, and had to serve out my sentence. But I decided to roll the dice. At least I was looking at a more hopeful outcome than I got in April. That's when Saul, my attorney, went back to Conti's court to motion for a reduction of sentence. My best friend Terry was in his final year at Hastings Law School getting ready for the bar, assisted

Saul by contacting my friends and work associates for letters of support. Ken Whelan, producer of "The Cage," attended as the only witness to let Conti know I had a guaranteed job. This was Terry's letter to me before the court appearance, dated April 5:

Dear Bruce,

Talked to Saul personally yesterday morning and your motion was to be filed that afternoon. If everything goes as planned, he should see Conti on April 17th on the 10:00 am calendar. The written motion is four-pronged: 1st it mentions the accompanying letters making you out to be J.C. reincarnated and concludes God will strike Conti down if he doesn't free you; next it talks of your volunteering for the NASA program and its patriotic ramifications; thirdly, it explains about "The Cage," your previous work with it, and that they want you back. There is all kinds of "Cage" literature attached to the motion; and finally, it says if all this isn't enough, super judge, please contact your supervisor at Safford and he will tell you Bruce doesn't belong.... I honestly believe the motion for reduction of sentence presents fair, equitable alternative. Saul is still rather pessimistic because of his past relationship with Conti. I wish there was something I could do to insure our success—This is really frustrating because everything depends on Conti's state of mind.[48]

Well, Conti couldn't wait until the 17th. That was a Monday and he didn't want to fuck up his weekend. He wanted me out of the way. And so, on Friday, April 14th, his "state of mind" was right where it usually is. As my friend put it: "He was ice cold. It was as if we weren't even in the room." And Saul wrote me as soon as he got back to his office. Dated April 14, 1972:

"*My dear political juggernaut:* [that was my closing salutation whenever I wrote him]:

I am sitting here pondering if there is any way to gracefully break the news to you that Judge Conti has once again run true to form. I expect you probably have guessed as much from the fact that I have not telephoned or at least wired you the good news. If there was some way of avoiding telling you the bad news, I would; if there was some way of making the bad news more palatable, I would likewise do that. But realities being what they are, we must accept the facts as they have occurred. With his usual eloquence, Judge Conti had naught to say but 'I have reviewed the file and my notes of the trial and the material submitted in connection with the motion. The motion is denied.' Bruce, this terminates what may be done for you as far as judicial remedies are concerned. It has been a long road, but we are now at its end as far as my abilities to do anything professionally... When your matter comes before the parole board I will be delighted to write you a letter and offended if you don't ask me to participate, but that this is as a friend and not as a lawyer.... I will be delighted to correspond with you on a person-to-person relationship. For the time being, all my best. Most sincerely, Saul."[49]

Pretty classy of Saul, I thought. But it didn't lessen the sting I felt when I read the letter, even though I knew Conti would turn us down. But by now my emotional wounds had healed, and I couldn't wait to write Saul and tell him to get that letter ready. But that would come after my initial meeting here with the Parole Board, when they went back to Washington. We'd send them all the material Conti got and hope it would fall on more objective eyes.

And the final reason my 'tripping out faze" ended: Someone came along to add further hope and inspiration to my life.... Colette.

Chapter Forty-six
My French pen pal...

S till living in New York, Colette flew into San Francisco one day
to start laying groundwork for her eventual move out to the West
Coast. She came by my apartment to say hello, and that's when she
found out I was in prison. Amy had moved out but Marcia had rented
it out to another friend, who put her in touch with Marcia. Colette
called her and got the full story of what had happened. Marcia gave
her the prison phone number and my address. She was on her way
back to New York and sure enough, as soon as she got home, the
letters started coming in starting with:

"What the hell are you doing in there?!"

I immediately responded, giving her the back-story of my
incarceration, then explained to Colette that I was up for parole in June
with a slim possibility of getting out in August, and if not, a NASA
bed rest program that I could take part in, which would bring me back
to San Francisco. I tried to explain what NASA and the bed rest study
was, what with her being relatively new to the country. I figured it
wouldn't really draw much of a response. After all, we hardly knew
each other. I thanked her for her concern, little realizing we were about
to become pen pals.

June 8 finally arrived. I just couldn't get a pulse on how it would
go, given the current political climate. It was election year, and George
McGovern was close to becoming the Democratic nominee who would
go against Nixon in November. He had just won the California
primary two days earlier, and all that remained was to have the
Democratic National Convention in July, and the nomination was his.
Ted Kennedy was supposed to have been the Democratic hopeful to
win the nomination, but failing to negotiate a bridge at
Chappaquiddick in 1969, put an end to that. Mary Jo Kopechne, one of
the former Boiler Room girls on Robert Kennedy's campaign staff,
drowned in the accident, and once again, yet another Kennedy changed
history.

McGovern was running an anti-war crusade, but Nixon was proclaiming that peace was at hand because of his policies – four years and thousands of more American dead since his 1968 plan to end the war. George had too much going against him. He wanted to grant amnesty to draft resistors; he was too honest and intelligent, and I think he scared the hell out of the rich, the corrupt, and the racists. Case in point: During a Senate floor debate in September of 1970, he tore into his colleagues for not supporting a bill he co-wrote with Mark Hatfield calling for complete withdrawal from Vietnam.

"Every Senator in this chamber is partly responsible for sending 50,000 young Americans to an early grave... This chamber reeks of blood... It does not take any courage at all for a Congressman or a Senator or a President to wrap himself in the flag and say we are staying in Viet Nam because it is not our blood that is being shed."

He blamed his colleagues for having contributed *to "that human wreckage all across our land—young men without legs or arms or genitals or faces—or hopes."*[50]

Needless to say, Senate Armed Services Committee Chairman John Stennis blasted him, and again McGovern retorted with blatant honesty.

"I'm tired of old men dreaming up wars for young men to fight. If he wants to use American ground troops in Cambodia, let him lead the charge himself."[51]

Too bad he couldn't have said all that in 1968, when he sought the Democratic nomination after Bobby Kennedy was assassinated. Hubert Humphrey got the nomination, even though anti-war Democrats didn't trust him. What hurt McGovern was Eugene McCarthy, also running on an anti-war platform. He split votes with McGovern, and Humphrey sailed into the nomination... Then got creamed. I feel to this day that that was the beginning of the end of the Hippie, anti-war generation. The October 15, 1969 Moratorium Day antiwar demonstrations were the last hurrah for the "peace and Groovy

Love-Flower Generation." I was amongst the thousands of protestors in San Francisco that day, and now it felt like the only real protestors left were those of us in prison who had no choice but to play it out. And not knowing the political makeup of the Parole Board I was about to face two days after McGovern won the California Primary, I didn't want his platform screwing up my chances of "early withdrawal." I was paranoid the members of the parole board were all Republicans.

There were about five parole board members present that day, and they were surprisingly cordial. Of course, I entered with a smile and a pleasant "Good morning," undressing the room of any veil of stoicism or coldness. Mr. Cunningham and Correctional Supervisor, Tom Lanier, were present. They had my records in front of them, and the parole board was impressed with my history and good standing. They knew I was a professional actor and asked what my plans were if I got an early parole. I told them I would once again tour with "The Cage" were I granted permission from my parole officer. I explained it was a prison reform program; that we'd performed at the Great Hall of Justice in D.C., hoping one of them had maybe seen the play—they hadn't. Mr. Cunningham complimented my behavior and attitude. I felt comfortable in the room and didn't sense any attitude of superiority. They wanted to understand where I was coming from, why I did what I did, and I explained as best I could without sounding like a far left radical, which I wasn't. It didn't have to be said, but everybody in that room knew that for me and my other CO inmates, that this was a complete and utter waste of time.

The interview lasted about fifteen minutes, ending with one of the parole board team telling me they'd be getting back to me with a decision in July. I left the room feeling pretty good about things.

I was on the list along with twelve other inmates to meet with the U.S. Public Health doctors on Thursday, June 15th. I wanted to make a good impression even though I'd decided not to go for the July-December study. In addition, I wanted to recommend Sean, because I knew he'd be perfect. He was a writer, a poet, a very laid back guy—and I knew he wanted to be part of this study in the worst way.

Then, one week after my parole hearing, I received my second letter from Colette. Jesus, who the hell was this girl!? She wanted to bring in her friend Andrew, a high-powered attorney from New York who had many connections in Washington DC. The letter was dated June12, 1972, as partly stated:

She gave me his name and address.

"He is definitely interested...Take advantage of this now. If nothing else, whatever mild noises he might make on your behalf could be useful with the parole board. At least try it, okay?"[52]

Colette concluded her letter assuring me that Andrew wanted to take my case for free. That of course was important, and I jumped on it because earlier that day, hours before I received Colette's letter, the two Project Directors from the NASA Research Project - Drs' Lockwood and Wilson—arrived to conduct interviews with CO's interested in volunteering for the bed rest study. And they changed it to a three-month program, not five, but because I could be eligible for parole in August—I was turned down. But depending on my parole date, they'd consider me for the next one. I walked away from the interview with very mixed feelings. Three days later, when the mail came that afternoon, mixed feelings turned into being just plain pissed off!It was letter from Pete, who had finished the study in March, came back to prison, paroled in late April, and was now back in San Francisco... Where I wanted to be. The mailing date was June 15, the day I'd had my interview. He wrote:

"Dear Bruce, Got your mail today and am trying to call the hospital now. Dr. Lockwood's secretary told me that the doctors are there in Safford now doing the interviewing and hopefully you will make it. I'm sure that Rick and Steve will also help you and also give a good word... The new study sounds like a very interesting one...not as arduous as ours was... More up and down and not as long. It is really a good deal to get on and the people to have near you are all okay. It's hard to tell what impact it has on the parole... It just can't hurt and at least you are in SF. Have stopped by to see your friends

at the Wine Shop on Chestnut. They have turned Beth and I on to some good stuff. Especially Shramsberg champagne and some Freemark Cabernet that we haven't cracked yet. They await your return as we all do.[53]

Well, shit! Did I fuck that up?!An easier study; a combination of sitting up and lying down; and not for five months but for three, ending September 26!That meant that even if I did get paroled on August 26, the study ended one month later. Hell, I'd have given them an extra month. Volunteers were paid $100.00 a week. I'd have walked out of the hospital a free man, with $1,200 cash in my pocket. The more I analyzed it, the angrier I became. Maybe I'd have gotten paroled in September! Talk about perfect. I might have missed "The Cage" fall college tour, but now I didn't care. Who knows? Maybe I'd have gotten film-TV work, a couple of national spots; I'd have been back in my apartment in time for Indian Summer and watching the sunset from the Cliff House in San Francisco or the Trident in Sausalito, while sipping on a Tequila Sunrise!

But I could still have that. It was just a matter of following up with Colette's attorney friend. And damn if Andrew didn't call me from New York within days after my first letter from Colette. He was sorry he didn't know about me when I went up for my parole hearing, but wanted me to send him whatever relevant information I had about myself, so he could present it to his connections in D.C.. I was only allowed to talk for a few minutes so we couldn't discuss too much. Colette was with Andrew in his office but the attorney decided it was best that she didn't get on the phone the first time. I was totally blown away that she was even there. I'd spent a few hours with her months ago and no communication since. And now there she was, pacing in the background, very upset that I was in a state of self-inflicted exile. I immediately sent off a letter to Andrew, telling him that I'd have my transcripts sent. I included a biography on myself. Within the week I had a letter from him saying he'd received my letter. He wrote:

".... I have been in touch with friends, including Willard Gaylin, whose book Colette is sending you and I hope we may

be able to be of some help. Frankly I don't know until I have looked into things further. All I can say is that the dignity and courage evident in your letter is a good example for us all. Best regards, Andrew. [54].

A few days later, I received a book from Colette, "In Service of Their Country – War Resistors in Prison," by Willard Gaylin, M.D..

The following week, Sean and two other inmates were on their way to San Francisco. I was glad that putting in a good word for Sean paid off. He promised to do the same for me in three months if I needed it. But I would miss him, because he was such a great guy, so soothing to the spirit. And the more I thought about it, the more pissed I got that I wasn't going. Anything past September for an early parole date was not going to make me a happy prison camper.

Chapter Forty-seven
June and America's Pastime.

On the national front, a historical moment had occurred two days after my NASA interview... at the Watergate Hotel complex in Washington D.C., on June 17, 1972. Five men were arrested for breaking into the Democratic National Headquarters. We didn't have a whole lot of information during the early stage, but this bungled burglary would ultimately lead straight to the White House, Richard Nixon, and his loyal staff. And by the time the FBI finished conducting their investigations, this man, who hired the judge who threw me in prison, would be accused of cover-ups, illegal payments, illegal wire-tapping, campaign fraud, secret slush funds laundered in Mexico and payoffs to the crooks who broke into the Watergate Hotel. This is shit that would bring a huge smile to my face on August 9, 1974, one day before my birthday, when Dirty Tricks Dick would resign from office.

However, there were other things happening in this country—the election and a major Democratic screw-up; updates from Vietnam; and the normal everyday tensions here. But now, with Colette and the intervention of her lawyer friend in my life, my morale was pretty good as I awaited the results of everyone's efforts for getting me early parole, although trying to match Colette letter for letter, was an impossible task. Considering she was still looking for the right location for her showroom in San Francisco, introducing herself around, connecting with business and social networks–she was struggling and frustrated. I guess writing to someone who was in a worse situation helped alleviate all that angst. I encouraged her in my letters, even suggesting she check out Union Street.

Other than that, nothing to do now but play softball, read, avoid trouble... and go rattlesnake hunting with Gordo. Here are some of my prison reflections, though not necessarily in chronological order, though softball season lasted from June through August.

Safford Prison Camp had a softball team, and we were allowed to play in the Safford City Softball League. I was fast, had a good glove, and could really cover the outfield. So I made the team. And we were great, thanks to one man—our pitcher. His name was Hal. He was in for bank embezzlement. And it just so happened that he'd also taken his softball team to the state championship for about seven years in a row. And we're not talking "lob-pitch." We're talking underhand fast pitch, and that fucker could throw. And now we had him. During practice games at camp, I didn't get one hit off of him. The rival teams all hated us because we were so good. Hal probably threw a half-dozen no-hitters; ten one-hitters—I don't think one team ever got more than four hits off him. We ended up with a record of 30-1, losing only to an all-star team from Phoenix—all of those guys were Hal's friends, most of them former teammates, or guys he'd played against. Our league consisted of a couple of other prisons, several teams from Safford, and the local college. I was a defensive star but couldn't hit worth a damn. Hal captained the team and most of the time, sent me up to bunt. I doubt if I got more than ten hits all season, and one of the few hits I got was a double that I tried to stretch into a triple, but got tagged out sliding into third base. Unfortunately, I didn't keep my right arm up and landed so hard on my elbow that I reinjured it again and ended up missing half the games in July. But it was great getting into baseball uniforms, feeling somewhat normal, climbing in the back of a truck, and heading into town for games. Officer Kenske, in his 60's, who coached basketball, was also the baseball coach. But he didn't really coach. He was a guard. He and one other guard just had to make sure we didn't run off. It was small town all the way, and lots of people showed up. Even though they knew we were prisoners, the folks of Safford were very courteous. For sure, the local ladies liked to flirt with us. We were the best looking guys in town. Besides, it was safe. The most grating thing about those games was the concession truck with a loudspeaker that played "Candy Man" by Sammy Davis Jr.– about this guy who combined sunrise, dew, miracles, chocolate, and love. Mix together and presto a world that tastes good. Between each inning that song came blaring out. We probably heard it 500 times during the season. It was like being pecked to death by a duck. To this day it haunts me.

In spite of that song, we won the league championship. From there we went on to win a regional championship which was a drag because it was a 4- hour round trip to the town where we played. Every other team stayed in the local motels, but because we were prisoners, we had to drive back and forth from Safford. I don't remember how many nights we did this, but getting back to the prison at midnight riding in the back of a truck was a bitch. But the great thing about being on that team was that almost all of us were CO's, so we had a nice three-month stretch of time where we connected with each other. That team brought us together more than the prison. Because without the team, we all would have tried doing our own time, afraid of making friends lest we keep having to lose them and feel that much more alone.

Chapter Forty-eight
"Meester Neekles...
Would ju like to go a-rattlesnake hunting?"

His name was Ray Sanchez. Everyone called him Gordo. He weighed at least 350 pounds. Probably in his late 30's, he had a black flattop haircut and looked like a Mexican Buddha sumo wrestler. His arms, chest, and back were covered with blue and green tattoos. In fact, he was a hell of a tattoo artist and made a nice living at Safford designing the flesh of many an inmate. He also had one other past-time: killing rattlesnakes... with his bare hands. But he didn't do it as a sport. It was another way to earn commissary money, and send money back to his family in Mexico. And with the raw leather and string, buckles, beads, and curing oils which he had mail-ordered in, he made purses, wallets, and belts. Rattlesnake skins were the decorative touch. They were sold to friends and families who visited inmates every weekend.

The first time I was even aware of Gordo's vocation, was one day in March when he went rattlesnake hunting and came back with two of the ugliest fang bites on his forearm. It wasn't a Diamondback that bit him, but the bites were deep and big, and he was on his way to get stitched up. I asked him how he felt when that poison hit his system.

"Ohhhhhh... I get a leetle dizzy, but I've been bit so many[tines], it don' bother me."

I looked at Officer Perkins, the guard assigned to these Gordo outings – asked if he'd witnessed the biting incident.

"Yeah," Perkins replied. He closed his eyes and slowly shook his head, as Gordo calmly walked into the infirmary.

#

There are at least fifteen different species of rattlesnake in Arizona. Several rattlers that I remember are the Mohave, Hopi, Southwestern Speckled, Arizona Black, the Colorado Desert Sidewinder (who liked to hang out in Arizona). But the superstar of all the rattlesnakes was the Western Diamondback. This bad boy can measure out at over seven feet long. He's known as King of the Southwestern rattlers, and the venomous bite from this son-of-a bitch produces the highest mortality rate by snakes in North America.

The first Western Diamondback rattler that I saw while at Safford prison was one that I smelled. It was April, and someone was barbecuing on the other side of the powerhouse. I didn't think much of it at first, because next to the powerhouse was the kitchen. Since I was allowed to enter that area, I decided to see what was going on. And there was Gordo with one of the daytime-shift powerhouse inmates named "Tex," barbecuing chunks of rattlesnake meat on a grill, made in the machine shop (located to the left of the powerhouse) out of a garbage can and soldered strips of metal. Normally the grill was brought out whenever an inmate chef would smuggle steaks to Tex. But today was a special day. Gordo had just come back from a rattlesnake hunt. On three different sawhorses, were three rattlesnake skins, stretched out, oiled and tanning. This kept the skin from discoloring and also made it very soft. One of these skins was at least six feet long. It belonged to a Diamondback rattlesnake. I can't even imagine how Gordo caught and killed this monster, but thank God the rest of him was over a fire in about thirty pieces. During the first three months, Gordo and I had become friends, so I wasn't at all an intruder.

"Meester Neekels, have ju ever ate rattlesnake?" He asked.

I said no but that I that I'd like to try some. Gordo picked one off the grill, put it on a paper towel and handed it to me. It was white meat, which Gordo boiled first to get it off the bones. I'd always heard that snake tasted like a cross between chicken and seafood. But this particular snake was quite gamy to me... And a little stringy. I wouldn't say it tasted like seafood—more like frog legs. Amazing what the sense memory can do, because decades later, I can smell that snake grilling on the barbeque. Just plain ol' snake. I mean, they were right there by the kitchen. Would it be asking too much to have marinated those chunks in olive oil, thyme, garlic, a pinch of cayenne? My whole snake-eating experience would have been much more enriching. I didn't ask for seconds. Gordo could tell I wasn't that excited about it, and let out with his high-pitched cackling laughter.

"Meester Neekels, next [tine] I go a'rattlesnake hunting, I take ju with me."

And without thinking, I said, "Hey that'd be fun. Yeah, I'll go." What the hell, I thought; I'm an actor. This would be another one of life's great experiences. Besides, he wouldn't be going out for a couple of months. He had enough skins to make two dozen purses, wallets, and belts.

It was sometime in June, after my parole hearing, that Gordo needed to go rattlesnake hunting again. Guard Perkins, known as the best tracker at Safford Prison, was always the one who took Gordo into the desert. Not that Gordo would ever try to escape, but whenever someone did try to bolt, Perkins had him by EOD (end of day) and took him to Florence prison where there were cells and bars. Anyway, Gordo would be going out early in the morning—for three hours. Snakes move around when it's cooler. They hide under rocks and bushes during the hottest part of the day.

"Okay, Meester Neekels, ees tine! I already talk to Perkins. He says you can go eef ju get permission."

Well, I didn't want to chicken out, but what lousy timing. I was up for parole; I still remembered those two fang marks on Gordo's arm. It'd be my luck to get bitten by a Diamondback. But there was still a chance that Correctional Supervisor, Tom Lanier, would not allow it. He had to consider liability issues, didn't he? No, and if he did, he didn't. Me and my big mouth. He gave me permission to go out with Gordo the next morning. I immediately went over to the machine shop and grabbed a garden hoe - not the kind that was bent at the bottom, but one with the blade straight down. Tex worked in there and I asked if he'd mind turning on the tool sharpener and putting a razor edge on my hoe. I was not going out there to face those prehistoric beasts with a dull blade.

And I didn't have to. This was my week off from the powerhouse, so I was asleep when a Mexican inmate bolted after the 2:00 a.m. count. Since Perkins was the man to go out after escapees, Gordo couldn't go out on his snake hunt... And neither could I. I remember it was a Friday. And with weekend visits, all guards, including Perkins, had to be on standby at the prison. The following week, he took Gordo out. I couldn't go because that was my work week. Gordo came back with enough skins to last two months. I wouldn't have to address this subject again.

I've mentioned Lanier, Perkins, Bob, Ron, Kenske – Here are my experiences with some of the guards. What I failed to mention thus far, is that, according to some of the older inmates who'd done time in other prisons, Safford was known the "armpit of the federal prison system, and the guards at Safford were there because they couldn't cut it in a maximum security prison." I remember wondering why a human being would even want to be a guard in a maximum security prison, unless they truly enjoyed being sadistic, pitting inmate against inmate, gang against gang. Because that is the only way guards can control a prison filled with murderers, rapists, drug dealers, and gangs. Since prisoners far outnumber the guards, divide and conquer is the name of the game. Not so at Safford. You had 70 percent Mexican; 40 CO's; a few old timers finishing out their sentences; several drug dealers, and a half dozen white collar embezzlement convicts. So guards at Safford were assholes as long as you allowed them to play that role. And in order to see that side of them, you in turn had to be an asshole.

Western Diamondback rattlesnake

Chapter Forty-nine
Keepers of the Gate Stories

I can't say that I really had any bad experiences with the guards. I was no kiss-ass by any means. I rarely spoke to most of them, but when I did, I never let them get to me. Nor can I say that they even tried, with a couple of exceptions. In fact, I don't think they really hassled anyone—couple of guys: One of them, who mouthed off to some of the guards, and showed no respect for the front office, was given his parole date for October 7th. A couple of nights before he was to be released, they called him into the office to let him know they'd made a "mistake" and miscalculated. His new release date was set for November 7.Another inmate was so uncooperative, that he served out his whole time. Yes, that may have qualified him as the most sincere, anti-government, anti-war candidate in Safford, but why spend a minute longer in that place than necessary?

Lanier...

So, let's start at the top. That would be Tom Lanier, the Correctional Supervisor. Very thin, pale complexion, reddish blond curly hair, wore glasses, and had an upper register pitched voice... Not quite as mousy as the Captain in "Cool Hand Luke," played by Strother Martin. It had to be frustrating for Tom because there really weren't any life lessons or rehabilitation programs this guy could implement for us CO's, because we already "had our heads straight. "So he was reduced to some very banal decisions.... Like when he wouldn't let me have an Easter basket.

Just before Easter Sunday, I was called into Lanier's office. He was sitting behind his desk. With him was an assistant supervisor. On Lanier's desk was this huge Easter basket filled with jelly beans, chocolate bunnies, marshmallow eggs, and candy bars - all from See's Candies®, with headquarters right there in San Francisco! The cellophane which covered the basket was off, and the empty box the basket came in was on the floor. They had inspected it for contraband.

"Neckels, you got a package from your friends in San Francisco."

"Right... my friends Al and Marcia. They wouldn't tell me what it was"

On March 30, I had come to Lanier with a request form: a surprise package.

"I can only guess it's a head-band and some sheet music - maybe books."

Lanier signed off on it. "Approved. Keep this as your approval. T.E. Lanier Jr., Corr Supv."

"Well, I guess it wasn't books and sheet music." I said.

"No, but I can't let you have this because we don't allow food to be sent in here except for Christmas. I'll have to send it back."

Well, I was pissed... somewhat. It seemed so stupid to box this up and send it back. At the same time, I wondered how ridiculous I'd look, walking through the prison compound carrying an Easter basket filled with chocolate bunnies and jelly beans. So I offered Lanier an alternative.

"Sir, instead of sending this back and wasting taxpayer's money, why don't you just keep it here and share it with your staff?"

I don't think he expected that. He stared blankly at me for a couple of seconds—I mean, God forbid he should take the advice from an inmate.

"Thanks, Neckels, but we're not allowed to keep items sent to the inmates."

I wouldn't let him off the hook.

"Okay, well here's a better idea," I said. "Isn't there a guard here who has a small child? Give the basket to him. I mean, where's he going to find an Easter basket like this in Safford?"

Both Lanier and his assistant broke out laughing. First time I'd ever seen Lanier smile, let alone laugh. I continued.

"And if there's no guard here with children, certainly you must have friends in Safford who have children. Give it to one of them."

Again, Lanier stared at me for a moment, then surprised me.

"You know, I just might do that. Thank you, Neckels. That's very generous of you. I appreciate your offer... You can go."

But before I turned to leave, I just had to see if I could take it a little further.

"Mr. Lanier, there are several small bags of jellybeans in that basket. Think we might be able to break one open and sample it?"

Lanier didn't answer. He reached for a bag of the jellybeans, tore it open, extended them to me. I held out my hand, he poured a few in my hand, offered some to his assistant, then popped one in his own mouth.

"Thanks again, Neckels."

"Wait'll you try the chocolate," I said. I could hear them laughing as I went out the door. Don't know whatever happened with that basket....

The significance of that story is: This happened in April, and I don't think Lanier and I ever spoke to each other again. But while he was there, never was I denied anything sent to me from the outside, even if it was sent without prior authorization—including a subscription to Playboy Magazine, a good segue to the next guard. But to wrap up Lanier, one day in early June, he was gone. Nobody knew why he left, but the air around Safford Prison was lighter. No question the guy was a jerk. We were all happy to see him go, though he was replaced by a Supervisor who also never smiled. One month later, in July, Lanier died of a brain tumor. Perhaps the knowledge of his own inevitable demise, which he bore in silence, is what made him so angry... Or not. As my friend Mike said to me in a letter after he'd been released and heard the news: *"Probably one of the only men to die out of pure hatred for the human race. Somewhere in this universe is an awful lot of hatred floating around."*[55]

Bob....

Sergeant and head guy at the front desk. He made all the announcements, opened and checked out the mail—everything went through him. And not too many people liked him either. Remember, he was the guy who found me when I was on escape alert. I guess he started liking me after that. He knew damn well I hadn't tried to escape. In fact, he told me he was the one who stopped Lanier from over-reacting and immediately contacting the FBI. Bob had made the extra effort to find me. And he knew how badly I felt about falling asleep and missing count - even made a couple of jokes about it. In fact, late one morning he saw me through the window, walking toward the library. As I mentioned, I was one of very few inmates at the prison during the day, since I worked graveyard at the powerhouse. Suddenly I heard from the loudspeaker, in a very soft voice:

"Neckels, there will be a count time in ten minutes." I laughed, waved at him, then he said in a normal voice.

"Neckels, report to control."

I walked into the building, and Bob was leaning back in his chair, thumbing through a Playboy Magazine.

"Did you put in a request for a Playboy Subscription?"

"No, I didn't... But I'll sure take it." I said.

"Well, normally, we're not supposed to allow this, but Lanier says go ahead and let you have it."

All right! Let's hear it for the Easter basket! My generous offer had paid off. Bob closed the magazine, stuck it under the opening in the glass window.

"Here you go... And you might as well take the rest of your mail."

Now that was a big deal. Mail gets handed out in the late afternoon, just before dinner. And for him to give me mine early was great. I didn't have to wait all day to see if I still had links to the outside world. I thanked him, and then thought, what the hell, I'll extend a generosity to him.

"Bob, if you want to hang on to the Playboy, I can come get it later."

A simple little offer that he declined, but again, just a normal, human touch - not prisoner to jailor - and from that day on, if he remembered, he always set my mail aside and gave it to me early.

Weeks later, toward the end of June, I was off that week from the powerhouse. During breakfast, I got a call to report to the Control Center. I had no idea what that was about. I was hoping the parole board had contacted the prison to inform them that I was getting paroled. No such luck. Bob was standing in the lobby with the new Correctional Supervisor, Mr. Ulibarri, to whom I hadn't yet spoken since his arrival. I suddenly got nervous. Something was up. Bob introduced me to Ulibarri who gave me a curt hello.

"You're going to El Paso with me," said Bob.

My heart was racing, and now I was scared.

"Am I being transferred to another prison?" I asked.

"No, Neckels, that's where the federal prison warehouse is. We're going for kitchen supplies. We'll be gone all day."

Ulibarri just wanted to see who I was, then he turned and left.

"We need to take one more inmate, so go pick one of your buddies I can trust, and let's get going."

Well, not only was I relieved, but blown away that he let me pick out the inmate. So I went and got my buddy, "Spinooch," a nickname I gave him. His name was also Mike. We were on the softball team together and he only had a couple more months to go on his sentence. Really a good guy.

I remember a funny moment. Neither Bob nor the Correctional Supervisor felt it necessary to handcuff us during the trip, but while we were waiting for Mike to get to the truck, I happened to see Bob wrapping his gun-belt around his holstered revolver, and putting it behind his seat. I don't think he realized I was watching.

"Bob, seriously," I asked. "Do you really need to take a gun?"

"No," he said. "But we're required to when we have prisoners."

"Well, if it'll help your peace of mind, I could wear that fucking thing and you'd have nothing to worry about."

It was indeed an all day trip and hotter than hell. No air conditioning in the truck, going through Arizona, New Mexico, into the tip of Texas. We stopped in a restaurant along the way and had breakfast. It was great to actually feel civilized. We got to El Paso by noon, loaded up the truck with bags of potatoes, flour, rice, canned goods - and headed back to Safford. Bob called the prison to let them know we were on our way back, and again once we got to the Arizona border to let them know where we were. Only this time he found out there'd been a little trouble back at the prison. One of the inmates who'd been doing time on a drug bust - came back from road duty and had taken some peyote. When the guards noticed his strange behavior and started to question him, he went totally ballistic and started fighting them. It took four guards to pin him down and get him into solitary - one small room with bars.

We got back to camp late that afternoon and unloaded the supplies into the kitchen storage room. We inquired about the inmate, but he was long gone. The FBI came in and took him to a maximum security prison. Stupid shit. He easily added another two years to his sentence.

One final story about Bob: As soon as I was given a graveyard position in the powerhouse, I was moved to a three-man room toward the entrance of the dorm. That move alone saved my sanity. No more sleeping in a 80-man dorm with the noise, noise, noise. I had two roommates: Tom, who worked swing shift, and James, my graveyard shift partner (who actually came up with the idea that there didn't need to be two of us working in that powerhouse at the same time). Because we had a door that we could close, we had privacy whenever we wanted it. We had a desk and chair, a small cabinet, a lamp, our own coffee pot, and we could have a radio playing all night long, as long as we kept it down. And we didn't have a "lights out" time, like in the dorms. And that was great, especially during my week off. To be able to have that kind of quiet time, to read and write letters. It was a Godsend.

And so I immediately wrote my dad and asked him to send me a portable radio, which he did - a Seminole AM radio, which I still have. Well, one night, about two months after I got it, there was a horrible lightening storm, that blew out my radio. It was gone, finished. For some reason, the next day I had to go to the main building where Bob was on duty, and I told him what happened to my radio. I didn't make a big deal out of it. Later that day, I was sitting in my room, when somebody gave two quick knocks on my door, and walked in. It was Bob, just getting off duty.

"Let me have that radio," he said. "I like to tinker around with electronics. Maybe I can fix it. I can't promise when I'll get it back to you."

I didn't care. It was broken anyway. I thanked him for even considering it.

Two weeks later, early one morning before he started his shift, Bob walked into my room and handed me the radio.

"Turn it on," he said. I did, and it worked perfectly. Bob said he replaced the shorted-out part, and soldered the new piece in. I offered to pay him for the part and his time, with money I had in my commissary account.

"Don't worry about it," he said. "It was only a few bucks."

He smiled and walked out; obviously proud that he had managed to fix it, and he knew how much I appreciated it. You can imagine the razzing I took from my COhorts, all in fun.

"How the fuck were you able to get that asshole to fix your radio?" "What's going on, Neckels? You giving that guy head?" "You gotta be his punk, Bruce!"

No. Not at all. But I never once related to Bob, or any of the guards in a "Me slave, you master" mentality. No doubt that was indeed the situation, but I didn't buy into it. And I must say, neither did most of my COhorts. We knew what we were about, and no-one was going to change that. Only time after incarceration would tell what kind of effect it really had on us. But again, I reiterate, though it must seem we didn't have it so bad, the fact that I did go to El Paso, stop for breakfast in a restaurant along the way; then lunch on the way back; playing softball in town; umpiring Little League games in Safford during the month of August; Bob fixing my radio— and a couple of other experiences, made it all the more difficult to understand why the hell we were here! Why our lives were being wasted and put on hold. Why one inmate would lose his life; and why another would lose his family.

Roy...

He was really a nice guy - good looking, along the Tom Cruise mold. About 5'8" tall, he walked the prison grounds with his chest puffed out, and his arms slightly away from his sides - like John Wayne. The Marine Corps would have been proud to have him. Maybe he was a Marine at one time, I don't remember. But his "tough guy" gait was almost amusing. I'm not sure exactly what month he showed up at Safford. He might have been transferred in from another prison. I just remember that one afternoon, there he was walking

263

through the compound and I said hello to him. Couldn't say what we talked about, but I never felt threatened by Roy. Not for a moment. And even though he was the shortest guard there, he didn't have a little man complex. He was married; not sure if he had children. But after a couple of months, he was gone. A week later he came back. I asked where he'd been and he told me that his wife's father passed away and left her his 700 acre farm in Ohio, and they went to check it out; secure the deed; and they were considering selling it.

So now, here we are, the day of the El Paso trip and the "peyote attack" - and here comes Roy walking my way. The whole left side of his face was red from catching one hell of a punch. I told him I'd heard about what happened and asked him if he was all right. He said he was... couldn't believe how strong the inmate was. But no doubt about it, Roy was shook from the incident. I actually felt bad for him.

"Roy, can I say something to you and let's forget that I'm a prisoner and you're a guard... Just a friend to friend talk?"

I don't remember waiting for an answer, then I went on a diatribe. And again, it may not be verbatim"

"What the fuck are you doing here? What do you need this shit for? Every day you come to work in a hostile, angry, and now, dangerous environment... and you take it home with you. And look what you'll be taking home to your wife tonight - a story about how you almost got your ass seriously hurt... Or killed. You told me a couple of months ago that your wife inherited 700 acres of land in Ohio. Have you sold it yet?"

He shook his head. "No."

"Then go live on it. Go be a farmer and grow corn, raise cattle, or whatever the fuck else you can grow there. Have a family, be your kid's little league coach. You're a good guy, Roy. This place is fucking depressing!"

"Yeah," he said. "My wife and I have been sorta talking about it. But I can retire in ten years and have a nice pension..."

"Fuck the pension! Ten years? You want to waste ten years of your life just to earn a pension? That's bullshit. Do you know what great things you and your wife can accomplish in ten years? You gotta leave, man."

One month later, in early August, I heard someone calling from behind me.

"Hey, Bruce! Wait up."

I turned, and saw that it was Roy. He walked up to me.

"I just want to say goodbye. Today's my last day. My wife and I are moving to Ohio. Thanks for the concern you showed that day."

I told him how proud I was of his decision. We talked briefly, then shook hands. He wished me luck, and hoped my parole would come soon, and that I'd get out early. He turned and walked away. Now that was truly rich. Of all the things I imagined could happen to me in prison, helping a guard to escape this misery was not one of them.

#

Ed... Mr. Shakedown.

For Ed, we go back to the end of March, when I finally got my graveyard shift job at the powerhouse, and a room. I'd been warned about this guy bursting into the private rooms at any given time looking for contraband which he knew wasn't there. Just his way of messing with the inmates.

After about a week being on graveyard, I still hadn't seen him. Then early one evening, I was in my room lying on my bunk, reading a book. It was still hotter than hell outside. I remember it had been our day of the week to go to the commissary. Besides my usual staple of snacks and sundries, I bought a case of warm Coca Cola, but had a few cans soaking in big bowl of ice on my desk. Because of my access to the powerhouse where the main ice machine was, I was always able to get ice. There were two smaller machines on the compound, but they only filled them once a day. And if you weren't one of the first 50 guys in line, you were out of business.

All of a sudden, the door burst open, scaring the crap out of me. I knew who it was, and lowered my book. There was Ed, cold-staring me. I sat up in my bunk and said:

"You must be Ed."

He stood there for a moment.

265

"Yeah, I am," he said. "How'd you know?"

I put it as non-offending as possible.

"One of the inmates mentioned you as the head guard who checks out our rooms for contraband."

I immediately extended my hand.

"I'm Bruce Neckels, Ed. I work graveyard shift in the powerhouse."

He nodded and we shook hands.

"You want me to go outside while you check my room?"

"No," He said. "You don't have to do that."

So he looked around a bit. Didn't pull the sheets off the beds or dump locker contents onto the floor and make a big mess, like I'd been warned. I noticed he had beads of sweat on his forehead.

"Still hot outside, huh?"

"Yeah," he said.

"Well, I got some Cokes on ice over there on the desk. Why don't you grab yourself one?"

"No, thanks," was all he said.

"Maybe next time, then."

He didn't respond and walked out the door. Once again, I'd defused any negative confrontation by meeting him on neutral ground. But then I wanted to kick myself in the ass for being so stupid. I mean, asking him if he wanted me to wait outside while he searched my room? How fucking lame was that? He could've planted drugs under my mattress, then busted me, and it would've been my word against his. But he didn't. Still, I wondered if he wasn't setting me up for the next time he busted in. You know the old saying: "Just because you're paranoid doesn't mean someone ISN'T following you."

But several nights later, I was sitting on a bench out at the playing field, watching some of the inmates playing soccer. Just me on that bench, no one else. After a while, I heard someone walk up behind me. I glanced over my shoulder and saw that it was Ed. Now understand that you have to go out of your way from the main compound to the playing field. So I assumed he came over to tell me to get my ass back to my dorm room. But instead he sat down on the bench a few feet away from me.

"Hey Ed... How's it going?" I asked. He nodded hello.

We both stared out at the soccer game, and after about a half minute I was starting to feel a real uncomfortable silence, when:

"That guy's really a good soccer player," He said, indicating the guy moving the ball. I was taken aback that he was trying to start a conversation with me, so I went along.

"Yeah, I've been watching him. He's fast."

And the ice-breaking conversation about soccer ended. Now there was an even longer silence. I was thinking about asking him how long he'd been a guard, when suddenly he said:

"You see that mountain right there?"

He was referring to Mt. Graham, straight ahead behind the soccer field, but a few miles away.

"Yeah," was all I said.

"I'd like to build a home right.... there."

He seemed to point to a specific area of the mountain.

"I'd never come down again." He concluded.

Now that threw me. Ed was no more than 35, and already he'd had it with the world... or at least his job. And why's he telling me this? All I could come back with was –

"Yeah, I'll bet it's great view from up there."

I don't remember a damn thing else about that conversation. The next time I saw him, I was on my way to the patio. It was rock music night. To get there, we had to go through the administration building. Ed was leaning against the counter that outlined the sergeant's glassed-in office. Apparently Ed had done some checking on me.

"Hey, Neckels! I hear you're an actor."

"That's right," I said.

"Have you been in any movies?"

"Two" I said. "I've done several commercials, but mainly theatre."

Once Again, I overestimated him, thinking he was going to follow up with something snide, like:

"I hear there's a lot of homos in show business. You a homo, Neckels?"

But no. He didn't say anything snide at all.

"I got a cousin in LA who's a film editor."

"Oh, yeah? Movies, television?" I asked.

He wasn't sure, but for the next few minutes we talked about show business, then I went into the courtyard.

From that point on, he would on occasion drop by for a cold can of Coke, and we'd talk about movies, sports, whatever. The one moment that I remember was the second time he came into my room, he looked around, then opened up my desk drawer about two inches, peeked in, then closed it. He looked over at me with a smile as if to say, "Well, I've got to at least act like I'm doing my job." In all the months I spent in prison after that, he never once bothered me, and never once ransacked our room. But he sure made a mess in a couple of other rooms.

So those four, plus Cunningham were really the only guards with whom I had any real communication. Kenske, the "coach" and oldest of the guards, walked with a limp, was close to retirement and just trying to get through his final couple of years. Bob had a brother, Doug, who was also a prison guard there. This guy never shot a mean glance at anyone, was very soft-spoken. He might as well have been a curator at a museum.

Still, no matter how often pleasantries were exchanged, and they really weren't that often, there was never a doubt who was the guard and who the prisoner. I may have played the role of a prisoner fighting for neutral ground, but they weren't acting. And I never dared show disrespect.

Chapter Fifty
Say it ain't true, Cat Ballou!

I n 1965 Jane Fonda played the role of Cat Ballou in a fictional movie of the same name. And as Nat King Cole sang in the theme song, Cat Ballou was out to make this country bleed. Well, seven years later, it was Jane Fonda, in a real-life drama, out to show how America was bleeding.

The month of July was an emotional up-and-down period, starting with reinjuring my elbow. But it was hot and dry. I'd already been here for five months. My friend, Mike, had been released in June and was now a free man living in Tempe, Arizona. He had a friend who worked in the public library and was always able to send me books. Colette wrote volumes, sent me books, and subscriptions to Rolling Stone, Time, and New York Magazine. I also had a subscription of the aforementioned Playboy, sent to me by another friend. So I had all the reading material I needed. What was interesting was how I changed my mind about where I was. When I first got to prison, I was relieved to see that there were no high walls, cells, or bars - only that wall about four feet high that surrounded the prison. But after five months, those same walls became degrading. They might as well have just painted a yellow line around the place, with the words "Go ahead! We dare you to cross that line." That's about how pointless, how meaningless, this all started to feel. And what happened on the outside during that month of July, made it even more frustrating: The Democratic National Convention.

The convention ran for three days, from July 10-13 at the Miami Beach Convention Center. McGovern got the nod; that wasn't the problem. But choosing his running mate was. And we all felt that if George even had a shot at beating Nixon, he'd need a great Vice-president. And at least 70 candidates were put into nomination, including the Berrigan brothers, Archibald Bunker, Mao Zedong, and Jerry Rubin. It was such a mess, such a circus, that many Democratic delegates even supported Richard Nixon. It took so long to hand out the votes, that acceptance speeches were finally given on July 14, around 3:00 a.m. in the morning, Miami time. And the Vice Presidential nod went to Thomas Eagleton, the great "depression" Senator from Missouri. Depression... as in manic depression. Two weeks after his nomination, a story broke that he had undergone electric shock therapy for depression and hadn't told McGovern about it. McGovern went on public record that he was backing Eagleton 1,000 percent. Three days later, after much negative attention, he asked Eagleton to withdraw. The Republicans were already having a field day with that, painting a picture of McGovern as an indecisive turncoat. [56]

For the next week, McGovern went around like a pregnant high school girl I once knew, who at her Senior Prom was begging someone, anyone, to marry her. After being turned down by half a dozen prominent Democrats, including Kennedy, Mondale, and I think even Hubert Humphrey; he finally got Kennedy's brother-in-law, Sargent Shriver, to say yes. But the damage was done. McGovern's poll rating, which started out at 41 percent, sunk to 24 percent.[57] It was pretty obvious the November election would be a cakewalk for Nixon. It was over before it would even start. How would this play on a parole board who must have known that one of the items on George's platform was to grant amnesty to draft evaders?

And if I wasn't being paranoid enough, one more thing happened in July of '72 on the Vietnam War front. Something that I felt at the time put the entire Anti-War movement in jeopardy: Jane Fonda's visit to North Vietnam. While celebrities like Ike and Tina Turner and The Osmond Brothers were taking their acts to Germany, Jane Fonda took hers to Hanoi. However, her main stage was the seat of an NVA anti-aircraft gun, smiling, looking through the sights as though getting ready to shoot down an American jet. It was not a sanctioned U.S. Government propaganda trip, but rather a private citizen trip to denounce America's political and military involvement. At the time, I didn't know she had prearranged visits with American POW's. It wasn't until she returned to the U.S. that she claimed the POW's were being treated humanely and not being tortured. Well, we know what bullshit that was. She even called them "war criminals." [58]

I was following my usual routine when I got off work: Breakfast with the COhorts; then after everyone left for work detail, I took a shower and went to the library. I liked to get the first crack at the daily Arizona Republic. When I saw the picture of "Hanoi Jane," sitting behind that gun, with these Viet Cong soldiers standing around her,[59]I got very angry. I mean, it's not like Jane hadn't done or said anything inflammatory over the last few years anyway. At several major colleges, she had declared herself a socialist, advocated communism, and called for an overthrow of the U.S. Government. If she'd tried pulling this during the McCarthy witch-hunts, she'd have been burned at the stake. But this was a different America and we had progressed a few notches above McCarthy's slime level. Jane was exercising her First Amendment rights, and putting up her own money to do it. Hell, I did what I had to do, too. But looking at that picture just set me off. How many American planes were shot down by that gun, or guns like it? How many fathers, sons, and friends had been killed or taken prisoner? Yes, there's the flip side - how many innocent Vietnamese men, women, and children were murdered by collateral damage? How much of the beautiful countryside had been napalmed or bombed back into the prehistoric ages? But there was a difference between wanting to stop the war and cease all this slaughter and showing support for the enemy. One need only read Mark Twain's "War Prayer" to see the twisted dichotomy of war - that when we pray for victory and safety of our soldiers, that we're also praying for defeat and death of the opposing soldiers—leaving THEIR guts and blood all over the land. Praying for THEIR mothers, fathers, sons, daughters, friends, and relatives to get the news that THEIR loved one has been slaughtered on the field of battle.

There were many right-wing factions accusing the anti-war movement of treason—of aiding and abetting the enemy by protesting the war. I also think our American corporations flooding into Saigon to profit from the war, with billions of dollars of our products going out into the black market - that's what was helping North Vietnam win the war. No doubt the antiwar movement here was fuel for North Vietnam to hold out, but it wasn't treason. And neither was what Jane did. It's not like she gave away secret information or war plans, money or materials to aid in the NVA's war effort, but this was one photo-op we didn't need. It was a bad move—totally insensitive to the thousands of American men who lay dead. But she broke my heart. I'd had a crush on that lady ever since I saw her in the movie "Cat Ballou." Why didn't she come visit us CO's in prison? She'd have made my visiting list!

But years later, she did finally apologize, admitting it was about the worst thing she could've done—that she'd go to her grave with regret over that photo of her sitting on the seat of an NVA anti-aircraft gun. Reports had it that POW's tried to palm her secret messages on small pieces of paper, as she greeted them, and that she handed them over to an NVA officer; that the POW's were subsequently beaten, and three of them died. But years later, however, several of the American soldiers who were supposedly part of these incidents, stepped forward and denied that they ever handed over secret messages to Jane, or that those beating deaths ever happened. According to Ret. Col. Larry Carrigan, who was shot down over Vietnam in 1967 and spent time in a POW camp, "It's a figment of somebody's imagination. I never met Jane Fonda." Two other former POWs, Mike McGrath, President of NAM-POWs, and Edison Miller, a former marine Corps pilot held captive for over five years, also disclaimed the story. [60]

Jane Fonda – as Cat Ballou - 1965

1972 – "Hanoi" Jane sits on the seat of an enemy anti-aircraft gun.

Chapter Fifty-one
Happy Birthday Blues

Y es, July had been a bitch of a month - a roller coaster ride of emotions. By then I had written many letters to Colette, and she'd written many back. In several of them, she commented on how I really should write a book.

She had saved every letter I wrote to her, and I'd been sending her a lot of material, knowing that at any time, if Cunningham, or the guard at the front decided to read what I was sending out, there could be bad repercussions. Letters written by inmates were never sealed in their envelopes. Guards inspected the contents first, then they sealed the envelopes. And when letters came in from the outside, they were opened and inspected for contraband first before inmates ever got them. We never knew whose letters were being read, and when. I was rolling the dice. Then on July 18, Colette sent me the craziest damn letter, that I prayed to God would not be read by the desk sergeant on duty:

> *"... Perhaps when I come visit you, I can get some kind of press card and try my hand with a camera...do a little on-the-spot coverage."*

Well, as long as I imagined her writing this with a French accent, I stayed amused. Fortunately she ran this idea by Andrew, who told her not to make waves – that I'd been given glowing notices for my good attitude, and let's not piss anybody off.

She then went on to mention Andrew and his quest to want to help me.

> *"He's very powerfully connected to the Republican Party, also went to school with Thomas Eagleton, McGovern's running mate..."*[61]

Well, that was encouraging - until around July 28, when the story broke about Eagleton's electric shock therapy, then his resignation three days later.

It was now the end of July and still no word from the parole board. All my friends on the outside were extremely anxious, including the guys at the Public Health Hospital and a couple of other inmates who'd already been released. This was pure torture. I know I hadn't heard anything by August 2, because that's when I got a letter from Colette, hoping I would hear good things from the parole board. Talk about incredible timing. I received her letter on Monday, August 7th, and that afternoon, all my paranoia and fears were for naught. McGovern didn't hurt me, and neither did Jane in the eyes of the parole board. Cunningham called me into his office. When I got there, he looked up at me with a smile, and said.

"Congratulations. You got your parole. I believe you've set a record for the shortest time served by a CO on a two year sentence."

My heart was beating so fast. I could feel myself getting choked up. I was already packing my bag. Still with that August 26 date etched in my brain, I asked:

"What's the date?

"December 4th," said Cunningham.

I know I should have been thrilled that I'd be home before Christmas, but goddamn it, it wasn't August; it wasn't September; it wasn't even October. I would be in that prison for another four months. Lot of time for bad shit to happen... for something to go wrong. Now I could harvest up a whole new set of paranoia in my mind. But I smiled back at Cunningham and told him how thrilled I was, and that I appreciated what he had done to assist in my early parole. A month earlier, on June 30, Cunningham wrote the following letter which was submitted to the parole board:

"... Concerning Mr. Neckels' adjustment to the institutional setting. In my opinion, Mr. Neckels has displayed an unusually fine attitude toward his confinement. He behaves in a mature, responsible manner. He is assigned to our powerhouse and his supervisor describes him as being 'very dependable.' He has

*not been the recipient of any type of disciplinary action. Mr.
Neckels appears to me to have a rather strong pro-social
orientation; the offense is obviously situational in nature. It is
extremely doubtful that he will ever run afoul of the law again.
I hope my comments will prove useful for your purpose. If we
may assist you further, please contact us. Very Truly yours,
William Cunningham, Senior Case Manager."*[62]

I certainly couldn't vent any anger toward him. After all, I had just
set a record! So I went back to my room and just alternated between
anger that I'd have to be there another four months, and relief that I
wouldn't be there until June 2, 1973. But I still had that one card to
play... NASA. I wrote Sean at the Public Health Hospital and gave him
the news about my parole, and asked for any info he could give me on
the next study. I also sent a letter to Colette. But she had already found
out from Andrew. She was in San Francisco on her way to Hawaii.

*"I know about the parole, love, and I know it's a long time off,
but it's a hell of a lot better than two years.... Andrew wanted
me to make two points to you. 1) [Bruce] did not get the parole
through any 'connections' in any way. He got it on the basis of
his behavior as a model prisoner.... the second point is that
since you got parole on the basis of model prisoner-ship, keep
it up.... parole is a very fragile thing, so be just as model as
you've ever been and hang in. As for NASA, I still feel lousy
about that idea, but I defer to your presumably greater wisdom.
It 'don't' enthuse me though, I can tell you that."*[63]

I should never have even mentioned it to her until I got the facts,
because if the next study was going to go into January, I wouldn't
participate. The next day I got a letter from Sean.

*"These here doctors will be returning to Safford for more
interviews probably around the middle ofSeptember."*[64]

That was all the info he had for now. So that meant, if they
interview in the middle of September, the study would begin at the end

of September - three months takes it to the end of December. Did I want to give the government three extra weeks of my time; miss a great Christmas celebration with my friends, and maybe New Year's Eve? I knew I'd be going out on tour in January, and that my legs would be weak from being off my feet for three months. I know, because when the other volunteers came back in June, they could barely walk. I had five weeks before I'd have to make a decision. Would the doctors even select me with that amount of time between my release date and the end of the study? That's all I needed, was more to think about; more future uncertainties, while trying to exist in an uncertain place where personal decisions were not allowed, save my commissary choices and what books to read. At least I still had a whole month of softball to play. Besides, this news came three days before my birthday. I guess you could call that a gift. In fact, after the news got around camp that I got my December parole, one of the inmate COhorts, who worked in the kitchen, made me a birthday cake and a bunch of us celebrated. And after receiving cards and letters from friends on the outside, I was starting to feel a little better. I even decided not to do the NASA project. The sooner I got out, the better. I was willing to gut it out here until December 4.

Chapter Fifty-two
That is, unless...

U nless it just got too depressing. And the end of July through August brought me two months' worth of that, starting with the Apache Indian. I think we called him "Chief," but never to his face.

#

Chief...

Was rugged-looking, with features like Charles Bronson. When I arrived in February, he was already there, doing a five-year stint, nailed in a major drug bust. While being pursued by the FBI in a high-speed chase, Chief decided to hide the evidence - tiny bags of cocaine and LSD capsules - by swallowing them. Unfortunately, the cocaine baggies burst, and the LSD capsules dissolved, leaving Chief with a fried brain. He was totally gone - a walking zombie. During the entire time I spent at Safford, he never uttered a single word. Not one. He didn't have a single friend, nor did he want one. He kept to himself, and even though he had to eat with the rest of us, almost always found an isolated spot to sit down. And if he did sit near us, didn't look at anyone or say a word. And when he put his food on his plate, he just piled one thing on top of the other - meat, mashed potatoes, jello, pudding, beans - didn't matter. And Jesus, he was disconcerting! We'd try to carry on a normal conversation, whether it was about politics, philosophy, a certain book, the Vietnam War, and all of a sudden, he'd just start laughing - not out loud - but that quiet, clinch-your-gut laughter - as though what we were saying was so stupid, so ignorant, so shallow. Then he'd get up and walk off, as if to say, "I can't stand to even be around you ignorant fucks!"

But that wasn't it at all. We weren't even in his realm - in his world. The fact is, when he was walking alone, or squatting down on his haunches - which he seemingly could do for an hour before getting up - he would all of a sudden erupt in that same silent, hysterical laughter. And when he wasn't laughing, he had this weird smile on his face, like he knew something that no one else did, which now that I think about it, was probably true.

And his dress code was not to be believed. I think the average temperature during the summer months was around 110 degrees, and yet every day he wore the exact same clothes: boots with shoelaces untied, wool socks, pants, t-shirt, long-sleeved shirt, wool sweater, and heavy jacket, topped off with a cap that had earmuffs. It had to be 200 degrees inside that wardrobe, and I don't think I ever saw him sweat.

Story has it from a couple of inmates who actually witnessed it, that when he first arrived, an inmate started to make fun of Chief the way he conducted himself - the way he dressed - and like a bolt of lightning, Chief damn near beat the life out of him before guards were able to pull him off. Instead of throwing Chief in solitary, the guards just let him go, and he walked away laughing, probably unaware of what had just taken place.

I spoke to him one time. He was sitting on a bench one evening in the main compound, smoking a cigarette, and he had that smile on his face. I sat down a few feet from him and said, "Good evening..." And that was it. After about five minutes of dead silence, he got up and walked away. I never went near him again. Who knows? Maybe with all that LSD in his brain, he was in constant touch with his forefathers, who were talking him through the remainder of his life. A tragic story... Here are three more.

Chris....

He came in about three months after I did. Blond-haired, baby-faced, in his mid 20's; very soft-spoken guy who kept to himself. I think he was from Utah. Emotionally, he was in deep pain, having been convicted for opposing the war in Vietnam. His sentence was only six months. But to him, it was unbearable because he had a wife and baby. He always walked around the compound smoking cigarettes. I used to watch him, and I mean, he wore his loneliness on his sleeve. A couple of weeks after he arrived, I finally started talking to him. I tried telling him to look at the good side: the fact that he only had six months meant that after the first month he immediately qualified for weekend furloughs, meaning he could go into the town of Safford Friday nights with his wife and baby, stay in a motel, and return to the prison by 6:00 p.m. Sunday. During his first month, I happened to also have a visitor, so he introduced me to his wife in the visitors' patio. Very pretty lady. On the second month, his furloughs began. She came to visit him a few times, and things went smoothly... until one Friday night, when she and their baby came to the prison to take him away for the weekend.... And never came back. I don't know what possessed her to do this, but from the report I got, she later confessed that when they got to the motel, she informed Chris that she couldn't stand their current situation and was seeing another man. Hearing that, Chris lost all common sense, put her and the baby in the car and drove home to Utah or wherever. So when he didn't report back to prison on Sunday night, and was not found at the motel in Safford, he was immediately put on escape alert and the FBI was summoned. That now meant an automatic five years added to a six-month sentence - and Chris only had three months left to go. Three fucking months. We were in shock that he would do that, and at the time didn't know why. So for the next few days, I'd go into the Administration office and ask Bob or whoever was on duty, if they'd heard any news. No... nothing... until the following weekend. We got the news that Chris, while walking along the midway of a County Fair in his home town with his wife and baby, was apprehended by the FBI, or the local police who had been put on alert by the FBI.

Now this part's hazy, so I stand corrected: Either at the fairgrounds, when he knew he was about to be apprehended - or after they handcuffed him and hauled him off to the county jail. Without bothering to shake him down - they took the cuffs off Chris once they arrived at the police station. During a moment when the officers took their eyes off him, Chris reached into his pocket, took out a small pistol, and blew his brains out. And the fact he had a wife and baby, our justice system couldn't have given him a suspended sentence and allowed him to perform alternative service?

Earl....

Not his real name. I've long forgotten it. On occasion, I used to see him walking alone, sometimes pausing to look off into the distance. Who knows what he thought about, but sometimes he would just start crying. He was the James Whitmore character in "Shawshank Redemption." In his early 70's, Earl had been in prison since the 1940's. I don't know if he'd been a mafia hit-man or a racketeer, but whatever felony he committed was some pretty heavy shit, because he started out on The Rock - Alcatraz Island, and stayed there until they closed it down. He spent time in a few maximum security prisons, before ending up in Leavenworth; and with five years left to go on his sentence, they brought him here to minimum security Safford, as sort of a debriefing period before turning him out into society. In fact, I think it was Earl who said that of all the federal prisons he'd been in, Safford was the armpit. The best prison food was in Alcatraz. I asked why, and he said:

"Because we were the worst of the lot; and the best way to keep us quiet was to feed us good."

Made sense. And in just a few days, after 30 years in prison, Earl was about to become a free man and start eating in restaurants. And he was terrified. Why? Because there was no-one out there for him anymore - no family, no friends, no home. And since he had served his entire time and wasn't being paroled, I'm not sure if he even had to report to a parole officer. Once he got on that bus in Safford, he could go where he wanted. But where was that? He had no job prospects; no driver's license, not that he'd want one. No Social Security card. He'd never used a credit card, and would never be able to get one. But he did have a plan. And he told me about it the night before he left.

It was still early evening, and I didn't have to be at the powerhouse for a few hours yet, but I dropped in early to give Tom some company. Next door was the aforementioned machine shop and someone was in there. So I walked over, and there was Earl with Tex. Earl was running a fine grain sander or buffer over something he was holding in his hand. I stepped in for a close look and saw that it was a ring... A huge ring... for his finger. Earl had made it himself and the face on it was a sharp-cornered heavy piece of metal that he'd soldered onto the band.

"Jesus Christ, Earl," I said. "That thing must weigh a pound. You actually gonna wear it?"

"Yep," was all he said.

"Looks like a fuckin' weapon."

"It is..." he replied. He wasn't joking, either.

"What are going to do?" I asked him.

"Neckels, I'm gonna go to a state that I think has the best prison with the best food, and I'm gonna knock the shit out of somebody so I can get thrown back in the joint. I'm too old to start over. I've got nothing. We'll see if I can do better in my next life."

Earl had become institutionalized. The wall had become his mama, and all he wanted was "maximum security." How depressing is that?

Charlie Simmons

I believe Charlie was doing a five-year stint for an IRS offense, and his time was finally up. He was very soft-spoken, wore glasses; he had thin hair on the sides, bald on top; smoked a pipe, and held bridge club every Thursday or Saturday night. Because of his filing and accounting skills, he worked in the administration office and ran the library. Charlie was in his 60's.

It was toward the end of August, and Charlie was so glad to finally be going home, and we were all very happy for him. We had a going-away party for him around 7:00 p.m. that evening. One of our kitchen chefs had a made a big sheet cake for him, so we sat around eating cake and drinking lemonade. His mother, in her 80's; his wife, and sister were on their way to pick him up. He'd be gone the first thing in the morning. So we all shook hands with Charlie and wished him good luck in case we didn't see him.

About two hours later, around 9:00 p.m., we heard a guard calling for him through the loudspeaker.

"Mr. Simmons, please report to control. Mr. Simmons, to control."

Mister Simmons? Usually, it was just your last name, followed by your prison number, and harshly called out. This call was different. It was more sedate. We figured it was the respect now given to someone who was no longer a prisoner. So Charlie walked up to the Administration building, figured he had some release papers to sign. But that wasn't it. Charlie was informed by Supervisor Ulibarri that earlier that evening, his mother, wife, and sister had been killed in a head-on collision. I don't remember how many of us walked away in separate directions, and just started crying. I don't doubt that some of the guards were crying, too. Charlie immediately left the prison with an officer, and driven to a town nearest the accident, so he could identify the bodies. I don't know whatever happened to him. It wouldn't surprise me if he died of a broken heart.

And that's when I decided that I wanted the fuck out of Safford Prison. It was time to stop ignoring the prevailing sadness that swept through that place. Charlie, Earl, Chris, Chief, and the CO who couldn't handle prison after a couple of weeks, so paroled himself into the army - I wondered what hell they put him through in basic training. I wondered if he was still alive.

I went in my room and immediately sent off a letter to Sean at the U.S. Public Health Hospital and told him I wanted to do the next study. I didn't care if I had to give them an extra month! Then I wrote to my friends, and told them about Charlie and how I felt so helpless knowing that if something tragic happened to a loved one, I wouldn't even be allowed to go to them, to assist them, or to even grieve for them, except from a distance. I told them I planned on volunteering for NASA, and at least being home. I didn't want another friend driving down a two-lane highway to pay me a visit.

Every one of them wrote me back, voicing their disapproval. On August 30, Colette wrote back to me, and again, I could hear that French accent.

"You and that goddamn NASA thing! I worry about you, dummy, and I've never been enthused about the program."[65]

Susan wasn't happy about it either; neither were Al and Marcia. I guess I forgot to tell them about the deal-breaker: My homosexual encounter in early September.

Chapter Fifty-three
And here I thought nobody cared....

Homosexuality at Safford prison was practically nonexistent. And what there was of it was consensual. Only once, did I ever see it occur, and that was one Sunday afternoon, when I came out of my room. Across from my room and to the left were two long rooms. One lined with toilets; the other, with showers. I needed to drop off a book to one of my COhorts in the main dorm. He wasn't in, so I was just going to put it on his bunk. To do that I had to walk by the shower room. I heard running water and glanced over to see two inmates going at it. They were positioned to where they didn't see me walk by. I quickly stopped, made a u-turn, and walked out the front door.

The second case of homosexuality involved an African-American in his 40's, and a Caucasian in his early 20's. The kid had red hair, cut very short. He was about 6'1" and probably weighed 130 pounds. Very fair complexion, with a million freckles. His lover was about the same height, had a thick mustache - a distinguished looking man, soft-spoken, very articulate. Both were very friendly and didn't hide their love for each other. They were inseparable. And after the 8:00 p.m. count was taken, they'd wait for the sun to go down, then casually make their way toward the bleachers to the left of the baseball diamond. They lived in the same dorm, and their bunk beds were next to each other. Some inmates claimed that on occasion, while everyone was asleep, one would climb into bed with the other, make love, then sneak back into his own bed.

The third case involved me. It was early September, and I was on duty at the powerhouse. At 2:00 a.m. sharp, the phone rang and it was the front desk, time for count. I picked up, checked in, and hung up. I had already done my water testing and sample tasting, so I sat back in my chair, closed my eyes, and tried to go to sleep. I'd been lying there for about ten minutes, when suddenly I felt the presence of someone in the room. I opened my eyes and was startled to see a Mexican, about

6'3", 250 pounds, standing a few feet away, just staring at me. I jumped out of my chair, and stood there facing him.

He smiled at me.

"Hey, Neekles," he said

"What are you doing in here?" I asked him.

"Oh, I just thought I'd come by a spend some time with you."

I told him that the power house was off limits to any inmate not working here, and to leave before a guard came in and caught him.

"No, they jus' had count. No guard going to come in here. We be all right."

"You're wrong," I told him. "They come in all the time to check up on me."

"Then I jus' stay for a leetle while," he said. This guy wasn't going anywhere. I slowly ambled my way toward the workbench where I kept the beakers and several tools.

"What exactly do you have mind?' I asked.

"Ah, you know... I thought maybe we get to know each other, and... you know..."

"No, I don't know. Tell me..." I was scared, but now I was pissed off.

"Well... you're a good looking man, Neekles."

I cut him off.

"I'm into women, not men. I'm not a queer." I said. Don't forget this was the early 70's. I didn't know if he knew what "homosexual" meant, and I wanted to make goddamn sure he understood. And he did.

"Hey, Man - I ain't no queer neither," he said.

Suddenly I spotted this ugly looking tool on the counter. It was a steel handle with a metal ball and spike. It looked like something with which you'd puncture a hole in tin. I grabbed it, then turned around a faced him.

"Then go do what the rest of us do. Lock yourself in a bathroom and beat off! But you're not getting anything in here."

He glanced down at the metal club I was holding. He interpreted what I was hoping - that if he was going to try and fuck me, he'd be wearing this club in his brains. He held his hands up and backed off.

"Hey, Neekles - come on, man. I don't want no trouble. I jus' wanta be you friend."

"And I want you to turn around and get out of here."

"Okay, okay," he said. "I'll see you again, Neekles."

He left. My legs were shaking. And now I was wondering just what the hell that would mean for me the rest of my stay in prison. Was he going to come back again one night after the 2 a.m. count and bring five of his buddies with him? Was he going to try and pick a fight with me in the mess hall? Was he going to sneak into my room when no one was in there, and put a scorpion or rattlesnake underneath my covers? That had happened once before at Safford, when two inmates got into it. One put a scorpion at the foot of the other one's bed. And when then inmate got under the covers, the scorpion stung the hell out of him. Yes, I avoided a physical fuck. But I was now being mind-fucked instead.

When my shift ended, I went into the cafeteria to have breakfast. Sure enough, there was that Mexican, staring at me, and whispering to a couple of his amigos sitting at the table. I went and sat with my COhorts and told them what happened. Fortunately, an inmate nicknamed "Cyclops"- because he was about 6'7" tall and cross-eyed – was sitting with us along with one of his drug buddies. Both of these guys were buffed out and spent a lot of time in the weight yard.

"Don't worry, Bruce," said Cyclops. "If you have another problem with that guy, just let me know. He works out in the weight pile with us. I'll drop a 50 pound weight on his face."

That made me feel a little better, but I didn't want to be going through this for three more months. So I wrote another letter to Sean at the U.S. Public Health Hospital and told him I was ready to leave, and please let the NASA doctors know that I wanted in on the next study. On September 16, Sean wrote me the following letter.

"Bruce - Flash! I know this much after having talked to Dr. Schneider yesterday: The next study will start approx. 9/26 with interviews taking place approx. 9/19 with a variable on both those dates being one day - again approx.

Also you should definitely go for it - definitely: You have been recommended to Schneider by both Lockwood and Wolton (the doctors who came last time but won't this time).

> *Also I assured Schneider that you would do the study even though it might extend past your release date. He assured me that your release date (Dec. 4) would not be a factor in his decision to accept you as one of the subjects - It looks like you're home free and if I don't see you in passing at the bus depot or airport - see you in Nov.*
>
> *Later/sooner – Sean* [66]

I cannot even describe the feeling inside me - the last time I'd felt so happy. And I received that letter on Tuesday, September 19, the same day the announcement was made that on Sept. 20, doctors from the NASA project would visit our center for purposes of interviewing conscientious objectors who may wish to volunteer for medical research. I went to the administration building, and asked to be put on the interview list. Mr. Cunningham knew my sentence would be up before the study ended, but had no problem if I wanted to give the government two extra weeks. I was the first one on the list. My roommate Tom decided he wanted to try for it, too. Since I was almost a slam-dunk, I promised I'd put in a good word for him.

The next day the NASA reps arrived bright and early. We had to fill out medical forms, describing our current health status. The interview was conducted in the Protestant Chapel, and again, I was the first one in. I was greeted with a big smile from Doctor Evelyn Bues and I believe one of the nurses. She obviously knew who I was. So I just came right out and said it.

"Dr. Bues, you couldn't have a better candidate than me. I live in San Francisco. It's my home. You have my word that even though my sentence is up on December 4, I will see the study through. The timing on this just couldn't be better - that after the study is over, I'll be able to put on my clothes walk out the door and be home, and not have to come back here. I wouldn't jeopardize the program by walking out early. My friends live there, and the only problem you'll have is throwing them out when visiting hours are over."

There was no doubt they appreciated my enthusiasm.

"Bruce, you've been very highly recommended. Let's just go over your medical history, and then we'll make it official by the weekend."

Without telling me in certain words, I was in. I then pushed the envelope and told them about Tom. I mentioned that he'd been my roommate for several months and that he was a very mellow, passive guy - that this study would be very suitable for him. They promised they'd consider him. When Tom finished his interview, I was waiting for him outside. I told him I really pitched the hell out of him. I didn't tell him that I had already been selected, but he pretty much guessed that I was. I immediately went to my room and started sending off letters to Colette, Susan, Al and Marcia, and told them I was a coming home. I was hoping they'd get the letters by Saturday, and told them I'd definitely have more news by then and would try to get permission to call them around 7:00 p.m. I asked Colette to try and be at Marcia's when I called.

Three days later, on Saturday morning, September 23, a call came over the loudspeaker:

"Neckels, Obannon, and Biederman, report to control."

I swear to God, all three of us came bursting out into the compound at the exact same time, from whatever room we were in, and broke into big smiles. I pretty much knew I'd made it, but to see the smile on Tom's face; the surprised stunned look on Gary's - we knew why we were being called to control. Once inside, we were directed to Ulibari's office.

"Just got a call from the U.S. Public Health Hospital. You three have been selected for the next NASA study. We'll have your travel instructions ready on Monday. Looks like you'll be leaving here either on Tuesday, the 26th, or Wednesday, the 27th."

When we walked out of that office, Tom was as giddy as I'd ever seen him. He gave me a hug, thanked me for going to bat for him. That evening after dinner, after all the visitors had left, I went to the office and asked if I could make a phone call. They okayed it, so I called Marcia to see if she'd gotten my letter. But there was no answer. Damn! I figured no one had even received my letters yet, and now wouldn't until Monday. I'd used up my phone call, but that was okay. I'd call from the Safford bus depot.

289

The following Monday, we were called in and told that transfer papers were being prepared for us to leave Wednesday morning, September 27th. The next day, we went in, had pictures taken that were attached to each individual Memorandum: I have it framed on my wall to this day:

> *"Under Public Law 89-176 you are authorized to go to the U.S. Public Health Service Hospital, 15th and Lake Street, San Francisco, California via unescorted furlough.*
>
> *You will depart this camp on Wednesday, September 27, 1972 in time to board the 8:45 Greyhound bus at Safford, Arizona destined for Phoenix, Arizona. The estimated time of arrival in Phoenix is approximately 12:40 PM the same day. You are to go immediately to Sky Harbor Airport in Phoenix where plane reservations have been made via TWA Flight #561 departing Phoenix at 2:00 PM. You are to pick up your plane tickets at the TWA ticket counter at Sky Harbor Airport prior to the 2:00 PM departure time. The estimated time of arrival at San Francisco Airport is 3:40 PM where a USPHS Hospital staff member will meet you and transport you to the Hospital.*
>
> *You are to save all receipts (bus, plane, meal, taxi) as you will be reimbursed by the hospital for these expenses. In the event of any difficulty arising en-route you are to call either the Hospital, [xxx-xxx-xxxx,] or this Camp, [xxx-xxx-xxxx.]*
>
> *You are reminded that willful failure on your part to abide by the instructions outlined in this memorandum and/or failure to report to the USPHS Hospital in San Francisco shall be deemed a violation and result in your being placed in escape status and is punishable as prescribed by Chapter 35, Title 18, United States Code."*[67]

Having fully read and understood the above instructions, I happily signed my name. This was really happening!

That night, we had a major going away party with all the COhorts plus Cyclops and a few other guys. It was sad, in some ways, to be saying goodbye to guys I knew I would never see again, but with whom we'd shared the most incredible experience.

The next morning, Wednesday, September 27, 1972, immediately after breakfast, we were called into the laundry room where I took off my prison clothes for the very last time, and put on some real hokey-looking civilian clothes. Since my boots had been sent home, I was allowed to wear the Puma running shoes I'd been given months ago. My wallet and driver's license had been sent home in February, so the only ID the three of us had were those memorandums with our pictures attached. They also gave us zip-up carry bags to put whatever belongings we had - toothpaste, toothbrush, hairbrush, deodorant. I filled a box with the bundles of letters I'd brought with me from S.F. County, plus all the letters I'd received at Safford - most of them from Colette - and a few books that Mike and his library friend sent me from Phoenix - that I wanted to keep; I took the one Andrew and Colette sent me, Willard Gaylin's *"In Service of Their Country - War Resistors in Prison."* I also had a couple of songbooks, and my Martin guitar. I took a two-tone blue windbreaker off the rack and stuffed it in the bag, knowing that the San Francisco weather could be cold and windy. After that, we went to the Administration Building where we were given what commissary money we had left. I had about $70.00.

A very funny side note on that $70.00: On the morning of September 23, the day I had found out I was part of the NASA program, Nebraska was playing Army. Bob Devaney was the coach of Nebraska, and Johnny Rodgers was their star running back who would win the Heisman that year. Nebraska had just come off back-to-back National championships in '70 and '71, and were still a powerhouse. So I sat in the auditorium waiting for kick-off. There were about a dozen inmates in there, when I blurted out, "Nebraska's gonna win this game by sixty points."

An inmate jumped on that and offered to bet me ten bucks worth of commissary if I'd give him Army plus sixty points. I thought, what the hell. I'm leaving in a few days. I don't really need the money. Plus I still had a bank account in San Francisco with about $900.00 from my 1971 income tax return. So I bet him. Well, other inmates heard the bet and wanted in on it. I had just become a sucker cash cow. So I bet two other inmates ten bucks each and gave them Army and sixty points. Now everybody wanted to bet me, but down to $40.00, I only bet four more times in five dollar increments, and I was only giving Army and fifty points. I figured I'd better keep $20.00 for the trip in case I lost.

Nebraska won, 77-7. And as pissed off as the inmates were, they were all relieved when I told them I'd be leaving next week and wouldn't be needing their commissary money, and to just use it on themselves.

Bob was working at the desk. We shook hands and said goodbye. He wished me the best of luck. I kind of think he was sorry to see me go. Mr. Cunningham also wished me luck and let me know that I'd be receiving my release papers on December 4 but would then have to contact a parole officer in San Francisco. Then one of the guards ushered us to a station wagon, me carrying my handbag with books: a box of letters, and guitar in case. And as we pulled out of the driveway, and headed down the road, I turned for one last look at Safford Federal Prison, and just stared until it disappeared into the desert. I may have only spent nine months there, but the ordeal, which wasn't quite over, had lasted for four years - eight if you consider college as a sanctuary rather than a higher place of learning. But the hard part was over - the physical part anyway. The emotional scars would reveal themselves over the years. Maybe there wouldn't be any at all. Maybe I could work them out through acting, through touring with the "The Cage"- or through just plain facing the beast and saying, "Fuck it. I did what I felt had to do. Time to get on with the rest of my life."

But first, I still had to get through this NASA thing.

Chapter Fifty-four
Homeward Bound....

With a couple of hiccups, however, bus trip to Phoenix, no problem. Cab to Sky Harbor Airport, no problem. Got there about an hour before flight and went to get our tickets. Tickets were waiting, but there was no plane. It was still in San Francisco with technical problems. Our departure time had been changed, and we wouldn't be leaving until 5:30 p.m. So instead of arriving in San Francisco at 3:40 p.m., it was now going to be more like 7:10 p.m. Still early enough to have my friends over to the hospital for a reunion.

I immediately called Safford Prison and let Ulibari know the situation. He understood, thanked me for calling in. I then contacted the U.S. Public Health Hospital, but they were already on top of it and knew we'd be arriving much later. Okay, so now we had four hours to kill. And it just so happened that I had called Mike from the Safford Greyhound Bus Depot. Mike was living in Tempe, just a few miles outside of Phoenix. And he was standing right there with us, having driven in to say hello and goodbye. He had a car, and there was nothing in the memorandum that said: "In case of a flight delay, you are to remain at the airport, AND you are not to fraternize with ex COhorts." So, the three of us hopped in Mike's car, drove to his place in Tempe, and sat there for a couple of hours, drinking wine and listening to music. I called Marcia collect, and let her know what time I'd be home. She was as excited as I've ever heard her but would be without a car. She told me Colette had contacted her the day before wondering when I'd be home, but had to fly to New York. Marcia told me she'd call Susan and give her the news. I then told her I'd be in touch as soon as I got to the hospital. By 4:30 p.m., Mike had us back at the airport, and we said goodbye. One hour later we were on our way to San Francisco.

When we arrived at SFO, the head nurse was waiting for us. Can't remember her name. Let's call her Julie. Nice lady. Since all we had were carry-on bags and boxes (my guitar had been stored in the cabin), we walked to her car and headed off. But no more than one mile down the 101, we had a flat tire. So we pulled off to the side and changed it. The night air was crisp, and the wind was blowing in the fog off the bay. At one point, I just looked up into the sky and stretched out my arms, taking in every drop of mist. It felt fantastic, like I was being reborn.

By the time we arrived at the hospital, it was 8:00 p.m.. We met the staff of nurses and doctors. I believe Evelyn was there, and we thanked her profusely for selecting us for the program. Thinking we were going to get settled in, we were shown to our rooms. Tom and I would share a room. Gary would either have his own or share with another inmate from Lompoc Prison, I don't remember. But we asked what the procedure was as of that moment and got the great news. For the rest of this week, we would meet with the doctors, do a full medical examination, draw blood, select our breakfast, lunch and dinner menu for the next three months, and just go through an indoctrination as to what would occur during the study. As for now.... We could just stay here at the hospital or we were free to go. We didn't even have to stay at the hospital that night if we didn't want to, as long as we reported back the next day by 8:00 a.m. to meet with Dr. Schneider.

I couldn't believe it! I jumped on a telephone and called Marcia and told her I was home. News was flying everywhere! Knowing that Marcia was without a car because Al was at Gatsby's in Sausalito with the Jean Hoffman Trio, Susan was on standby to come pick me up. I was free for the night and on my way over. Marcia was thrilled. It just so happened that my friend Sig was informed about my arrival.

"Call him and tell him to come over. Let's all go to Gatsby's!"

Ahhh, the freedom ball was rolling. Susan was at the hospital in less than a half hour. We hugged and kissed. By that time, Tom was caught up in the joy of it all and wanted to come with us. Gary just wanted to kick back and enjoy his private bed without noise and 79 other inmates in the same room with him.

We got to Marcia's place and more hugs and kisses were exchanged. Sig was already there. I mean, we were ready to party. Marcia and Al had been storing my clothes and my wine there. So we cracked open a 1966 BV Private Reserve. My God, was it great! I quickly pulled out a pair of my own jeans, plus a shirt and jacket, and off we went to Sausalito. As we approached the entrance to Gatsby's, I could hear the Trio. And when we walked through that door, I went into an immediate time warp. It was beginning to feel as though I'd never left. When Jean Hoffman looked up from her piano and saw me, she broke into big smile and let out a scream. I walked over to the Trio; Al and Nat broke out with big smiles; Jean had tears in her eyes as I gave her a kiss. After the song, we all hugged. I introduced them to Tom, and before Jean played her next song, she announced to the Gatsby's crowd: "Sorry, but I had to say hello to Bruce and his friend Tom. They just got back from spending time in prison for being against the Vietnam War." The place erupted with applause, and for the rest of the night, Tom and I drank for free. It was grand. I was only sorry that Colette couldn't have been there to share in the moment.

But we were wise and didn't drink everything that was set on our table. We wanted to show Dr. Schneider some respect and not meet him the next morning with hangovers. Since I really hadn't expected that we'd be able to have a night of freedom, I'd made no arrangements to stay with anyone. So I went back to the hospital with Tom. I couldn't wait for the weekend, so I could show him San Francisco. At that moment, there was no doubt that I had made the right decision. Whatever I was going to endure for these next three months would be worth it. I thought....

The next morning, Friday, September 28, Dr. Victor Schneider was there by 7:00 a.m. A nice man, soft-spoken, dry sense of humor, and very intelligent. We were given a brief indoctrination of what the study would entail. One of the first things we had to do was decide on what we would eat during the next eleven weeks. We were handed a menu with a multiple choice of foods for breakfast, lunch, and dinner. We could choose three different meals and we all had to agree on the same food, i.e., the same three breakfasts; the same three lunches; the same three dinners. I believe we actually got to have a small glass of red wine with one of our dinners, and a white wine with either one of the lunches or one of the other dinners. So we picked our favorite meal to have three times a week. For breakfast, it was the French toast; lunch, the hamburger, fries, and strawberry shortcake; dinner, I believe was whatever came with the red wine. Plus, we had to select three different snacks, to be served at 9:00 p.m. We were then handed an information sheet - "GENERAL INFORMATION FOR SUBJECTS ON METABOLIC BALANCE DIETS." And the guidelines were strict. To wit:

1. Mealtimes are as follows: Breakfast - 8:00 a.m.; Lunch - 12:00 Noon; Dinner -5:00p.m.;Snack - 9:00 p.m. approximately.
2. Eat all food and drink that is served to you.
3. Do not eat anything other than what is served to you by a member of the Metabolic Staff.
4. Do not chew gum.
5. Drink only distilled water from your water pitcher.
6. Clean dishes well and rinse glassware with distilled water from your pitcher. Drink the rinsings.
7. The salt which you receive at the breakfast meal is your supply for the day; therefore you should use it accordingly. All salt should be used by the end of the dinner meal.
8. Three pepper packets per day will be given. The pepper may be used or not, as you so choose.
9. Eat your meals when they are served to you. Do not save food or beverages for "later." Do not remove food from your tray and place it elsewhere.
10. All food and drink should be consumed by no later than 11:00 p.m.
11. If you should drop or spill any food, report it immediately to a member of the nursing staff.DO NOT wipe up any liquid which may have spilled. The amount must be estimated and replaced
12. Visitors are not allowed in the room when you (or they) are eating.
13. Please inform your visitors that you are on a controlled diet and not to bring you anything edible.

Regarding item 13, they forgot to include the word "smokable."

We would start officially on Monday, October 2. The program would end on December 18. During the first two weeks, we'd be alternating between sitting in a chair and lying in bed at two-hour intervals, beginning at 8:00 a.m., thru 8:00 p.m., then to bed until the next morning. We'd always be off our feet but at least sitting in a chair for some part of the study was good news. But from that point on, it was strictly bed rest for the next nine weeks. Dr. Schneider advised us to go do a little shopping and find something to occupy our time while in bed: books, puzzles, some kind of hobby. Don't forget - this was 1972. We didn't have laptops, video games, i-Pods, or CD players. In the room, we had a television and a record player.

After doing what needed to be done at the hospital, we were once again released for the day. And the first thing we did, was head down town to some novelty store. I bought a Calligraphy set; a wire sculpture kit, and a couple of crossword puzzle magazines. Dr. Schneider said I could bring my guitar if I was willing to play in a prone position. So I went to a music store and picked up some songbooks with the guitar chords -"Songs of Don McLean," and "Crosby, Stills, and Nash/CCNY Deja Vu" -along with matching record albums so I could play along with the music. I also had some sheet music stored away in box at my old apartment back in the storage shed, so I got in there, and took those, plus the music books I had at Safford. So by the time I laid out all my activities for the next eleven weeks, I had a library next to my bed. I was good to go. Let the study begin.

Chapter Fifty-five
And now... In service of my country.

T he NASA project was a weightlessness study. When astronauts are up in outer space, no matter how active they are, they're still operating in zero gravity. Therefore, their bones and muscles weaken. There's a loss in bone marrow, and bones in space can atrophy at a rate of 1% a month. Muscles also atrophy because in zero gravity, the body perceives it doesn't need muscles. Muscle mass can disappear at a rate of 5% a week. And the main muscles used to fight gravity, the calves and spine, can lose 20% of their mass if you don't use them. That's why after splashing down in their space capsules, being picked up by helicopter, then brought to an aircraft carrier - instead of hanging around doing a press conference, astronauts were whisked away because in just a matter of days or weeks that they were in outer space, they now had to adjust to the pull of gravity. And they could barely stand. Some had to be carried away on stretchers. So imagine what a trip back to the moon; several weeks in a space shuttle; a three-month stay in a space station or a six-month trip to Mars - could do to their bodies. Sure, you can exercise or work your ass off in outer space, but you don't have that gravity component. On Earth with the gravity's pull, you get resistive force that maintains muscles and bones. According to Dr. Schneider, it could take a couple years to regain that lost bone. Another thing about that journey to Mars. Mars gravity is 38% of Earth's gravity. Those astronauts need to be in pretty damn good shape when they get there. Also, there's a shift in fluid and blood flow. In space, you float and so does everything inside your body. So if the blood leaves your feet and equalizes throughout the body, and sends higher blood pressure to your head, an alarm goes off, telling the brain that your body has too much blood. And that sends a faulty message to the heart, saying, "Slow down, heart. You don't have to pump as much." And what happens? Your heart starts to atrophy. And if astronauts are in space for three or more days, they can actually lose at least 22% of their blood volume. Then suddenly they get down to gravity, and the body now tells them that there's not enough blood in their vessels. So how do you solve the bone and muscle loss problem? What kind of exercises can they do that will offer resistance and mimic body weight? And how do you keep the blood pressure gradient normal? [68]

That was the purpose of the weightlessness study at the hospital. And lying flat in bed with your head tilted down at a 6-degree angle, or on your side with your head never raised above the shoulders, was the best way in a gravity situation to find answers.[69]I understood the risks involved, but I wasn't overly concerned about my health for several reasons. One, even though we were trying to assimilate weightlessness, we were still operating in gravity. Two, our vitals would be carefully monitored; our blood, stool, and urine would be analyzed on a daily basis, to make sure we were adhering to our diet. I saw Pete, Rick, and Larry hobbling back to prison, so I knew the legs and feet would be my weakest links, and that I'd have to work out big time in order to be ready for a rigorous "Cage" tour that would start in the middle of January - should Ken and Rick need me.

We enjoyed our final weekend of freedom before being taken off our feet for good. I had promised to send one of the inmates at Safford some books, so I took care of that. I had received a few letters that had been sent to Safford, which Bob immediately forwarded to me, one of them from Colette sent, written in flight on September 26, 1972.

"What A mish-mash!" She wrote. *"I got your letter too late to get to Al and Marcia's for your phone call & and so did they. So nobody knows when you're coming. I called them at 8 a.m., before this flight so I could steal one more day, if you were coming in! I wouldn't care if the sky fell in over NY—for your arrival, I'd have stayed. But since no one knew, I split. I guess I can see the appeal that the NASA program has for you, love, and I have to concede to your judgment. I just hope it's okay, I really do!"*[70]

I wrote her back, letting her know I had arrived, but didn't describe in any detail what this study was about - only to tell her it was going to be easier than I had thought. Okay, so I lied.

And on Monday morning, at 7:00 a.m., Metabolic Ward, 6-E, was jumping with excitement. There were six of us involved: three from Safford Federal Prison, and three from Lompoc.

The first two weeks of the study were okay. Alternating between bed and chair, I became very creative. I learned to write in Old English, which I used in all my Christmas cards. I created several pieces of wire sculpture, which I gave away as Christmas presents; and learned a number of songs on my guitar, which was rather amusing. Whenever I needed to put a record on the turntable (yes, records), I'd buzz for a nurse who would put it on for me. And if I was trying to learn a particular song, for example "Three Flights Up" by Don McLean, and wanted to play it fifteen times, a nurse would come in and replay the song fifteen times. No, she didn't stay in the room, or she'd have gone crazy. Tom, too. Whenever I got into one of these moods, he'd get on a gurney and wheel himself out of the room and go visit the nurses or the other volunteers. We always gave each other our private time. For me personally, I had a lot of visitors, mostly girls... at night. And there was a curtain attached to a ceiling rod that could be pulled to separate one half of the room from the other for my more intimate moments—and yes, there were several. Tom would again be escorted out on a gurney, or move himself out as long as he moved in a prone position. I too, could move.... As long as I was in a prone position... usually on my back. But those times really were few and far between.

Colette and I wrote back and forth. Her second letter to me was much more enthusiastic.

However, she went on to say that she wouldn't be back in San Francisco until November 1, which really bummed me out. I wanted to actually hug this lady who'd saved my sanity for the last four months. But she was going through emotional hell, wanting so badly to move to San Francisco, but suddenly torn about leaving New York. Her letter went from joy to pleading:

"Will you please write me, bug me, cajole me, encourage me...anything....Just get me out of here. You're the only one I can talk to about it. Please... Help!!!And you can't begin to know how much I mean that."[71]

Funny how things change. She now needed my encouragement and I was only too happy to help. Obviously stuck in bed, I could only send her an inspiring quotation. It came down to two choices: "Get your ass back to San Francisco and stop your fucking sniveling," or... "What paralyzes life is the failure to believe and the failure to dare." I wisely chose the latter and it worked. She let me know that she kept it pinned to the lamp next to her bed. By the time I saw her, though, I'd be flat out in bed.... And on that subject, I guess now's as good a time as any to talk about going to the bathroom flat out in bed - not the transition I'd planned to segue from Colette.

It was a little embarrassing at first; having the nurse bring in a metal potty pan, then close my curtain for privacy. Providing stool while sitting on it in a chair wasn't so bad, but in bed, lying down with that thing under me, was no fun. Also, we had to urinate in a plastic bottle first, so as not to mix the two "samples," as both were analyzed after each discharge. Urinating while lying down was slightly more difficult because we had to roll over on our side, tilt the bottle at an angle. Now, since we were encouraged to drink a lot of distilled water, we obviously had to use the bottle more than the metal stool pan. But since this was a critical part of the study, and the nurses had to do this for six of us, it didn't take long to get used to it.

On Sunday night, October 8,I called Colette in New York. We must have talked for a half hour. Apparently, through a friend, I had helped find her a nice apartment in lower Pacific Heights in the Cow Hollow area next to the Presidio. She would be out in a couple of weeks to check it out, but had gone solely on trust. One week later, October 16, 1972, we were totally confined to our beds, and it now began to sink in that we'd be in this position for 74 days. Remember earlier when I talked about my second trip back to SF County Jail - how staying in my bunk as much as possible, confining myself to a smaller space, was preparation for an even smaller space to come? Well, this was it. And the only thing I kept thinking about to get me through this, was that the next time my feet touched the floor, I was going to be a free man.

Chapter Fifty-six
Medicinal Marijuana – The Early Days

I look back at it decades later and ask myself, how the fuck did I get through it? Eating while lying down, though we were allowed to prop our pillows up and at least have our heads slightly above our shoulders, was okay. The meals, which were weighed to the milligram, held up pretty well, except for the spaghetti and meatballs with green beans and jello. After a while, I just mixed it up altogether and ate it. Drinking the rinse from that meal was horrendous. Hey, if Chief could do it, so could I.

Since we were allowed to lie sideways, on our backs, on our stomachs, we didn't get bedsores. But what helped to that end was that every night, nurses came in and gave us body-oil massages. That made it tolerable.

I can still remember what we watched on television over 35 years ago. Tom was very amenable. He didn't care. And remember, we only had ABC, CBS, and NBC. But we were mainly looking for laughs, given our situation, and for that, we had plenty from which to choose: "Rowan & Martin's Laugh-in," "The Flip Wilson Show," "The Carol Burnett Show," "Sanford and Son." Saturday night had the best comedy line-up with "All In The Family," "The Mary Tyler Moore Show," and "The Bob Newhart Show." This was sprinkled of course with some drama, including "Mod Squad" given my prior connection to Michael Cole - and a dose of Monday Night Football, after a lot of football during the weekends.

And given the climate on the national front and in Vietnam, we needed all the diversion we could get, because it was depressing. Those of us who had gone to prison were pretty much forgotten, and those who took our place on the anti-war front by the end of 1971 and '72 were the military deserters and the thousands of veterans who fought in Vietnam and were now staging the demonstrations, the sit-ins and speaking at the rallies - many of these veterans in wheelchairs and on crutches. According to the Department of Defense, there were

305

503,926 "incidents" of desertion between 1963 to 1973.In 1971 alone, there were close to 80,000 military deserters, compared to under 14,000 draft resistors who were prosecuted for draft evasion in a ten-year period from 1963-1973. [72]

By October of 1972, the election was over before a single voter went to the polls in November. McGovern finally chose Sargent Shriver as his running mate, and even though he promised to end the war in 90 days after his election, he was dead in the water. Henry Kissinger would take a variation on a theme from Richard Nixon. Remember how Nixon proclaimed in 1968, "I have a plan to end the war in Vietnam," and didn't have anything? That lie was enough to barely squeak-out a victory the first time around. Now Kissinger was going to make sure Nixon won his second term by saying, "Peace is at hand." For "security reasons" Kissinger couldn't really elaborate, except to say that right after North Vietnam signed the agreement, our boys would be coming home. Why wait until next March, after McGovern took office, for the boys to come home? Nixon was going to get them back before the election!

And once again, the voters bought it. However, Kissinger had no finalized peace deal when he made that announcement. What was drawn up was months away from signing.[73]Nixon slaughtered McGovern in November. Of course, having committed a felony, I wasn't allowed to vote. And in 1972, only 55% of the registered voters did, the lowest turnout since 1948.Talk about depressing.

But for me, life was beginning to show normalcy. Toward the end of October, Ken Whelan visited me at the hospital to guarantee me a job as tour manager for "The Cage," and once again playing the role of "Hatchet."

And sight of all sights, Colette finally walked into my hospital room. After all this time, I finally got to look at her, hug her, thank her personally for her support throughout these arduous months. She had been to see the apartment I found for her, and absolutely loved it. She was now an official resident of San Francisco, even though she'd be making a few more trips to New York to tie up all the loose ends to her personal and business life. However, being an interior designer, she couldn't help notice how drab our hospital room looked, and by the next day, had it decorated with several very colorful and chic posters: A Picasso; van Gogh's "Starry Night"; an Erte, and of course the iconic "War is not healthy for children and other living things" poster. And so until my release in December, Colette paid me many visits, updating me on her progress; thrilled about setting up her design studio on Union Street, just blocks from her apartment. She bought a car for local use only. The steep hills and streetcar tracks of San Francisco scared the shit out of her, so she chose to learn the bus lines. She was distributing cards and brochures to architects and real estate agents all over town. But she couldn't have gotten better advertising than that day in early December when she walked into Perry's Bar and Restaurant on Union Street, just down from her studio. Well, damn if she doesn't strike up a conversation with a guy who frequented the place all the time. She talked to him for about twenty minutes, telling him all about herself, unaware that the man was Herb Caen, columnist for the San Francisco Chronicle. Herb was the voice of local and social gossip, political stuff – his comments always filled with anecdotes and puns. If you were mentioned in his column, you were an official part of the San Francisco scene. Two days later, there she was, leading off his column, and it was instant fame. Once people dropped into her studio and got one look at her, heard that French accent, and browsed through her design catalogue, she was the talk of the town. Her visits were more scarce, but our phone calls at night, increased, tying up our three-room "community" phone between me and Tom in one room; Gary in another; and the two guys from Lompoc.

I mentioned earlier there were three other inmates from Lompoc. One of the inmates was taken off the project and sent back to prison because of a bout with hepatitis. That left Rodney and Jack, and here's where the "Early Medical Marijuana" story comes in. These two guys had a much more intense study, because every Saturday, they were driven to Moffett Field - North of San Jose - to the NASA Ames Research Center, where they were strapped into a centrifugal force machine - the ultimate merry-go-round. When these guys returned, they did not always look good, and oftentimes could not walk off the elevator and into their beds without assistance. However, once they revived themselves, they were well taken care of late in the evening...

307

not by the doctors or the nurses, but by a couple of hippie free- spirited girlfriends. That is until they finally got busted.

Yes, every scrap of food, every drop of water, the stool, the urine, were all scrutinized in the lab with test tubes, and on slides under the most powerful microscopes. But what had been totally overlooked was all the marijuana these guys had been smoking.... every day since day one! Compliments of these hippie holdovers. We were always allowed private time at night. The nurses would close our doors, pull down the shades, even pull a curtain around our beds. And that's when Rod and Jack would kick back and get wasted. The girls would open the window nearest one of the beds, light up, and blow the smoke out the window. Jack, who was furthest from the window, would take a huge hit, then exhale it into his girlfriend's mouth, and she'd go right up to the window and blow it out. Rodney would simply lean toward the window and exhale. And that worked really well every night for about six weeks. Then one night, as fate would have it, the ill wind decided to change directions, and blew all that smoke right back into the room, and there was no way they could get rid of the smell. Not long after the girls left, a male nurse came in with a fresh pitcher of distilled water and almost fell on his ass, asphyxiated with this marijuana smoke. He knew exactly what it was.

The next morning, every doctor and nurse affiliated with the study, was in their room.

"How long have been smoking the marijuana" "How many days?"

"Approximately how much marijuana did you smoke every day?" "And tell the truth!"

Rod and Jack were busted; as far as they knew, the FBI had been contacted and they were about to be sent back to Lompoc handcuffed and leg-ironed. And their girlfriends? Interfering with a U.S. Government project; smoking dope on government property; possession of an illegal drug - Some federal prosecutor was about to have a field day coming up with the number of counts to lay on these two. They were looking at prison time.

But that's not what happened. Because of the money invested in the study; the amount of information gathered, and the fact that Randy and Jack had been smoking weed for almost two months with a month left to go, they weren't about to pour all that down the drain. So they were told that they'd have to continue smoking approximately the same amount of marijuana that they'd been smoking throughout the study. Can you believe that shit! One more month of being stoned and here we were - Tom, Gary, and I - playing it straight, literally - and these two guys get rewarded with cannabis. And I think the girls were still allowed to supply it. I don't know if they were put on payroll. Probably not. And I don't believe Rod and Jack were allowed to have it before taking their ride on the merry-go-round. Only at night.

During that time, Rick Cluchey, author of "The Cage," paid me a visit to stoke my enthusiasm even more. He wanted to know if I'd do the play in Europe when I got out. I'd leave in January. However, there were sticking points: One, there's no way my parole officer would let me go to Europe. I didn't know if I'd even be allowed to leave San Francisco to go on a national tour. Two, I'd have to pay my own way to Europe with no guarantees we'd have a lot of shows. I just didn't want this costing me money. Three, I still wanted to find out what the sentiment was with college students all over America regarding the Vietnam War. And this Watergate thing was starting to pick up steam. James McCord, one of the original five burglars involved in the June 17 break-in, was on Nixon's payroll. In fact, the FBI found a check for twenty-five grand in his bank account that was supposed to go toward the Nixon Campaign Fund. So McCord was indicted. And soon to follow were E. Howard Hunt and G. Gordon Liddy. Liddy's indictment was big because he was the general counsel for the Committee to Re-Elect the President. And yet, the people working for Nixon were so brazen that instead of throwing caution to the wind, Daniel Ellsberg's office was burglarized in September by the White House "Plumbers" unit. They were still pissed because Ellsberg leaked the Pentagon Papers, but let's not get stupid about it! Also in September came a report from the Washington Post that Attorney General John Mitchell controlled a secret Republican fund to finance intelligence-gathering operations against the Democrats, including the bugging of Democratic headquarters at the Watergate Hotel. The FBI concluded that the Watergate break-in stemmed from a massive campaign of political spying and sabotage conducted on behalf of the

Nixon reelection effort. But that didn't mean Nixon was personally involved. And the fact that Nixon beat McGovern in a humiliating landslide - 60% of the vote - the nation didn't seem to care about the break-ins. McGovern couldn't even win his own state! Besides, months earlier, Nixon had sent his White House Counsel, John Dean, out to investigate. Dean concluded that no one at the White House was involved. We were to find out later that Nixon and his cronies were into the cover-up of the Watergate Hotel break-in six days after it happened. But as of early December there still wasn't enough information to involve Nixon.[74]

But I didn't care, because my big day had finally arrived.

Chapter Fifty-seven
Free at last.... Let the celebration begin!

D amn, what a great feeling that was - to wake up on Monday morning, December 4 at 7:00 a.m., knowing I was a free man. Were I still at Safford Federal Prison, I'd just now be getting into civilian clothes, and heading for the bus depot. I'd be strong and in good shape. There would be no recovery period, other than emotional. But I'd also be walking out with about $60.00 instead of the $1,200 tax free I'd be getting for the NASA study. And looking back, who's to say what shape I'd be in leaving Safford? According to reports I received later, there had been a clash between the Mexicans and Caucasians. The prison was having new drainpipes put in and there was a long ditch that ran right down the center of the compound between the administration office and the cafeteria. There were mounds of dirt and rocks next to the trenches. Apparently, it started out with an argument between one Mexican and one Caucasian, then deteriorated into a rock fight between a couple dozen inmates. Several were hurt pretty badly. I have no idea what the tension must have been like after that. Knowing me, I'd have stayed out of it. The idea of a rock coming at my face at seventy miles per hour.... But it's the aftermath I would've been nervous about - working at the powerhouse late at night, wondering if the guy who came to visit me a few months ago would have reappeared and brought a few of his friends with him.

No, the way I'd done it was fine with me. I was happy to give NASA two extra weeks. I mean, what the hell - the day I set foot into the courtroom, I had offered to do alternative service. I just didn't want to do it at the back end of a prison sentence, that's all. But c'est la vie, and my whole attitude, which I felt was pretty good anyway, was even better on December 4. Doctors and nurses came in and congratulated me on being a free man.

"Thanks - now get me my clothes because I'm outta here!" They knew I was joking. Around 10:00 a.m., Judy walked in carrying a cake with the words "Congratulations! Free at Last!" Of course, I wasn't allowed to eat a single crumb because it wasn't part of my diet. But the staff and all of my friends who came to visit me that day, ate it up. I received numerous telephone calls from friends. I even received a call from Mr. Cunningham, who congratulated me on my freedom and wished me luck and success.

"I have no doubt that you'll do very well in life," he added. He then told me he'd contacted the San Francisco parole board, informing them I was still doing a NASA volunteer study, and that I'd be calling him to make an appointment. He gave me the name of my parole officer and suggested I call him today. I said goodbye to Mr. Cunningham forever, hung up, and immediately called my parole officer. His name was Pat. I let him know where I was and that I'd be finished on December 18. We arranged for me to come see him the next day, on the 19th. Later that day, when the mail came, I had a note from Bob, the guard at Safford, wishing me good luck. I was actually very touched they he even cared enough to send me a message like that.

I sailed through the last two weeks. The food tasted better; television was better; the NFL playoffs had started - the year of the "immaculate reception," when Pittsburgh was playing Oakland, and Franco Harris grabbed a ricocheting football, which looked like it was about to fall for an incomplete pass, and ran it in for a touchdown—a play I loved to watch back then when I was a Steeler fan, but hated to look at a few years later when I became a Raiders fan. And on December 7, I felt a real part of the NASA program when Apollo 17 was launched. Ron Evans, Gene Cernan, and Harrison Schmitt were the last manned mission to the moon. On December 11, Cernan and Schmitt had the honor of setting foot on the moon once again. No one had taken the American flag put there three years earlier by Armstrong and Aldrin. They spent twelve days in zero gravity, and I'm sure they felt a hell of lot better than I did when their feet touched down on planet Earth on December 19, one day after my feet touched the floor after 80 days, on December 18.

I don't know what I was expecting, but it wasn't to see my legs shaking violently three seconds after I stood up. The leg muscles had gotten very weak in spite of any dynamic tension exercises I tried to perform while lying down. And the bottoms of my feet! The callous had turned soft and I could feel the bones against the floor. And it hurt! Within fifteen seconds, I had to sit back down on my bed. This was not going to be easy. And Tom wasn't doing any better.

After receiving our final examinations, we got dressed and ready to go. I wasn't totally free of the hospital. I would have to come back in a week for one more check-up. Tom was supposed to go back to Safford Prison, but the hospital arranged for him to remain free for Christmas, for rehabilitation. But he didn't stay at the hospital. He had already made reservations to fly back to his hometown in another state for the holidays. But when Tom arrived back in San Francisco, he was offered the opportunity to apply for the very next study, which he did in an instant. He would be doing this bed rest all over again. I don't know that I could've done that.

I don't remember who picked me up and helped me load up their car with my belongings. I don't know exactly where we took them either. I had no home. What I did own in the way of furniture, clothes, kitchen items, my records, wine, stereo - was scattered in three different homes and one, small shed. But I did have $1,200.00 from NASA, plus a few hundred dollars in my bank account. There was no point trying to find a place to live since I would be going on tour in less than a month. I would get one when I came back to San Francisco in late May after our final show. By that time I would have made several thousand dollars. So during the month of December I stayed with Colette for a couple of days. While she was working, I started getting my strength back with walks around Marina Green; It was great spending time with Colette and reflecting over the past several months. She had saved all my letters and asked if I wanted them back. I foolishly declined. I didn't want the reminder, and I'm sorry I didn't look ahead. They would have been a great addition to this book, adding my true feelings, moods, depression, and humor at the time, as opposed to the rough edges, which have been softened over the years.

Since Colette was preparing to host several holiday cocktail parties, I figured I'd better leave. Her place was right out of Architectural Digest, and these parties were an opportunity to showcase her talent. And just in case her potential clients were wealthy, right-wing Republicans, she didn't need a fresh-out-of-prison-antiwar actor as part of her décor. So I stayed with other friends – a day here, a day there, happy that I could afford to buy them all Christmas presents for the trouble of taking me in.

On December 22, singer/activist Joan Baez and Human rights Attorney Telford Taylor visited Hanoi to deliver Christmas mail to prisoners of war. They arrived in time to see Richard Nixon's gift to Le DucTho and the North Vietnamese via air mail: A Christmas bombing, 24-7, for two weeks. This resulted in criticism of Nixon and the U.S. from all over the world. The Prime Minister of Sweden compared the bombings to Nazi massacres. Well, Nixon showed him. In a "gutsy" move, he broke diplomatic contact with Sweden.[75]Nixon claimed that this bombing was really what sent Lee DucTho back to Paris to resume the Paris Peace Accords, which had fallen apart earlier. I hate to admit it, but I think he was right. In January of 1973, a cease-fire plan was made giving the North Vietnamese what they already had anyway. We still had 24,000 troops there, but the polls showed Americans wanted them all out. Nixon and Kissinger made secret promises to South Vietnamese President Thieu, promising him that even though American troops were pulling out, they wouldn't be too far away. They assured Thieu of their commitment to fighting communism in Vietnam. But the American press was suspicious as hell and questioned Nixon and Kissinger, and the two of them went after the press, denouncing their questions and demanding they be more supportive. Nixon asking to be trusted... that's rich. Thieu further tried to convince the Americans that everything was cool. He set up an Office of Tourism, and suddenly we were all invited to hop on a Korean Airlines and visit tropical Vietnam. They really did it up, making travel brochures, TV spots. I don't really know if they sold one ticket. Americans weren't buying into it. And they were smart. All the troops were out of there except for 9,000 American advisors—well, okay, a few thousand were soldiers... and CIA agents, and they sure as hell weren't running tour buses or opening restaurants. Nor was the newly created Development Office successful in getting American investors to build hotels—not with guns blazing and cease-fire violations occurring between North and South Vietnam.[76]The final, pathetic end was still two years away. But for the returning American soldiers, it was over, leaving them to deal with the scars of that war pretty much on their own. And just what the hell did it all mean? What had we done, other than lose 58,000 of our men, thousands more with limbs missing; minds missing? And in the years ahead, thousands more would die from Agent Orange disease and suicide. The anti-war movement which had started almost ten years ago with a few students wearing tattered jeans, granny dresses, fringe, and headbands, sent a message to the American Government and the American people, that patriotism and love for country could be demonstrated in other ways. And though the American people finally got it, I doubt if they ever realized how we'd betrayed Vietnam and Ho Chi Minh to wind up in the position we were in. This man had come to our rescue during World War II, when the country - the entire country, was called Vietminh. They had rescued our downed-pilots, saving them from capture by the Japanese. We gave them weapons so they could fight for their independence. Then after the war, while using our Merchant Marine troopships to take Americans out of Vietminh, we secretly used some of those ships to transport French troops into the country to try and take away their freedom. Then, when that failed, we took our turn, backing several puppet leaders, and slaughtering millions of their people.

But Vietnam was almost a back-burner issue in 1973, because lurking in the shadows was Watergate. As for me, my service wasn't quite finished. I had met with Pat, my parole officer, on Dec. 23. He was a young, stoic man, used to seeing new parolees enter his office with pent up anger and resentment. I wasn't at all what he expected. I greeted him with a smile; we shook hands. Of course from my file he already knew I was an actor. My difficulty walking reminded him that I'd given an extra two weeks to the NASA bed rest study. We talked a little about that experience. He wanted to know about my job plans. I told him that I had a job as an actor touring the United States and Canada. I asked if that would be a problem. He could've given a rat's ass.

"Just call me once a month and let me know where you are." I told him I'd be gone until late May, and he was fine with that. Hell, parolees should all be like me.

315

Before I left the Federal building, I had two more stops to make. I went up to the FBI floor. It was just as I'd remembered it: locked security door, and windows to see into the office area. I looked down the row of desks and there he was... Phil. The officer who'd taken me to Safford. I rang the buzzer. All the officers present looked up to see who was there. Phil looked up and I smiled and waved. At first he didn't know who I was, then suddenly broke into a smile. I could see he was mouthing to the other officers that he knew me. He hit the buzzer and I walked down the long room separated by the security windows. When I approached the office security door, he opened it. And I remember how the other officers wouldn't take their eyes off me, in case all of a sudden I was some whacko ex-con hell bent on revenge. They had nothing to worry about.

"Hey, Phil... Remember me? Bruce Neckels"

"Welcome home." He said, as we shook hands.

He noticed I was limping badly and inquired. I told him about NASA. I probably fed him the same information I gave Pat. I reminded him about having lunch at Tommy's Joynt when I got back, but it was too early for lunch; and with Christmas two days away, and my upcoming tour plans, we took a rain check. I never saw him again after that day.

Stop number two... Samuel Conti's courtroom. I just had to take one more look at the judge who threw me in prison with no bail. Only now I knew that he had not been appointed to the United States Supreme Court. I'm sure one of the reasons was his inability to show leniency or compassion.

I entered his courtroom and took a seat. Conti was listening to an attorney presenting his case. He actually glanced up at me as I entered. I wasn't at all worried that he'd recognize me because he never looked at me for one second the day he sentenced me. I sat there and just stared at him for about fifteen minutes, then he called for a recess. As I watched him leave the courtroom, it struck me that I and the other COhorts who faced him, were partly responsible for derailing his trip to the Supreme Court because of the way he treated us. I left the courtroom having closed the chapter on that part of my life. Now my tour with The Cage would open a new one, only this time I didn't have prison looming in front of me.

IRONIC FOOTNOTE: In 1985, a law clerk working in San Francisco for Judge Conti, made the following assessment: *"...His humble background as a self-made, first-generation Italian-American who served in World War II, then attended Stanford Law with two future U.S. Supreme Court justices, was likely among many reasons the judge was especially sensitive to the plight of "little people" who found themselves pitted against the government, large corporations, or other entities or people with superior resources and power."* [77]

Too bad he couldn't have felt that way in the early 70's, when he was throwing all the "little people" in prison. But then how could he when he was appointed by one of the biggest crooks who ever sat in the White House? The late Judge Sanford Levin was also appointed by Nixon. Levin too, was a Republican, but because he showed compassion, I doubt Nixon shed a tear when he died. Then along came Judge Conti, exactly who Nixon and his cronies needed to come down hard on draft dodgers and marijuana smokers. In a speech given in 1995, these were the words given by John Ehrlichman, Domestic Policy Chief for President Richard Nixon when the administration declared its war on drugs in 1971, the same year of Conti's appointment.

"The Nixon campaign in 1968, and the Nixon White House after that, had two enemies: the antiwar left and black people. You understand what I'm saying? We knew we couldn't make it illegal to be either against the war or be black, but by getting the public to associate hippies with marijuana and blacks with heroin, and then criminalizing both heavily, we could disrupt those communities, we could arrest their leaders, raid their homes, break up their meetings, and vilify them night after night on the evening news. Did we know we were lying about the drugs? Of course we did." [78]

Me, at the US Public Health Hospital, just before my 74-day bedrest study.

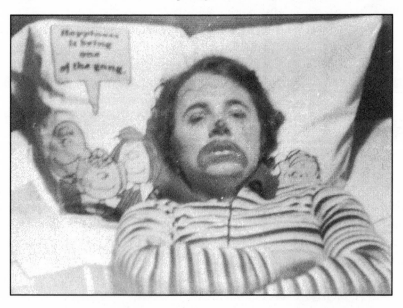

Nurse Judy painted my face – a sad clown – about 40 days into my bedrest.

Chapter Fifty-eight
Full circle to Belfield

During the time I was in prison, Rick and Ken had downsized The Cage. It was no longer a six-character play. They'd eliminated the two guards, lots of luggage, and therefore we only needed one vehicle. Don was the only actor I knew from my tour in 1971. One was a guy named Sonny, from Oakland. He was a nice guy, but very volatile. I think he might have done time in San Quentin. I have no idea what the other actor had on his resume. But he was quiet and easy to get along with.

By the second week of January, my legs and feet were stronger. I was getting my muscles and calluses back. My final checkup at the U.S. Public Health Hospital gave me a good-to-go report, and I was outta here! As much as I loved San Francisco, to be on the road again with The Cage was the therapy and debriefing I needed. I figured a few months of playing that madman character "Hatchet," lecturing in classrooms; question and answer sessions in theatres and auditoriums in some of the finest colleges in North America; the many coeds I imagined would help me relieve my year of frustration, and I would have that prison poison all out of my system. I was now quite knowledgeable about the prison system. I felt I could contribute so much more this time around, aside from just being an actor who'd spent one month in jail. I'd read several books on prisons; knew my prison statistics; and I'd spoken to other prisoners about their experiences. I had their stories to tell as well as mine. But there was one thing that made me somewhat apprehensive about my second tour: The new students at the colleges, and I don't mean those fresh out of high school. I'm talking about the students who were fresh out of Vietnam. These men had come back from hell. Some were missing body parts; others were angry; some ashamed that they didn't have the courage to say "no;" and many who admitted the war was wrong and were now members of the Vietnam Veterans Against the War. Even though I'd gotten approval and standing ovations in 1971, how would these men treat me for the stand I took?

For the opening leg of the tour, we started out in the Pacific Northwest. My worries were dispelled after the first college, Washington State, in Spokane, when a Nam vet came up to me after a classroom discussion and shook hands, thanking me for at least having the balls to choose prison. I thanked him for the sacrifice he made. Next was North Idaho College in Coeur d'Alene, Idaho. Idaho's about as conservative as you can get, but not necessarily the students. No problems. From there we went into Canada, back to the University of Winnipeg. Going through the Canadian Rockies with the snow gently falling; listening to the radio with John Denver singing "Rocky Mountain High;" Roberta Flack singing "Killing Me Softly;" Al Green's "Let's Stay together," it was nothing short of magic. I met many of the students at the college who were there in 1971 and we had a real celebration. And this time, I had a hell of lot more to talk about.

The tour wasn't even one week old when we left the University of Winnipeg, heading back into the states to do a show in Fargo, North Dakota. We were on Highway 75, no more than twenty miles outside of Winnipeg, on a two-lane stretch of dangerous road, and caught in a blizzard. It was a 223-mile trip. Nothing but white out there and the snow was falling hard against our windshield. It created a sensation of not even moving. But we were—at 40 miles per hour because we couldn't see the hood of the car and we didn't know the highway. But a man and his wife, heading for Texas, did. And they were coming up behind us at 55 miles per hour, and we got slammed from behind. They went off the road into a ditch, and we were sitting there in the middle of the highway, and the car was stalled. I was riding shotgun; Sonny was driving. We were all pretty shook up. I asked if everyone was okay, then suddenly it occurred to me:

"Sonny, see if the car will start. We'd better get off this highway."

Sonny turned the key and the car started. He pulled off to the side of the road and three seconds later; a semi-truck pulling a trailer came barreling by doing about 50. That's how close we came to being killed.

It took about two hours before we were on our way again. After filing an accident report, the couple who hit us were towed back to Winnipeg. Both were a little banged up but didn't need an ambulance. We hobbled into Fargo, getting there about four hours before show time. We immediately called Ken in San Francisco and let him know what happened. We were a week from our next show in the mid-west, and since our rear door and one side rear door couldn't be opened, Ken told us to dead-head back home right after the Fargo show and pick up another car. Though the school had reserved dorm rooms for us, we packed and left right after the question and answer session. It was a 1,840-mile trip, and we had no idea which way to go. Nobody wanted to drive in this storm. But that's when Providence stepped in.

We stopped at the nearest gas station and asked the attendant what would be the best route back to San Francisco? Should we take Interstate 29 all the way to Nebraska and catch the 80 Interstate right into San Francisco?

"No, do that and you'll be following the blizzard," said the attendant. "If I was you, I'd take 94 all the way across the state and pick up highway 85... through a little town called Belfield..."

Belfield.... Where I grew up with my grandmother for the first ten years of my life... where she was now buried. A town I hadn't seen since I left it twenty years ago. I turned to the other three cast members.

"Guys, I'll drive all the way to Belfield, if once we get there, you have breakfast somewhere and leave me alone for about two hours. It's where I grew up."

They had no problem with that. It was a 313-mile trip that should've taken four and a half hours. But with the snow falling and black ice on the freeway, it took me almost seven hours to get there. Driving over black ice is a terrifying experience. There were times when I realized that my wheels weren't rolling down the freeway; they were sliding down the freeway! I had absolutely no control over the car, except to keep the wheels straight and keep that fucking car between the ditches. But sometime around 7:00 a.m., we arrived at a highway diner on Highway 94, just a mile outside of Belfield. I let the guys off and proceeded down highway 85 into my hometown.

"Welcome to Belfield - Population 925." When I left in 1954, the population was 900.

It was surreal. Nothing had changed. It was as though time had stood still for the last twenty years, waiting for me to come home again. I parked on the main street where all the stores were, and just started walking - past the post office, Prokop's Pool Hall, the Red Owl Store, John and Joe's Bar... And it was open! I walked inside, said hello to John... Or was it Joe? I don't remember. He actually had a customer sitting there at the bar having a beer. I told them who I was, how I'd once lived in Belfield, and spent a lot of time in this bar while my grandmother played cards. I left after a few minutes of small talk, crossed the street and walked past Mike's Bar, another one of my Grandma's hangouts; past Dick Snyder's Chevy dealership - and yes indeed, there was one change on that street: he'd added a used car lot next to his store. I passed a small café where my mother waitressed during the summer to keep money coming in between her teaching job; next, Thompson Hardware store where every Christmas season as a boy, I stood gazing at the bubble lights on the tree; the Lionel train going round and round on a display table next to the window, hoping that Santa would bring me one just like it. But it never happened. "Santa" was out of Lionel trains by the time he got to my house.

After that, I went by the Belfield Theater, then hopped in my car and drove a few blocks to where my Aunt Polly and Uncle Adolph used to live. Next to their house was the creek where had I played so many war games. With the water in the creek now turned to ice, the beautiful, white snow banks, and the bare branches covered with snow and icicles, it was right out of that opening scene in "Camelot."

From where I stood, could see the home where my Grandma and I lived. As a boy it was a long walk down a dirt road, past a very high water tower. But now, it was less than a hundred yards away, and the tower was not high at all. I was saving my Grandma's house for last. I drove to the front of the house and just stared at it. The front porch was in need of ... well, a new porch. The house itself had withstood decades of weather abuse and needed painting. But someone was living there. So I decided to see if maybe whoever was home would let me come in to just look around. By now, it was about 8:00 a.m.

The screen door in front of the main door was locked, so I had to bang on it pretty hard. As I waited for someone to answer, I turned around and looked across the street toward the railroad tracks where I used to play. Next to the tracks about a hundred yards east of our house was a big grain elevator. I think I was eight years old the summer when my Uncle Charlie, Aunt Ollie, and my two cousins, Butch and Roger, came to visit us, from Hayward, California. Uncle Charlie was actually there to install a toilet in my Grandma's house, thus rendering our outdoor toilet obsolete. Uncle Charlie was a real man - a former boxer, who'd taken too many shots to the head; owned his own fishing boat; a painter by trade, a master plumber - he could do it all. Cousin Butch was two years older than me and Roger, and he was as ugly as his dad - cauliflower ears, chunky, homely, and a real bully. We were playing by the grain elevator, and Butch just couldn't resist pulling down on a thick rope attached to what looked like a huge trap door. And down came two tons of grain spilling all over the ground. We ran like hell and hid under our house. But a witness had seen what happened, followed us home, and told Uncle Charlie, who came out with his razor strap and knew right where to find us. When he looked under the house and glared at us, we all started crying. Of course, Roger and I pointed the finger at Butch and he got the living shit beat out of him with that razor strap. Those were the days when child abuse laws didn't exist.

When I turned back to the door, a little boy about five years old was peeking out the window.

"Hi... Are your mommy and daddy home? Can I speak to them?"

The little boy disappeared, and after a few moments, the door opened just wide enough for a lady to look through at me. I had to look scary. I was wearing a black cowboy hat; a dark blue pea coat; jeans, boots, sunglasses, and I had a beard.

"Yes?" she asked.

"I'm really sorry to knock on your door so early, but I'm with a theatre group and we're heading back to San Francisco... And I used to live in this house with my grandmother twenty years ago."

323

"Wow, how cool," she replied.

I then asked her if I could come in and just look around.

"I'm sorry," she replied apologetically. "I really believe you, but my husband's already left for work, and I'm here alone with my son and baby daughter."

Good thing I didn't tell her I was an ex-convict.

"I understand," I said. And then I talked to her about each room.

"The room to your left is the bedroom. You're in the living room. Behind it is the dining room, and your kitchen's to the right of the dining room... Right?" She replied that it was.

"And the bathroom is next to the kitchen, just to the right of the back door. My Uncle Charlie installed that. Before then, we had an outhouse. And on the left side of the dining room is a staircase that leads upstairs where you have two small bedrooms and a closet."

"Yeah," she said. "I use one of those rooms as a sewing room. I really do believe you sir, and I'm sorry that I can't let you in."

I told her that I understood where she was coming from and thanked her for her time. She closed the door and as I turned to go, I looked up at the porch ceiling, and there was an old, rusty hook. There was no doubt in my mind it was one of the hooks to which my porch swing had been attached. If I'd only noticed it while I was talking to the lady, I'd have asked for a wrench, a ladder, and offered her ten bucks for that hook.

But before I went to my car. I walked around to the right side of the house, almost to the back yard, and stopped near a dormant Lilac bush, where my Grandma and I had buried our dog, Pudgy.

I really wanted to go to the Belfield Cemetery and find my grandmother's grave, but with two feet of snow all over the ground, it would've been impossible to find. I found out years later that she wasn't even buried there, but at a cemetery in Grassy Butte, 38 miles north of Belfield.

And so I drove back to the highway diner where the guys had been patiently waiting. Sonny took over the driving duties, and as we drove back down Highway 85, heading South. We went through Belfield one more time, passing the South Hill, where all of us kids - well, at least the bravest ones, dared go down on sleds. It was sure steep when I was a little boy; but now, not even a good bunny hill at a ski resort. As Belfield disappeared behind me, I felt like I'd been dreaming. And all it took to bring me home again was going to prison and almost getting killed in a car crash. I've never been back since. The population of Belfield today is around 1,000.

Chapter Fifty-nine
Near-death experience

We were a few miles outside of Newcastle, Wyoming. Don was driving. It was a clear day - the same day we left Belfield. Highway 85 was another two-lane highway. Don decided to pass the truck but suddenly the sun reflected off a large patch of icy road, and Don started to panic. Instead of taking his foot off the gas and getting back behind the truck, or speeding up and passing it, he opted to drive right off the road, and we went airborne into a ditch, landing in four feet of snow. The car was buried up to the hood and we had to crawl through the windows to get out. After walking to a gas station two miles away and getting a tow truck with a wench, we were towed back to the gas station where the car was inspected. We needed a new radiator. So five hours later and $200.00 poorer, we were on our way.

We stayed in San Francisco for two days, and then with a new car, headed back out on the road. But within a week, things had turned for the worst once again. We had to send Sonny home because he challenged a student to a fight during a classroom visitation. The student had made a comment to Sonny, which he took as an insult. As the tour manager, I had to make a decision. I might have only given him a warning, but for an incident a couple of nights earlier, in Crookston, Minnesota.

We'd just finished the play and there was a heavy blizzard. So we went back to the motel. The guys had been paid a few days before, but Sonny had to send most of his back to his ex for alimony and child support. He didn't have much left to get him through the week. And Don was almost broke, too. The two of them were rooming together right next to my room. The walls were thin, and I could hear them talking. I couldn't believe what I was hearing. They were discussing whether or not they should rob an all-night supermarket on Interstate 2. I immediately went outside and banged on their door. I was pissed.

"Guys, I could hear you through the walls - talking about robbing an all-night supermarket. Are you out of your fucking minds? How fast do you think the police would be able to make a connection between a robbery and the fact that a theatre group of ex-convicts were in town performing at the local college? You guys would destroy the Barbwire Theatre for good, not to mention I'm on parole and just being a part of this group, I'd be sent back to prison. So please... tell me you were joking."

And that's what they told me. But I could tell by their faces they had seriously considered it. I remembered that Sonny had driven back to the motel after the play. I took the car keys when I left the room, just to be safe. So with that incident, coupled with Sonny picking a fight, I called Ken. But thank God the school's Activities Director had already notified him about the classroom incident. Sonny was sent home and Ken flew out and joined us. He played Hatchet and I took over the role of Al. I was very relieved that Ken was with us.

In spite of all the opportunities I had with coeds, I spent more time with Vietnam vets. After the plays, they were always waiting to talk to me, hug, and shake hands. On many of these occasions, we went out together and had dinner. Or I'd go to their places and we'd sit around, get drunk, get stoned, listen to music, and talk, and never once was I angrily confronted or threatened. They asked me as much about prison as I asked them about Vietnam. But I learned a lot, too. I learned about the number of suicides committed in Nam by soldiers who couldn't take it any longer; the fraggings that happened. That's when a gung-ho lieutenant or commanding officer ordered his troops out on a sure suicide mission. As soon as the opportunity presented itself, a soldier would kill the officer, usually with a fragmentation grenade, making it appear like an accident. Of course, no one ever saw it.

Drug addiction was rampant in Vietnam. According to reports I'd heard at the time, one third of our American soldiers had tried heroin or opium, and addiction was epidemic. Thousands of our servicemen came home addicted. I got to meet one of them, and it damn near killed me.

One night after the play, a Nam vet and his girlfriend invited the cast to his house just outside of town. Two or three other vets were there with their girlfriends - the vets looking more like hippies than ex-soldiers. One of them had recently returned from Nam and brought with him some high-grade heroin. I guess because we'd all been to prison, with three of our cast being hard-timers, he had no problem shooting up in front of us. And apparently this heroin was so pure; you could actually smoke it if needles weren't your thing. One of the vets handed me a joint and said, "Here, try this. It'll kick your ass. "I figured it was probably some good hashish. I took a nice hit of this joint, and within seconds I was in another world. I felt as though my stomach was going to come crawling out of my mouth if I didn't get to a bathroom fast. So I stood up and walked to a hallway. There were two rooms on my left. Both doors were open. I stopped in between them, leaned forward and looked into one door. It was a bedroom. I backed up a couple of steps and leaned back to peek in the room behind me. The next thing I knew, I was hearing a loud thump, followed by a visual field of bright red. It was my head hitting the floor. I had knocked myself unconscious. But as I lay there on the hallway floor, my mind was analyzing the situation. I remembered saying to myself, "Bruce, you're dead. You dumb, stupid son-of-a-bitch. You're in a coffin, surrounded in a deep, red color, and this is what it's like to be dead." Then suddenly, I heard:

"Hey! Open your eyes!"

And just like that, I did. I was looking into the face of one of the Vietnam vets.

"Say hello," said the vet.

"Hello," I replied. "What the fuck was in that joint?"

The vet helped me to my feet. I walked back into the living room. Ken was calmly sitting there.

"You all right, Johnny?" He asked.

Two of the girls were crying because they thought I had died. I asked what that joint had been laced with, but they stayed with the claim it was just good marijuana. I didn't believe them, though at the time, thought the weed had been soaked in hash oil. But it certainly could have been sprinkled with heroin dust. We hung around for a while longer, until I literally got my head together, then left. That was the last time on the tour that I smoked anything.

What fascinated me most was how many vets felt they had to explain to me why they submitted to induction and fought in Vietnam.

Here are a few of those reasons - and these came from vet-students attending colleges mainly in the Midwest and the south:

"My dad, grandfather, and great grandfather all fought in wars. They told me I had to keep the tradition going."

"My dad told me if I dodged the Vietnam War, that he'd kill me."

"I was taught that when your country called, you went, right or wrong."

"I went 'cause I never thought my government would lie to me."

"If you go to Canada, you will shame your mom and me, and we'll have to leave town."

"I went because my dad said that if North Vietnam won, communism would spread throughout the world, and it was up to my generation to stop it."

"I was terrified about going to prison"- was the most popular answer.

But my personal favorite came from a Vietnam vet at a college in Iowa. After a classroom visitation, I was walking through the college grounds when I suddenly heard someone calling my name. I turned around, and saw a student approaching me. I recognized him from the class. He proceeded to tell me how he admired the stand I'd taken. I inquired as to why he submitted to induction, and this was his reply:

"I always wanted to know what it would be like to kill another human being legally and get away with it."

"And did you?" I asked.

"Yeah, I killed quite a few."

"How do you feel about it now that you're home?" I asked.

"Oh, I don't really sleep much anymore," he replied.

Chapter Sixty
Farewell Dick, the Draft... and Mark

During the tour, Watergate had gathered a full head of steam. E. Howard Hunt and Gordon Liddy were tried and convicted in January. By March, James McCord was spilling his guts; and within a month, John Dean, Counsel to the President, began cooperating with the Watergate prosecutors. And when Nixon dismissed Dean for doing too good a job, and accepted the resignations of H.R. Haldeman and John Ehrlichman, it was starting to look like a real cover-up with Nixon right in the middle. So there was plenty to talk about during the tour: Watergate, prison reform, my prison experience; the war; and the role I played in it as a CO.

My favorite subject was prison reform. I had done a lot of reading on the penal system during my own incarceration, and could quote Ramsey Clark, Dostoevsky, Murton, and Menninger. The prisoners of today (1965-73) were no longer the James Cagney type. With 45% of all inmates being black, "political prisoner" was a new term in the system. I'd heard it the first day I was taken to the main line at San Francisco County. And their grievances were more than about bad food and a demand for medical improvements, or the gang violence and brutal raping. They were questioning a social and political system that denied them equal opportunities; a discriminating bail system; indefinite incarceration before trial; unequal sentencing by prejudice judges; administrative abuse; cruel punishment. And they wanted to bring all this information to the public. However, the prison system, embarrassed enough by Attica, the Ohio State Penitentiary riots; and sadly a very peaceful demonstration at Sing Sing Prison - met the grievances with only harsher measures. And as far as the public was concerned, any negative response by inmates confirmed that these "animals" belonged where they were - in fact, build more prisons and make them bigger and the walls higher. And there I was, trying to give these future world changers the prison facts of life. They needed to know that 80% of all inmates would eventually be released, and within five years of their release date, at least 65% of them would wind up back in prison for committing crimes even more violent. Because that's what maximum-security prisons do.... create a more violent criminal. Pair that up with a parole system geared for failure and high recidivism, it was inevitable.

The question I hated the most was, "Well, what can we do?" So we'd advise them to send letters to their state and federal legislators, telling them to spend more of the prison budget on education and vocation, and less on the custodial end. Then give them decent paying jobs, help them regain self-esteem. I had all the answers to all the questions. Including a most defeating one that went counter to all my answers and opinions - one asked by a law student at Ohio State University.

"Do you think prison conditions will improve over the next few decades?"

"Never," I said. "It'll only get worse."

"Why do you say that?" He asked.

"Because it would take a movement as massive as the one that ended the Vietnam War. And are you ready to do that? After we leave today we'll be out of sight, out of mind, just like all those prisons out there. You'll move on with your lives, going for those college degrees. Then you'll travel or go after that high paying job, a family, and children... and that's fine. You should do all that. That's what I want to do."

On January 27, 1973, Secretary of Defense Melvin Laird had announced the end of the draft. By the end of March, hundreds of American POW's were released from North Vietnamese prisons; all combat troops were out of Vietnam. During the ensuing months, I was applauded as playing a major part in bringing the draft to an end. Truth is, I didn't play any bigger a part than the guy who showed up at his induction as a cross-dresser. In fact, the cross-dresser got to immediately go home and resume his life. My role was nobler, that's all. And over the years, that has counted for something.

By May, I was tired of talking about my prison experiences and myself. And talking about prison reform made me feel like I was still there. I had been able to survive on the road just through my per diem. My salary all went into my bank account. I was ready to get back to

332

San Francisco, find an apartment, get my furniture and belongings back under one roof, and resume a normal life, if there is such a thing for an actor as a normal life.

And it was surprisingly easy to get back into the flow. By now, Colette had a boyfriend, but she always had time for me and we became very dear friends. I immediately landed roles on "Magnum Force," "Streets of San Francisco," and several TV commercials. One of them, a regional spot for "Lone Star Beer," was directed by Haskell Wexler, who had directed the movie "Medium Cool," which was filmed at the very violent, Democratic convention in Chicago in 1968. When asked what I'd been doing lately, I told Haskell about my tour and spending 1972 in prison for being a CO. I really think that's why I got one of the principle parts. But the most interesting thing happened during that shoot - something that Haskell picked up about me: It was a barroom scene with everybody dancing and having a good time. We were rehearsing the camera movements during close-ups of me and my partner. Just before we started filming, Haskell came up to me and quietly said:

"Bruce, you need to have more fun. You have a lot of pain in your smile."

I never realized it before, but I guess I'd been hiding it more than I realized.

The Senate Watergate Committee had begun their public hearings. John Dean admitted discussing the Watergate cover-up with Nixon at least 35 times. A memo surfaced in which Ehrlichman described plans to burglarize Daniel Ellsberg's office. On August 29, 1973, just as I was heading out for the college fall tour of "The Cage," Judge John Sirica ordered Nixon to hand over nine White House tapes so he could review them in private. Nixon refused to cooperate. This guy was going down! But irony of ironies. In 1975, John Ehrlichman was found guilty of conspiracy, perjury, and obstruction of justice. After pretty much exhausting his appeals, he finally turned himself in and served 18 months.[79] Guess where? The Federal Correctional Institute at Safford. He even took my old job at the power house. Ain't life a grin?

But something else happened on August 29 that briefly took my attention from Watergate. The Boston police shot and killed an armed man, then apprehended his two accomplices in a failed attempt to rob the Brigham Circle Branch of New England Merchants National Bank, in the Roxbury District of Boston. One of the robbers was Mark Frechette, my 'ol acting buddy from "Zabriskie Point." The bank was several blocks away from the Fort Hill Commune, where the three robbers were living. Remember Fort Hill? Established by spiritual leader Mel Lyman? Apparently, Mel's teachings were a little short on substance and these three bandidos fell through the cracks. However, Mark justified his actions with the following statement:

> *"There was no way to stop what was going to happen. We just reached the point where all that the three of us really wanted to do was hold up a bank. And besides, standing there with a gun, cleaning out a teller's cage - that's about as fuckin' honest as you can get, man!" ...It would be like a direct attack on everything that is choking this country to death."*

His final comment, given today's current state of the banking system, was more profound now than it was then. A pathetic footnote to this: As Mark was trying to escape, he dropped his gun. When the police retrieved the weapon, they discovered there were no bullets in the chamber. Poor Mark. He never could get it right with guns. But then, no bullets in his gun may have reduced his sentence. He was sent to the Massachusetts Correctional Institution at Norfolk, where he was to serve a 6-to-15-year sentence. However, Mark barely lasted two years. He was killed on September 27, 1975. According to an article in Rolling Stone Magazine, Mark was found "pinned beneath a 150-pound set of weights, the bar resting on his throat. An autopsy revealed he had died of asphyxiation and the official explanation is that the weights slipped from his hands while he was trying to bench press them, killing him instantly. A source in the county DA's office, which is investigating the incident, termed the circumstances a little strange, especially since the bar left no mark on Frechette's neck."[80]

Mark's attorney claimed there was no foul play – that he was well-liked by the inmates. But how can a 150 pound barbell balance itself on someone's throat unless the bar is exactly spot-on dead center across his throat. According to Mark's attorney, he was too strong to have been subdued without leaving some sign of a struggle. Okay, if he was that strong, then why couldn't he have pushed the barbell off to one side? It happened to me at Safford one day while I was bench pressing about the same amount of weight. As I was pushing the barbell up, my right elbow locked on me. I could barely keep the weights from crashing back down on my chest, but was still able to guide the barbell off me with my left arm. My opinion, but somebody didn't like him.

Back to 1973 and Nixon. Finally, in October under subpoena, Nixon handed over a few of the tapes. Experts found five different erasures totaling an eighteen-and-a-half-minute gap clearly indicating the tapes had been tampered with. Soon Nixon was appointing Attorney Generals, Deputy Attorney Generals, special prosecutors - people who he thought could protect his sorry ass - but they couldn't. "I'm not a crook," he stated toward the end of 1973, but on August 9, 1974, one day before my birthday, he resigned rather than be impeached.[81] The man who hired the judge who threw me in prison was now leaving the White House in shame. I'm sure that's the day when the pain in my smile went away. Months later, just about the time that my parole ended, I received a letter from the Presidential Clemency Board.

"President Ford wishes to heal the divisions caused by the Viet Nam War to enable persons with draft-evasion or AWOL offenses to gain their way back into society... You must apply before January 31, 1975."[82]

A condition was that I be willing to do alternative service. I immediately responded by telling them about my participation in the NASA study during my incarceration. I included a letter of support from Dr. Schneider. Along with the application package was another letter describing how I had been on a national college tour with The

Cage and prison reform (I went out in the fall of 1973, and again in entire school year of 1974). I concluded by telling them that I had done my alternative service, and that I didn't feel more was necessary. I can't believe how brazen that comment was now that I look back on it. The Americans evacuated South Vietnam on April 29 and 30. Saigon fell to the communists, and the war ended. Months later, on August 14th, 1975, I received a second letter from the Presidential Clemency Board. which read as follows:

"Dear Mr. Neckels:

President Ford has accepted the recommendation of the Presidential clemency Board and has signed a master warrant which granted you a full, free, and unconditional pardon pursuant to Article II, Section 2, of the Constitution of the United States...... Congratulations and best wishes for the future. Sincerely, Charles E. Goodell, Chairman. "[83]

Talk about irony. August 14 was Colette's birthday. We went to "The Hippo" and celebrated with a decadent meal of banana fritters and vanilla ice cream.

I remember one of my friends saying, after I informed them of my pardon. "Oh, so then it's like it never happened."

Chapter Sixty-one
What did we learn and
where do we go from here?

W ell, we certainly didn't learn how to stop fighting senseless wars and I doubt if we ever will. But we did learn in my opinion the most important lesson of all:

During the Vietnam War, our soldiers were treated horribly by anti-war organizations waiting at airports to "greet" them upon their return from Vietnam. They were spit at, jeered; pig's blood or red-dyed water was dumped on them by protestors. They were called "baby killers" and "murderers." Today, antiwar groups still exist. But our feelings about the war in Iraq; our involvement in Afghanistan and Pakistan, what they learned - what we've all learned - is to never again demonize the American soldier. He or she is the tip of the spear. They join out of a sense of duty, family tradition, maybe they're looking for adventure; maybe they're lost and trying to find themselves; or maybe they just need a job. But these young men and women put their trust in their leaders that they are doing the right thing, and that their aim is righteous and necessary. So if we want to get angry and protest an unjust, immoral, undeclared war, we should be directing our wrath at the leaders who throw the spear.

In 1970, when accepting the Laurel Award from the Screen Actors Guild. Dalton Trumbo said these words:

"...a time of evil, [and that] no one on either side who survived it came through untouched by evil. Caught in a situation that had passed beyond the control of mere individuals, each person reacted as his nature, his needs, his convictions, and his particular circumstances compelled him to. There was bad faith and good, selflessness and opportunism, wisdom and stupidity, good and bad on both sides.

When you who are in your forties or younger look back with curiosity on that dark time, as I think you occasionally should, it will do no good to search for villains or heroes or saints or devils because there were none; there were only victims. Some suffered less than others; some grew and some diminished; but in the final tally we were all victims because almost without exception each of us felt compelled to say things he did not want to say; to do things he did not want to do; to deliver and receive wounds he truly did not want to exchange. That is why none of us – left, right, or center –emerged from that long nightmare without sin. "[84]

Mr. Trumbo was referring to the investigations conducted by the House of Un-American Activities Committee in 1947 – the McCarthy Communist witch hunts – into the Hollywood Motion Picture Industry. He could easily have been talking about the Vietnam War.

So why did I wait forty-seven years to tell this story? After all, it was the baby boomers born between 1946-1954 who were most affected by the Vietnam War. And we're all over 60-70 years old now. If a boy turned 16 around 1963, then he had a decision to make about Vietnam. Those born after 1959 never had to worry about it. Nor have they been tested since.

Still, I couldn't find the right time to tell this story. The 70's were too soon. The war didn't end till 1975, and this country needed time to heal. I wasn't ready to piss anybody off; and besides, I wanted to get my life back. The 80's? I had just moved to L.A., trying to get an acting career going. Reagan, who helped get that gun-toting judge appointed, was now President. And with Iran-gate and Oliver North swearing to God that he had nothing to do with illegal selling of arms to support the Contras, the climate still wasn't right. The 90's? A story about a C.O. wouldn't have flown then with The Gulf War, and America up in arms to stop Saddam Hussein from his illegal invasion of Kuwait. Saddam Hussein, who poisoned his own people to death - Hitler of the Middle East. Who on this planet was worse than him? We got that answer on September 11, 2001. And I certainly couldn't write my story after what Osama bin Laden did to our nation.

Finally, I had to just step back and face the fact that there would never be a right time. War is a staple on this planet; it's a lust; it's a tradition... perhaps even written in genetic codes. Violence and war. It's certainly what America does best. We promote it; we create, package, market, and sell it through movies, television, advertising, video games, and gun sales. The United States of America is the non-fiction version of "The Little Shop of Horrors." We're Audrey II, the huge plant that keeps screaming to be fed. Like Audrey II, we crave flesh and blood. And for that we need a steady diet of war. We don't lose wars because we don't know how to win them. We don't **want** to win. That's secondary to our main goal which is to profit.

But we do need a space on this planet for the peaceful people, the conscientious objectors; for those seeking the highest ideal... peace in the world. However, I have no solutions. I would never enter this project with such childish dreams. The greatest minds alive—writers, historians, politicians, scientists, theologians—since the beginning of mankind, haven't been able to find the peaceful solution. I would never portend to be a torch-bearer or beacon of light, but merely a window to peer into—An opportunity to look at the results of making a choice that you and/or your children may one day have to make: To follow the world's expectations of you, or your own conscience. It won't be easy. And you may be tested sooner than you think. How many more troops, and how many more years are we willing to sacrifice? In the sixteen years (and counting)that we've been in the Middle East, the longest running war in American history, young boys and girls from five to ten years old, watched their mothers, fathers, brothers, sister, friends, and relatives killed because of our presence and our bombs. That 5-year old is now 21; 6-year old, 22; 7-year-old, 23; 8 year-old, 24; the 9 year old, 25 –millions of potential soldiers. They haven't forgotten what they've seen. We have beget new enemy warriors, who will continue to hate us, fight us, and it will go on and on and on. Find an old copy of Newsweek Magazine, October 15, 2001. The cover shows a picture taken at an anti-war rally in Islamabad - of an Islamic boy, no more than six years old, holding an automatic weapon. The picture is worth a thousand words.

As of 2019, we're still in the Middle East, with no immediate exit plan; North Korea is testing a nuclear bomb; Russia and China are trying to make inroads in South America. And with drug cartels from

Mexico entering our country and committing acts of kidnapping, torture, and murder over drug deals gone bad; and the possibility of Al-Queda and ISIS terrorist cells here waiting to strike, we can never send our National Guard to foreign lands again. They must stand ready not only to protect our borders from enemies foreign and domestic, but we need them well trained and ready to lend disaster relief in whatever states they serve: Hurricanes, floods, fires , earthquakes, tornadoes – are stronger, deadlier, and more frequent that ever before. We need our National Guard here and actively involved. But then, we don't have enough volunteer forces to handle all our world-wide interventions. With a very small percentage of our total population on active duty or reserves, the result is multiple tours of duty; thousands more dead and wounded; more PTSD and brain damaged victims, and of course trillions of dollars spent with very few objectives accomplished.

However, the chances of reinstating the draft are slim – at least not the way we left it in 1973. Any Congressional member voting for it will be ending their career in politics. And would the Pentagon even want to bring it back? Wouldn't they rather train soldiers who are more career oriented, who want to be there?

But if we do bring back the Selective Service, then we need to redefine Conscientious Objector. A "Selective Objector" must be included, and the importance of a religious CO as criteria, be extremely downgraded. Why can't an atheist or agnostic believe in the First Commandment? Should students fresh out of high school who have no plans for college do at least two years of local, state, or national public service - if we can just figure out how to do it? For those who submit to induction, what will determine their decision to go? Does a young man or woman have the right to know the pros and cons of why they're going to war? Should they not be allowed that benefit before declaring their status as a CO, a Selective Objector, or a military inductee? And if they do choose to be drafted into the military, perhaps they, and enlistees, should be offered extra incentive. Corporations like Dick Cheney's former company Halliburton; a Halliburton subsidiary, Brown & Root; Shell, Exxon, General Dynamics, United Technologies, Lockheed Martin, BAE Systems, American Fluor Corporation, AMEC(UK), Bechtel, ET AL – should all set aside a percentage of earnings, based on their profits, and put that into a Military Death and Loss of Limb Fund. If a soldier gets killed while serving in a hostile nation, his immediate family is given a determined amount of tax free dollars, somewhere in the millions; loss of limb(s) in combat: another determined tax free sum. Those who are going insane or near suicide get free psychiatric service for as long as it takes to heal their emotional hidden scars. And ALL those who survive get a free college education, based on SAT or ACT test scores, to whichever college they wish to go. It's only fair that major corporations, who help plan these wars – who lobby to stay in wars, who put billions of dollars of blood money into their coffers while our soldiers come back in coffins, should compensate those who do the fighting in order to insure corporate profits.

For me, I just couldn't see getting my ass blown off in a war that was a mistake - getting false information about what was happening in Vietnam. "My country right or wrong" no longer filled me with a sense of pride and patriotism. Fighting a war that, according to the Christian Just War Theory, which goes back to St. Augustine in the 4th Century, was wrong. There are seven "just war" standards. But at the time, I only knew of one. Maybe if you knew all seven, it might alter your decision. Take it for what it's worth:

1. War must be the last resort after all other possible solutions have been tried and failed.
2. The reason for war must be to redress rights actually violated or to defend against unjust demands backed by force.
3. The war must be openly and legally declared by a lawful government.
4. There must be a reasonable chance of winning.
5. Soldiers must try to distinguish between armies and civilians and never kill civilians on purpose.
6. The means used in fighting the war must be "proportionate" to the end sought. The good being done by the war must outweigh the evil which the war would do.
7. The winner must never require the utter humiliation of the loser.

The Vietnam War violated six of them.[85]

And yet, it happened again - fighting an illegal war in Iraq, undeclared, with unstable regimes like Vietnam - a war that couldn't be won; a war that lost the United States respect throughout the world; a war that has led to terrorism all over the world. And even though we still have a few thousand troops in a "training/advisory" capacity, Iraq is in control of their own destiny. They can approve or reject our actions. That's what happened in Vietnam.

On Monday, July 6, 2009, former Secretary of Defense Robert S. McNamara, labeled as the architect of the Vietnam War, passed away – gone to that great war room in the sky. To those born long after the Vietnam War, McNamara's life and death may mean nothing to you. Unless you are a descendant of a dead soldier, he didn't affect your lives; But he sure had an effect on ours. Because of his decisions, our boys came home from Vietnam in a variety of ways: in body bags; as paraplegics; as heroin addicts; clinically insane; many committed suicide; and many were forgotten, living today in cardboard boxes, in tunnels, and on our city street sidewalks. In 1995, he finally admitted that "the war was wrong...terribly wrong." Now whether that mea culpa balances the scales with over 58,000 dead American soldiers, and millions of Vietnamese dead, is between McNamara and all those ghosts who were awaiting his arrival. In his book, *In Retrospect: The Tragedy and Lessons of Vietnam (1995)*, Secretary of Defense Robert McNamara made the following statement.

> *"We of the Kennedy and Johnson administrations who participated in the decisions on Vietnam acted according to what we thought were the principles and traditions of this nation. We made our decisions in light of these values. Yet we were wrong, terribly wrong. We owe it to future generations to explain why. I truly believe that we made an error not of values and intentions, but of judgment and capabilities."*[86]

In Errol Morris' 2003 Oscar-winning documentary, "The Fog of War: Eleven Lessons from the Life of Robert S. McNamara," McNamara presents an updated version of the Christian Just War

Theory, written centuries ago, with ten additional lessons added.[87] Unfortunately, those lessons were never applied to the war in Iraq, and Afghanistan. Bush, Rumsfeld, and Cheney learned absolutely nothing – nor did they want to - and now the young men and women returning from Iraq, Pakistan, and Afghanistan are joining the ranks of the Vietnam Veterans.

I don't remember the college in Ohio - maybe Cleveland State University. We arrived early for classroom visits, followed by the play that evening, then Q&A afterwards. But the school's Activities Director informed us that the local television station wanted two or three of us to give an interview at the studio around 5:00 p.m. So one of the other actors and I went. We met the news reporter who'd be conducting the interview, and of course he asked the nature of our crimes. It was a live broadcast, and during the course of the interview, I was asked several questions about my prison experience as a CO. That evening, after the performance and Q&A, I was standing by the stage area, signing autograph copies of" The Cage," and talking to some audience members. I had my eye on a coed who I wanted to leave with, when the Activities Director approached me.

"Bruce, sorry to interrupt, but there's a lady and her husband sitting over there. They want to talk to you."

I looked over and saw a man and woman, in their 50's, patiently waiting. So I excused myself and went over to the couple.

"Hello, I'm Bruce Neckels. You wanted to speak with me?"

The man stood, introduced himself and his wife, and we shook hands.

"We had no idea there was a play at the college tonight," said the lady. "But we saw you on the evening news, and when you said you were a conscientious objector, we just had to be here. We wanted to meet you."

I thanked them for coming to see the play, and asked if there was anything in particular they wanted to talk about.

"Our son was in the army and was killed in Vietnam two years ago. We've watched and read all about the anti-war protests and seen all the hippies on television, screaming about the war, making peace signs, burning draft cards, and we've been filled with such resentment.

Then tonight we saw you on television and you were so articulate and such a nice, young man. You reminded us of our son. So we just want you to know that we wish our son had done what you did."

It was humbling, yet so inspiring to hear that from parents of a fallen son - A son who died in a senseless war. And until the citizens of the world realize that all wars are a senseless waste of life, parents will continue to grieve over the coffins of their sons and daughters; and children, over their fathers and mothers. So if we do have a draft again that is strictly for military induction, we'll need to see a movement just like the one in the 60's.

In the meantime, stop listening to catch phrases meant to guilt you into fighting senseless wars.

"My country, right or wrong." Be careful on that one. Substitute the words "My President," or, "my government.," for "Country." Then it becomes, "My President right or wrong." When George Bush Jr. puts a young man's life on the line, sending him into Iraq because "[Saddam Hussein] tried to kill my daddy." – Nah, sorry, that's "My President, wrong!" You're not using my child to extract revenge.

When the Bush/Cheney Administration lied about Iraq having Weapons of Mass Destruction and sent American soldiers to their deaths, that's "My government, liars and wrong!" Because if we believe in "My country, right or wrong," then shouldn't young men in all countries believe in that catch phrase? There was a day when Hitler was Germany. Was every young man justified in helping exterminate 6 million Jews because Hitler ordered it? Remember – "My country, right or wrong." From 1969-1972, the most stressful period of my life, Richard Nixon was "my country." And in that time, instead of fulfilling his "secret plan" to end the war in Vietnam, we lost another 21,000 men.

"We're fighting them there so we don't have to fight them here." It's a different time in history. The enemy doesn't need to come here with armies and weapons. They come as individuals… as terrorists. And one brilliant cyber-snooping terrorist could alter the functionality of a nuclear weapon or bring down a U.S. power grid. How do we know they haven't been here for years, waiting for a command to strike? Just like they did on September 11, 2001.We had the most powerful military to ever exist since the beginning of time. And what good did all those planes, tanks, missiles, aircraft carriers, and armies, do? Nineteen men with box-cutting knives hijacked four of our commercial airliners and changed this world forever. So what do we do? We create Homeland Security, which hurts our country even more. Because now individual rights are taken away that we'll never get back again. I don't mind being inconvenienced at airports. I'll take off my shoes, my belt; I'll throw my change, cell phone, keys in a box. But what worries me are the millions of suitcases going into those planes and how soon before the wrong people are in position to start letting the wrong, unchecked suitcases go onto those planes. After 911, we all sat around in our living rooms with friends, created our own think tanks, and came up with a thousand different ways that terrorists could pull the plug on this nation's economy. So have the FBI, the CIA, and every law enforcement unit in every city in America. What most of us don't want to mention is the fact that neither Homeland Security nor the most powerful military on the planet would be able to stop it. We go on red alert at Christmas time; New Year's Eve; the Super Bowl – as if we're afraid they'll choose one of our holidays or events to strike again. They don't want our holidays! They'll create their own memorable dates. Americans know September 11 as well as they know December 25. The suicide bombings and terrorist strikes will continue. This will never end. Remember, in 2001 the Taliban and Al Queda were in Afghanistan. Today, along with Isis, they are in countries all over the globe.

"If we pull out now, our soldiers will have died in vain." But if we don't then it's possible more will die in vain. So did 58,000 American soldiers die in vain when we pulled out of Vietnam? Or did their deaths stop maybe another 58,000 from dying had we stayed and continued the war? And it's not just soldiers who die in vain. It's the millions of civilians who are killed or maimed; it's their land that's been destroyed in vain; and in the case of Iraq, an eco-system that's been destroyed. Fifteen years of war, the trampling of tanks and Humvees over fertile land; months of bombing during the first Gulf War by the United States and Great Britain left tons of ammunition fragments laced with depleted uranium. Add to this, two years of draught, horrible dusts storms, and Iraq is headed toward ecological catastrophe, which could take generations to mend. There was a time when Iraq's fertile land fed much of the entire Middle East. They now import 80% of their food.[88]How many more years do we want to add to that?

There's more to war than just soldiers dying in vain. Four students were killed at Kent State University on Monday, May 4, 1970; nine were wounded, including Dean Kahler who was permanently paralyzed from the waist down. That day affected national politics. It began the downfall of the Nixon Administration. If any one incident defined the division of this country during the Vietnam War, it was Kent State. So does that mean those four students didn't die in vain? Three of the four were in a parking lot over 300 yards away when they were struck with random bullets. Who speaks for the dead? Who decides what dying in vain is? It's a stock platitude made by generals, clergyman, and politicians to make those loved ones left behind, feel better. More polite than saying, "War is hell. He knew what he was getting into, right?"

Democracy: A "government of the people, by the people, and for the people." Our founding fathers, Washington and Madison, warned us against this. When's the last time any of us had a say in the President's decisions? On the Supreme Court's legal decisions; or what Congress legislates? It's an illusionary phrase fostered by the Congressional ruling class who are supposedly representing WE, the people. Because of our two-party system, half the country will always stay within party lines, striving to bring the other party down. We've worked at this democracy thing for over two hundred years and we still don't have it right. And we're trying to shove it down the throats of other nations? It's a difficult form of government, because it's driving force is capitalism. I like capitalism, but on a large scale, it turns to greed, and not everyone has an equal chance. Today, 2% percent of the people own 80% of the wealth. Our diminishing middle class and lower-class citizens have become indentured servants. How do you incorporate Democracy/Capitalism into a Muslim religion that's 14 centuries old? You don't.

So, to the Military Industrial Complex – the same one President Dwight D. Eisenhower warned us against in the 1950's:the major corporations; oil companies; the manufacturers who feed, clothe and arm our troops – your wars will still be safe. There's too much money to be made building weapons capable of destroying other countries – and an even bigger payday if- take Afghanistan, for instance – we can defeat the Taliban and rape that country of its rare natural resources worth an estimated one trillion dollars. It's been 43 years since the end of the Vietnam War and where are we? Once again we're riding a wave of disgust, resentment, and even fury about the cost of our involvement in Iraq and Afghanistan (somewhere between 4-6 trillion dollars), and the obvious déjà vu with Vietnam: being duped and paying with lives and suffering beyond mere statistics. Kennedy-Johnson-McNamera;Nixon-Laird-Kissinger;Reagan-Weinberger; Bush Sr.-Taft-Cheney; Clinton-Cohen; Bush Jr.-Rumsfeld. Obama-Hegel-Panetta; Trump-??????. The names change; the politicians change; but it's the same game. What can we learn by reexamining a previous war similar in the arrogance with which we committed ourselves, the cynicism of our appraisals, and the cost to our young?

But we have to be <u>willing</u> to learn. Unfortunately, there is a psychological need for the psyche of man to, pardon my choice of words, "erect" the ultimate phallic symbol: a missile that can shoot straight, far, and explode with deadly accuracy. All it will take is one power hungry tyrant to push the button; another to retaliate; and we will fight the war to end all wars. Mother Nature will at last begin to heal herself...without our interference.

"I don't think we can really afford to forget that we were political prisoners of the greatest country ever to exist on the face of this planet. Maybe that way we won't be so awed by the future facing both of us."

- May 1972

Note to me from a fellow CO on the inside cover of Herman Hesse's "If the War Goes On."

Epilogue
It's time... but what's missing?

I t's been fifty years since I went through my ordeal, but along the way, I've asked myself if the day would ever come again when our young men and women would have reason to mount a protest that would equal the individual and collective sacrifices we made to end the war in Vietnam. We were a generation of people finding ourselves at a time in history when we needed to take a stand - when we needed to give our "country" a swift kick in the ass and say - "Stop lying to us - stop killing us - stop making us cripples - stop driving us insane. Stop making our mothers, fathers, wives, and children, cry over the deaths of our loved ones fighting senseless wars. And this is how far we're willing to go to show you how wrong you are - to let you know you're not fooling us anymore."

In Chapter One, I wrote: "The decade of the 1960's was insane-Civil War, Part II." Sadly, the insanity continues today with "Civil War, Part III." Not since Vietnam has our nation has been so divided, so angry; so stressed out; so mean-spirited. God knows, our future architects and saviors of America have plenty of issues to protest.

The NRA and its staunch supporters need to be reminded that the second amendment is more than just the last fourteen words that justify their right to bear arms – that its original purpose was to provide for "a well-regulated militia, being necessary to the security of a free state" – i.e., a supplemental army of civilian minutemen to help the colonies' small army and navy to fight the British. We now HAVE a structured military, so we really don't need all those semi-automatic weapons and large capacity gun magazines circulating and easily attainable from your local gun shops, gun shows, the black market, or the internet by mentally unstable citizens and homegrown terrorists.

Climate change is probably the most important issue of all. It's no hoax. There are hundreds of wildfires all over America - heat records being broken all over the world. Bats – the ones that fly – are boiling to death in Australia and the Bonac Peninsula inside the Arctic Circle

349

hit 89.6 degrees. If we don't start solving this problem in the next 10-15 years, this planet is headed for catastrophe. And it won't just affect one party or the other. Hurricanes, floods, fires, tornados, pandemics and earthquakes could give a damn whether you're a democrat, republican, socialist, Christian, or atheist. And we still haven't dealt with the issues of prison reform; the homeless; general health care, and better health care for soldiers returning home with PTSD; the huge gap between the rich and poor; civil rights and race relations; immigration; foreign relations. But how can we accomplish anything if we can't unify the country?

So then what's missing? I realize this is a different time than the 60's – that most protesting is done through social media – the written word. But you need voices and faces for today's movement. Where and who are they? Where's your Martin Luther King, Tom Hayden, David Harris, Abbie Hoffman, Gloria Steinem, Betty Friedan, and yes, Jane Fonda? Thank God Jane and Gloria are still actively involved. Where's the music that ties all the causes together: Bob Dylan - Joan Baez - Simon and Garfunkel - Peter, Paul,& Mary–CSN&Y? I've heard quite of few of today's protest songs, but none of their music resemble iconic anthems like Dylan's *"The Times They Are a'Changin,"* Where's your political face of hope – your Bobby Kennedy, Jesse Jackson, or John Lewis? It's the different faces from each cause who become intertwined, which makes the movement stronger. And music is the lifeblood which gives the movement its courage, its heart and its soul.

"We did not inherit this land from our forefathers – we are borrowing it from our children." - unknown

But nothing is going to get accomplished if we don't take off those party hats – the red and blue ones. The party's over. It's time for "We the People," because we're all in this together. And that's what it's going to take to save this country. The Gen Y's, and Z's comprise millions of new voters. You can make an incredible change in this country if you get out there and vote with your conscience, not your party. It was very encouraging to see that over a 100 million people voted in the November, 2018 mid-term election – the largest in the history of mid-term elections. Yet the smallest percentages of voters were between the ages of 18-29. You can't do that anymore! The 2020 election will be the most important in our history. It will have a drastic effect on our country for decades to come. <u>You</u> are now borrowing this land from <u>your</u> children. Find candidates who you can get behind – younger candidates who care about the future - who aren't owned by corporations and special interest groups - who will bring solidarity to this nation. Because right now there is no solidarity. And if politicians – the ones whose own self interests are more important than their sworn duty to protect our country and serve its people – don't get their heads out of their… "litter boxes" and start smelling the truth and seeing the light, we're <u>all</u> going to wake up one day and find that while we've been sleeping, democracy disappeared. And if that happens, America and its empire throughout the world, will become the shortest-lived power in the history of the planet. America is your Vietnam War.

REFERENCES

1. "2-Year Terms For 4 Draft Refusers." San Francisco Chronicle, February 25, 1971. p.15

2. Lyndon Johnson quote – February, 1965

3. Perry, Charles. "The Sound of San Francisco." The Rolling Stone Illustrated – History of Rock and Roll. New York. Random House/Rolling Stone Press. Canada. Random House of Canada, Limited. Toronto. 1980.

4. Timeline of the Hippie Movement. (2004). Retrieved February 27, 2011 from: http://www.hippy.comtimeline.htm

5. Detroit Riots of 1967. Retrieved August 3, 2007 from: http://www.67riots.rutgers.edu/dindex.html.

6. "Waiting For the Light." Time. July 1, 2004: 16-23. Print.* Witnessed by B. Neckels on NBC News. February 1, 1968.

7. Dareff, Hal. The Story of Vietnam. New York. Avon Books. 1967. Pp. 17-38.

8. Mega, Timothy P. (2000) The Complete Idiot's Guide to the Vietnam War. Indianapolis: Alpha Books.

9. Dareff, Op. cit., pp.67-71

10. The Day The Earth Stood Still. Dir. Robert Wise. [motion picture]20th Century Fox. 1951.

11. Dareff, Op. cit., pp. 92-95

12. Confessions of a Pop culture Addict. (May, 2010). Retrieved June, 2010 from: http://popcultureaddict.com/movies-zabriskiepoint-html.

13. O'Brian, D. "The Sorry Life & Death of Mark Frechette." Rolling Stone. Nov. 6, 1975. p. 32.

14. Michelangelo Antonioni. Playboy Magazine Interview, November, 1967

15. Mega, Timothy P. (2000).The complete Idiot's Guide to the Vietnam War: The Battling Democrats and Campaign. pp. 231-233. Alpha Books.

16. Dareff, Ibid. pp. 235-241.

17. Ibid. Pp. 214-218.

18. Mega, Op. cit., pp 213-218

19. Zabriskie Point. Reviewed by Dennis Schwartz. (Jan.6, 2000). Retrieved Jan. 14, 2003 from: http://www.reviews.imbd.com/Reviews/227/22752.

20. Villella, Fiona A. (Feb., 2000). Here Comes the Sun: New Ways of Seeing In Antonioni's Zabriskie Point. Retrieved Jan. 14, 2000 from: http://www.sensesofcinema.com/contents/00/4/zabriskie.html.

21. Types of Draft Resistance. Retrieved Feb. 9, 2003 from http://www.seas.upenn.edu/~pws/60s/ethival.html.

22. Ibid.

23. Selective Service System. Order to report for Armed Forces Physical Examination. Retrieved from U.S. Government Printing Office March 3, 2003.

24. Lederer, William A. (June, 1968). Our Own Worst Enemy. WW Norton and Co., Inc., p. 56.

25. Selective Service System. Order to Report for Induction. SSS form 252.Retrieved from U.S. Government Printing Office. March 3, 2003.

26. Lederer. Op. cit. pp. 80-104

27. Dalton Trumbo (1905-1976). Retrieved March 27, 2003 from: http://www.kirjasto.sci.fi/trumbo.htm.

28. Trumbo, Dalton. (1939). Johnny Got His Gun. J.B. Lippincott Company. New York.

29. Linder, Douglas. The My Lai Massacre Trial. (March, 2000). Retrieved February 10, 2003 from: http://www.jurist.law.pitt. edu./trials3.htm.

30. Summons – Cr Form No. 13 (rev. July 1953). June 24, 1970. (Summons framed and hanging on my wall).

31. San Francisco Chronicle. Op cit.p.15

32. Lewis, Jerry M. and Hensley, Thomas R. (1998). The May 4 Shootings at Kent State University: The Search For Historical Accuracy. Retrieved May 13, 2010 from the World Wide Web: http://dept.kent.edu/sociology/lewis/LEWIHEN.htm.

33. Middleton, P., & Pilgrim, D. (2001). The African American Registry. Nigger (the word), a brief history! Retrieved Jan. 22, 2007 from: http://www.aaregistry.com/african American history/ 2420/Nigger the word a brief history!

34. Wikipedia, the free encyclopedia. Nigger. Retrieved Jan. 22, 2007 from: http://en.wikipedia.org/wiki/Nigger %28word%29.

35. American Vietnam War Casualty Statistics. (November 25, 2002.) Retrieved March 19, 2007 from: http://www.militaryfactory.com/vietnam/casualties.asp

36. George Jackson account. Neckels recollection from articles in San Francisco Chronicle and San Francisco Examiner. Week of August 22, 1971.

37. Pearson, Hugh. (1994). The Shadow of the Panther: Huey Newton and the Price of Black Power In America. USA, Perseus Publishing.

38. Cluchey, Rick. (1970). The Cage.[Stage Play].Barbwire Press.

39. Attica: The Official Report of the New York special Commission On Attica.(September 1972).Summary, p. 104;pp. 313-366.Bantam Books.

40. Ellsberg, Daniel. (2002) SECRETS: A Memoir of Vietnam and the Pentagon Papers. First published by Viking Penguin, a member of Penguin Putnam, Inc.

41. Zimbardo, Philip G.(1999).The Stanford Experiment – Slide Show. Retrieved from http://www.prison.org/slide-4.htm,March 12,2008.

42. Zimbardo, Phillip. (2007). The Stanford Prison Experiment: A Simulation Study of the Psychology of Imprisonment Conducted at Stanford University. Retrieved March 12, 2008 from: http://www.prisonexp.org/

43. Arizona Republic Story from March, 1972.Found written on a piece of paper with letters I'd saved from that time.).

44. Amy letter to Neckels dated February 20, 1972

45. Ibid. February 23, 1972

46. Ibid. April 19, 1972

47. Ibid. May 17, 1972

48. K. Whelan. Letter to Neckels dated, April 15, 1972

49. P. Maier. Letter to Neckels dated April 17,1972

50. George McGovern: Congressional career – Opposition to the Vietnam War. Extracted from Time Magazine article Plight of the Doves. September 14, 1970.Retrieved February 22, 2008 from: http://en.wikipedia.org/wiki/GeorgeMcGovern.

51. Ibid.

52. Collette. Letter to Neckels dated June 12, 1972.

53. P. Thomas. Letter to Neckels dated June 15, 1972.

54. Andrew. Letter to Neckels dated June 23, 1972

55. M. Feherty. Letter to Neckels dated August 11, 1972.

56. United States Presidential Election. Retrieved February 22, 2008 from: http://en.wikipedia.org/wiki/U.S. Election%2C 1972.

57. Ibid.

58. Snopes.com. (1999).Urban Legends Reference Pages: Jane Fonda and POWs. Hanoi'd with Jane. Retrieved February 20, 2008 from: http://www.snopes.com/military/fonda.asp.

59. (July 23, 1972). Jane Fonda's visit to North Vietnam. Arizona Republic. Page 1.

60. Snopes.com. Ibid. p. 7.

61. Collette. Letter to Neckels dated July 18, 1972.

62. W. Cunningham letter to Andrew Tuck dated July 30, 1972.

63. Collette letter to Neckels dated August 10, 1972.

64. Sean letter to Neckels dated September 2, 1972.

65. Collette letter to Neckels dated August 30, 1972.

66. Sean letter to Neckels dated September 16, 1972.

67. United States Government Memorandum. (September 26, 1972). Subject: Transfer to USPHS Hospital, San Francisco, California.

68. Miller, K. (August 2, 2001). Science. NASA. Gravity Hurts (So Good). Retrieved December 30, 2007 from: http://science.nasa.gov/headlines/y2001/ast02aug 1.htm.

69. Hutchison, A. (Oct. 17, 2001). NASA News Release. NASA Seeks Volunteers for Month-Long Bed Rest Study. Retrieved December 30, 2007 from: http://www.nasa.gov/centers/ames/news/releases/2001/01.html.

70. Collette letter to Neckels dated September 26, 1972.

71. Collette letter to Neckels dated October 2, 1972.

72. John Whiteclay Chambers II. "Desertion" The Oxford Companion to American Military History. 2000.Retrieved March 12, 2006 from Encyclopedia.com:http://www.encyclopedia.com/doc/3/128-Desertion.html.

73. Maga, Timothy P. (2000).The complete Idiot's Guide to the Vietnam War: Coming Home. 270-271. Alpha Books.

74. Anonymous. Book Rags. (2006). Watergate Scandal. Retrieved August 1, 2008from: http://www.bookrags.com/wiki/watergate scandal.

75. Wikipedia, the free encyclopedia,1972 in the United States. Retrieved August 3, 2008 from: http:en.wikipedia.org/wiki/1972 in the United States.

76. Maga, Timothy P, Ph.D., Op.Cit., Pp. 268-274.

77. Keckeissen, Gordon. A Judge Samuel Conti Christmas Carol. Dec. 20, 2016.The Recorder. https://www.law.com/therecorder/almID/1202775200416/?slreturn=20180206183939

78. Ehrlichman, John. Speaking in 1994, quoted by Dan Baum in Harper's Magazine, 2016.

79. Watergate Chronology 1973.Retrieved October 11, 2008 from: http://www.Watergate.info/chronology/1973.shtml. P.3.

80. O'brian, David. The Sorry Life & Death of Mark Frechette. Rolling Stone #199. Nov. 6, 1975.P. 32

81. Watergate Chronology 1973. Retrieved October 11,2008 from: http://www.Watergate.info/chronology/1973.shtml. P.6.

82. Letter from the Presidential Clemency Board. The White House. Instructions for Application for Clemency. Received early January, 1975.

83. Goodell, Charles E. Letter from the Presidential Clemency Board. Certified Mail No. 584901, dated August 18, 1975.

84. The National Archives Learning Curve. Dalton Trumbo. Retrieved March 27, 2003 from: http://www.spartacus.schoolnet.co.uk/USAtrumbo.html.

85. Copan, Paul. Jesus, Religions, and Just War.EveryStudent.com. Retrieved February 17, 2009 from: http://everystudent.com/wirres/justwar.html?OVRAW=just%20war%theory&OVKEY=J

86. McNamara, Robert S. & Vandemark, Brian. (1996). In Retrospect: The Tragedy and Lessons of Vietnam. New York, Vintage Books.

87. Morris, Errol, Williams, Michael, & Ahlberg, Julie (Producers) & Morris, Errol (Director). (2003). The Fog of War: Eleven Lessons from the Life of Robert S. McNamara. Documentary Feature. Sony Pictures classics.

88. Sly, Liz. (July 30, 2009).Iraq in throes of environmental catastrophe, experts say. Los Angeles Times. Retrieved August 1, 2009 from:
http://search.imesh.com/web?src=404&appid=575&systemid=1&q=http://www.latimes.com/news/nationwide/world/la-fg-iraq-dust30-2009jul30%2c3137832.st

MATTER OF CONSCIENCE INDEX

Made in the USA
Las Vegas, NV
06 March 2021